DEBATING

RACE, ETHNICITY, AND

LATINO IDENTITY

DEBATING

RACE, ETHNICITY, AND

LATINO IDENTITY

jorge j. e. gracia and his critics

EDITED BY IVÁN JAKSIĆ

COLUMBIA UNIVERSITY PRESS

New York

COLUMBIA UNIVERSITY PRESS

Publishers Since 1893

NEW YORK   CHICHESTER, WEST SUSSEX

cup.columbia.edu

Library of Congress Cataloging-in-Publication Data

Debating race, ethnicity, and Latino identity :

Jorge J. E. Gracia and his critics / edited by Iván Jaksić.

pages cm

Summary: "This book brings together some of the most prominent scholars in the philosophy of race and ethnicity in conversation about issues of ethnic and racial identity, nationality, and ethnic philosophy. The book contains the best defense by Jorge J. E. Gracia of his familial-historical view of Latino identity"—Provided by publisher.

Includes bibliographical references and index.

ISBN 978-0-231-16944-8 (cloth : acid-free paper)

ISBN 978-0-231-53772-8 (e-book)

1. Hispanic Americans—Ethnic identity.   2. Hispanic Americans—Race identity.

3. Latin Americans—Ethnic identity.   4. Latin Americans—Race identity.   5. Gracia,

Jorge J. E.—Political and social views.   6. Gracia, Jorge J. E.—Philosophy.   7. Ethnicity—

Philosophy.   8. Race—Philosophy.   9. United States—Ethnic relations.   10. Latin

America—Ethnic relations.   I. Jaksić, Iván, 1954–

E184.S75D42 2015

305.868'073—dc23

2014049267

Columbia University Press books are printed on permanent and durable acid-free paper.

This book is printed on paper with recycled content.

Printed in the United States of America

c 10 9 8 7 6 5 4 3 2 1

COVER DESIGN: CHANG JAE LEE

CONTENTS

PREFACE

The first decade of the twenty-first century has seen an unprecedented inter-est in, and development of, philosophical issues concerned with the intersec-tion of race, ethnicity, and Hispanic/Latino identity. The exploration of race by philosophers goes back a relatively long way. Leaving aside the confusing and often biased notions put forward by the likes of Immanuel Kant and David Hume, authors such as Alain Locke and perhaps most of all W. E. B. Du Bois probed deeply into issues of race and racism in the eighteenth and nine-teenth centuries. This was followed in the twentieth century by a plethora of work by black philosophers and philosophers of color, including Kwame Anthony Appiah, Bernard Boxill, Robert Gooding-Williams, Lewis Gordon, Leonard Harris, Bill E. Lawson, Howard McGary, Charles Mills, Lucius T. Outlaw Jr., Tommy Shelby, George Yancy, and Naomi Zack, and by white philosophers such as Robin Andreasen, Robert Bernasconi, Lawrence Blum, Joshua Glasgow, Sally Haslanger, Philip Kitcher, and Ron Mallon, to men-tion just a few of the most established, who have engaged the philosophy of race.

The exploration of ethnicity is connected to early discussions of race in-sofar as race and ethnicity have been thought to be closely related by some authors as early as Locke and Du Bois, although this has not been the norm. However, the first attempts at tying the philosophical discussion of race and ethnicity to Hispanic/Latino issues began in the nineties, with the work of Linda M. Alcoff, J. Angelo Corlett, and Jorge J. E. Gracia, who together with other philosophers interested in ethnic issues related to Hispanics/Latinos, such as José Medina, Eduardo Mendieta, Susana Nuccetelli, and Mariana

Ortega, and I, among others, constituted a strong contingent. But it is at the beginning of the twenty-first century that this interest undergoes a substantial expansion with the publication of many books and articles, in part no doubt influenced by the demographic explosion of this ethnic group in the country and its increasing influence in American culture and politics.

This book tries to capture recent advances in the discussion of these issues by gathering important exchanges between Gracia and other prominent philosophers who have engaged him in dialogue. Gracia has been a leader in the philosophical discussion of these topics and has been at the center of many of the most important controversies surrounding race, ethnicity, and Hispanic/Latino identity.

The foundation for Gracia's familiarity with these topics began with research on Latin American philosophy in the mid-seventies. This was helped by his personal friendship and collaboration with Risieri Frondizi, one of the most important Latin American philosophers of his generation, who acted as a mentor and partner to him. In Latin American philosophy, Gracia found some of the themes that he later explored and for which eventually he offered original theories and analyses. In collaboration with Frondizi, he compiled an anthology of philosophical texts from contemporary Latin American philosophers on the topics popular in the first half of the century, concerned with human nature and values: *El hombre y los valores en la filosofía latinoamericana del siglo XX* (1975, 1981). The editors intended to publish an English version of this volume, but given the American philosophical climate at the time, their efforts failed. Following this book, Gracia and I compiled a collection of texts in Venezuela (*Filosofía e identidad cultural en América Latina*, copyright 1983 but published in 1988), and he edited a volume with Eduardo Rabossi, Enrique Villanueva, and Marcelo Dascal (*Philosophical Analysis in Latin America*, 1984; Spanish enlarged edition, 1985), a *Festschrift* in honor of Frondizi (*Man and His Conduct: Philosophical Essays in Honor of Risieri Frondizi/El hombre y su conducta: Ensayos filosóficos en honor de Risieri Frondizi*, 1980), and a collection of Frondizi's essays titled *Ensayos filosóficos* (1986). In 1986 also Gracia published a substantially different version of *El hombre y los valores*, with the title *Latin American Philosophy in the Twentieth Century: Man, Values, and the Search for Philosophical Identity*, the first such work in English edited by a philosopher.

Encouraged by the publication of the anthology in English and the growing influence of the Hispanic/Latino population in the United States, Gracia convinced the board of the State University of New York Press in 1989 to begin a series devoted to the publication of monographs in the area of Latin American and Iberian Thought and Culture. The series was inaugurated with my book *Academic Rebels in Chile: The Role of Philosophy in Higher Education and Politics* (1989) and followed in 1993 by Ofelia Schutte's *Cultural Identity and Social Liberation in Latin American Thought.*

These events signaled that the field of Latin American philosophy was beginning to move and Hispanic/Latino demographics were helping, so that even the stodgy American Philosophical Association began to take notice. In 1991, Gracia became the founding chair of the association's Committee for Hispanics, an event that provided some impetus to the study of Latin American philosophy and Hispanic/Latino issues in the United States. Encouraged by these developments, Gracia published two groundbreaking books in 2000. *Hispanic/Latino Identity: A Philosophical Perspective* was the first book in English on Hispanic/Latino identity that was not a historical study of Latin American ideas on this topic but instead proposed an original philosophical theory. And *Hispanics/Latinos in the United States: Ethnicity, Race, and Rights,* edited in collaboration with Pablo De Greiff, was the first collection of philosophical essays focused on Hispanic/Latino issues and the relation between race and ethnicity in that context.

Until around 1995, Gracia's interest in Hispanics/Latinos hovered around topics related to identity and the history of Latin American thought. But working on his book on Hispanic/Latino identity he realized that he needed to turn to questions of race and nationality as well. This resulted in the publication of the mentioned anthology in 2000, a substantially revised edition of the 1986 volume on Latin American philosophy in collaboration with Elizabeth Millán-Zaibert titled *Latin American Philosophy for the 21st Century: The Human Condition, Values, and the Search for Identity* (2004), and, more significantly, the monograph *Surviving Race, Ethnicity, and Nationality: A Challenge for the Twenty-First Century* (2005b). In the last of these, he explicitly addressed questions of race, ethnicity, and nationality from a systematic perspective. Two years later he followed this with the publication of a collection of essays by leading black, Hispanic/Latino, and white American philosophers: *Race or Ethnicity? On Black and Latino Identity* (2007b). And a year later he published *Latinos in America: Philosophy and Social Identity* (2008b), which explores not only matters of identity but also questions of affirmative action, linguistic rights, ethnic names, and Hispanic/Latino philosophy in the United States. His latest book on related topics is an edited collection of essays by leading historians of Latin American thought called

Forging People: Race, Ethnicity, and Nationality in Hispanic American and Latino/a Thought (2011).

It should not be overlooked that, in addition to these publications, Gracia also has produced a substantial body of work dealing with Iberian philosophy. This includes a book on Francesc Eiximenis (*Com usar bé de beure e menjar*, 1977), two translations from the Latin texts, with commentaries, of three of Francisco Suárez's *Disputationes metaphysicae* (*Suárez on Individuation*, 1982, and, with Douglas Davis, *The Metaphysics of Good and Evil According to Suárez*, 1989), and many articles on such medieval authors as Ramon Llull, Gonsalvus Hispanus, Guido Terrena, and Averröes, in addition to contemporary authors from Spain and Latin America, such as Arturo Ardao, Risieri Frondizi, José Ortega y Gasset, Arturo Andrés Roig, Francisco Romero, and Leopoldo Zea.

Since the year 2000, Gracia has been at the center and forefront of many of the recent philosophical developments on topics having to do with race, ethnicity, and Hispanic/Latino issues in the United States, and many of the discussions in these fields have taken place in the context of public academic sessions devoted to his work. Indeed, it is not easy to find philosophical analyses of Hispanic/Latino/Latin American issues that have not touched in one way or another on his contributions. Every one of his books in this area has elicited panels at the American Philosophical Association and other professional contexts in which prominent philosophers have engaged his work and theories. These discussions constitute an important historical record of the evolution of the field in the United States and maintain a current relevance supported by the interest that they continue to elicit. Indeed, they provide a revealing panorama of the *status quaestionis* today in the United States and of the global leadership of this country in these matters.

Gracia's contributions in the areas covered in this volume are informed by his work in other philosophical fields. Particularly significant among these are metaphysics and hermeneutics. In metaphysics, Gracia has done pioneering work in meta-metaphysics, individuality and individuation, universals, and categories. In hermeneutics, he has written on the interpretation of philosophical texts, texts regarded as divinely revealed by religious communities, literature, and visual art. This work has made it possible for him to formulate new theories and to develop a careful methodology that he has used to address the questions raised and discussed here.

This volume gathers the most significant, critical, and controversial of these discussions, together with Gracia's responses. The topics range from the

nature of race and ethnicity to the relation of these phenomena to nationality, Hispanics/Latinos, linguistic rights, the way ethnic labels function, as well
as matters of identity and affirmative action, among others. The discussions
are gathered under three main topics: race, ethnicity, nationality, and philosophy; Hispanic/Latino identity; and Hispanics/Latinos and philosophy. The
pertinent panels, discussions, and articles on which these texts are based are
listed at the back of this volume.

The book begins with an introductory chapter that maps out in general
terms the exchanges in the volume, locating them in a historical and conceptual context. The rest of the book is divided into three parts that reflect
the three mentioned topics, although overlaps occur insofar as authors whose
chapters have been placed in one part often make reference to issues discussed
in the other two parts. Part I is concerned with race, ethnicity, nationality,
and the meta-philosophical question of the value of a philosophical inquiry
of these topics. Part II addresses Hispanic/Latino identity and related questions. Part III turns to Hispanic/Latino philosophy and philosophers in Latin
America and the United States. Within these general topics are integrated
discussions of many other topics, such as racial and ethnic identity, racial and
ethnic boundaries, the relation of nationality to race and ethnicity, the function of racial and ethnic labels, linguistic rights for minorities, and affirmative
action.

Part I includes contributions by four major philosophers of race and ethnicity: Lucius T. Outlaw Jr., Linda M. Alcoff, K. Anthony Appiah, and Lawrence Blum, in addition to Gracia's response. Their positions have to a great
extent determined the recent course of the philosophy of race and ethnicity
in American philosophy. They hold different and often conflicting perspectives with respect to both the topics of the section and the points they criticize in Gracia's position. Part II contains essays by six philosophers, three of
whom are known for their work on race or ethnicity and three who are known
for their work on Hispanic/Latino issues. J. L. A. García and Robert Gooding-
Williams have worked on ethical and political issues surrounding race in
particular, and Richard J. Bernstein has engaged wider topics concerned
with society and culture. Gregory Pappas works in the history of American
and Latin American philosophy; Eduardo Mendieta publishes in the history
of Latin American philosophy and thought and on social and political issues
related to Hispanics/Latinos and their identity; and Ilan Stavans is a commentator and essayist of American and Latin American cultures and litera-
tures. The section closes with Gracia's response to their criticisms. Part III

explores Hispanic/Latino philosophy in four chapters in addition to Gracia's response. Susana Nuccetelli adopts an analytic perspective in the characterization of Latin American philosophy. Renzo Llorente's Marxist point of view contrasts with Nuccetelli's in his analysis of issues having to do with labeling, language rights, and affirmative action. María Cristina González and Nora Stigol bring to bear a Latin American perspective to the issues. And Howard McGary considers affirmative action from the perspective of a black philosopher who is not Hispanic/Latino. The section ends with Gracia's response.

Gracia has revised and expanded his original responses to his critics in order to make them fit the book format, providing a coherent and topical account of the philosophical issues at stake, his proposed solutions to these issues, and his answers to the objections that have been brought against them. Although an effort has been made to preserve the original integrity of the pieces written by Gracia's critics, most of them have also undergone revision, sometimes substantial; the essays by Appiah and Stavans are published for the first time here. The book provides a point of departure for any current discussion of the fundamental philosophical questions that concern race, ethnicity, and Hispanics/Latinos, a way of deepening an understanding of various approaches to them, and the most important solutions that play roles in current discussions.

The volume can be read in various ways. If one is interested in Gracia's philosophy, one may begin by reading the introduction and Gracia's three responses to his critics. These materials are designed to hang together and stand by themselves. One may also read the introduction and the fifteen chapters critical of Gracia, followed by his three responses. Otherwise one may select some among the various topics discussed in the volume following a topical order in which essays are chosen from different parts of the book. Or one could follow the order in which the chapters are presented. To help readers, cross-references have been introduced by the editor as follows: "Blum, I:4" refers to Blum's chapter 4 in part I, and "Llorente, III:13" refers to Llorente's chapter 13 in part III.

This volume records important historical events that have taken place recently in the academy regarding significant concerns in contemporary American society. Eight features make it unique and especially valuable. First, many of the participants engaged in the dialogue are not Hispanics/Latinos. This lends the collection a perspective that is particularly useful and pertinent to the population at large. Second, many current philosophical discussions of Hispanics/Latinos ignore the important relation to race and ethnicity. This collection not only does not ignore it but also includes some of the best-known contributors to the conversation on race and ethnicity in the United States. This is in line with Gracia's pioneering work in this area and his focus on the relation between Hispanics/Latinos and African Americans in particular. Third, the contributors include philosophers from diverse philosophical traditions—Analytic, Aristotelian, Continental, Literary, Marxist, and Pragmatic—which is rarely seen in present-day American philosophy. This gives the volume greater appeal and allows the reader to be exposed to widely differing approaches.

Fourth, the diversity among the contributors themselves is wide, including women and men, blacks and whites, Hispanics/Latinos and non-Hispanics/Latinos, and philosophers born in the United States and others born elsewhere. This diversity is one of the strengths of the volume and should contribute to making the perspectives represented in it both versatile and useful to an understanding of the difficulties and intricacies involved in the topics discussed. Fifth, the very structure of the volume as a set of dialogues in which the authors engage in lively discussion, voicing with strength, but not venom, blatant disagreements on controversial topics, makes the volume an ideal point of departure for anyone interested in some of the most frequently discussed topics that affect not just American but also other, contemporary societies. It is also a good basis for introducing students to the discussion of these topics in the classroom. Sixth, the fact that the debates have taken place at the beginning of the twenty-first century gives the volume currency and sets the tone for future discussions of topics that will be at the heart of social philosophy for the foreseeable future.

Seventh, it is also significant that several of the fifteen philosophers who engage Gracia in these dialogues are among the most distinguished in contemporary philosophy, and all the participants are at the forefront of the discussions of the topics explored here and have put forward views and perspectives that have elicited attention. The sharp contrasts between their views and those of Gracia and each other constitute a unique testament to the vitality and diversity that characterizes the philosophy of race, ethnicity, and Hispanic/Latino identity today, not just in the United States but also in Latin America and elsewhere.

Finally, and perhaps above everything else, this book records an important and heretofore undocumented moment in the history of philosophy in general, and in the philosophy of race in particular, in which two different traditions meet and begin to interact. On the one hand, the American tradition initiated by African American philosophers in the nineteenth century, and, on the other, the Latin American tradition begun by Latin American philosophers in the sixteenth. They meet, first, in the philosophy of Hispanics/Latinos in the United States and subsequently in the philosophy of African Americans and Anglo-Americans in the United States and in the philosophy of Latin Americans in Latin America.

In closing I wish to thank my mentor Jorge Gracia, the authors of the contributing chapters, the journal editors and various press editors who have given permission to include previously published materials in the volume, Susan Smith for making some valuable suggestions for the introduction, and two very sharp and knowledgeable anonymous reviewers. I am particularly grateful to Wendy Lochner for her interest in this project and her support throughout the process of publication as well as to the other members of the staff of Columbia University Press for their attention to detail and help.

DEBATING

RACE, ETHNICITY, AND

LATINO IDENTITY

INTRODUCTION

IVÁN JAKSIĆ

From the very beginning, the philosophical understanding of race and its relation to ethnicity has been murky, and unclarity, confusion, and misinterpretation have been frequent. As late as the eighteenth century, Immanuel Kant and David Hume made appalling claims about race (Bernasconi 2001b; Rosen Velásquez 2008). And even as late as the first half of the twentieth century, such pioneering thinkers as Alain Locke and W. E. B. Du Bois proposed theories in which race and ethnicity were mixed sometimes indiscriminately. Moreover, although some philosophers in Europe and the British colonies that later constituted the United States paid some attention to race as early as the seventeenth century, their interest can be described as having been marginal at best. Most of those concerned with race were not philosophers but sociologists, anthropologists, biologists, and political scientists who looked at it through the particular lenses of their disciplines.

Several attempts at the beginning of the fourth quarter of the twentieth century were made that improved the situation. Scientific developments in genetics and biology helped insofar as they indicated that some views about race were mistaken. It became clear that there was no race gene and, therefore, that racial classifications were not strictly biological, as many had thought. This opened the way in the 1980s for some new developments. Some philosophers began to argue against the reality of race and to propose that racial labels and concepts should be eliminated or modified, whereas others continued to emphasize the need for them. And still others proposed the idea that race is a social construct.

The first important contributions to race theory occurred when two leading black philosophers selected race as a major focus of their attention. They
took opposite sides in the controversy over the need for, and the reality of,
race. K. Anthony Appiah (1992, 1996; Appiah and Gates 1995), who had been
trained at Cambridge in philosophical analysis, turned to race after having
made significant contributions to the philosophy of language and the
philosophy of mind. His moderate eliminativist thesis, according to which the
notion of race should be replaced by the notion of racial identity, encountered immediate opposition from Lucius T. Outlaw Jr., who argued that the
rectification of social inequities based on race required keeping racial terminology and concepts in the philosophical discourse. Outlaw (1996) had been
trained in the American philosophical tradition of pragmatism and was particularly interested in social issues. Appiah and Outlaw were soon joined by
Naomi Zack (1993, 1995), who focused on the importance of racial identity
and mixed race and argued for a more radical form of eliminativism, according to which all racial designations are racist insofar as race does not have
a scientific foundation.

At the time, most of the work of other philosophers dealing with racial
issues was related to social and political concerns, particularly those having
to do with racism and discrimination, a focus that, for obvious reasons, has
never left the field (e.g., Boxill 1984; Harris 1984).[1] Indeed, the very works by
Appiah, Outlaw, and Zack responded to strong social and political concerns,
and a good number of them were devoted to exploring such issues. It was not
until the very late nineties that other philosophers joined in the discussion
of race in contexts that went beyond social and political matters, as in the
work of Lawrence Blum (1999) on ethnicity, Sally Haslanger (1995) on ontology and social construction, and Charles Mills (1998) on the metaphysics of
race. In addition, the work of Berel Lang (1997), Robin Andreasen (1998), and
Philip Kitcher (1999) brought back concerns about the reality and biology of
race.

These developments mark the beginning of significant shifts in social philosophy in the last years of the twentieth century that continue into the
present. One is the attempt to understand the relation of race to ethnicity in
particular, and in some, although fewer cases, to nationality. Perhaps the most
widely accepted folk conception of these phenomena is that race has to do
with biology, ethnicity with culture, and nationality with the state. By the
first it is usually meant that race is a matter of descent, by the second that
ethnicity concerns values and customs, and by the third that nationality has

to do with social organization and government. These folk notions, however, have proven inadequate.

Another significant shift is the use of a metaphysical approach in trying to understand these phenomena. Whereas previously the common approaches used in the philosophy of race were largely social, anthropological, and political, an increasing number of philosophers realized that much that had been wrong in the understanding of race had to do with a lack of an in-depth analysis of the concepts involved. This led to the use of a metaphysical approach in which the reality of race became a central point of contention: is race something real, a product of nature, or is it something unreal, a socially constructed fiction, or a combination of the two?[2]

A third, and perhaps the most significant shift is the extension of the discussion of race and ethnicity to include Hispanics/Latinos, and an effort to understand how the situation of this social group helps in the general understanding of race. As a consequence, it has become increasingly difficult to focus exclusively on African and Euro-Americans in the treatment of these phenomena. The binary black/white, so common in previous discussions of race in America, was put into question, opening the way for a more complex grasp of racial and ethnic issues.

The year 2000 is particularly important in the history of the philosophy of race in the United States not only because it marks the beginning of a substantial increase in the number of books published on topics related to race but also and most significantly because it makes clear both the new shift in direction in the field and Gracia's contribution to it.[3] The new literature reflects the three developments mentioned earlier, but most clearly the third. The inclusion of Hispanics/Latinos in the discussion of race is quite novel if one considers that prior to the year 2000, only Linda M. Alcoff (1995) had made a significant reference to Hispanics/Latinos in the context of race. The great surprise is that in that year, two books were published that exemplify the new direction the philosophy of race was taking: a collection of essays by various authors titled *Hispanics/Latinos in the United States: Ethnicity, Race, and Rights*, edited by Gracia and Pablo De Greiff, and a monograph by Gracia, *Hispanic/Latino Identity: A Philosophical Perspective*.

Both books are groundbreaking and signal the change in the discussion of the philosophy of race in the United States. It is significant that the collective volume has a section devoted to "Hispanic/Latino Identity, Ethnicity, and Race," and some of its contributions explicitly address issues of race in the context of Hispanics/Latinos. It is also significant that the volume brings together a group of Hispanic/Latino philosophers for the first time with pieces relevant to Hispanics/Latinos but on subjects that had been largely the province of African Americans. That Gracia and De Greiff took the initiative to publish this book is not surprising considering that at the time Gracia was writing *Hispanic/Latino Identity*.

The difference between the pieces included in the volume edited by Gracia and De Greiff, on the one hand, and Gracia's monograph, on the other, is that the latter articulated a comprehensive theory of Hispanic/Latino identity and applied it to many of the questions that can be asked about the situation of this group in the United States, whereas the first offered a variety of opinions presented from many different perspectives. Once the doors were open to these topics and approaches, other Hispanic/Latino philosophers followed suit. One example was J. Angelo Corlett, who in 2001 published an article that, together with the piece he published in the volume edited by Gracia and De Greiff, became the basis for his book *Race, Racism, and Reparations* (2003). In this monograph, Corlett raised traditional questions concerning race, but, unlike most other philosophers, he couched the answers in terms of Hispanic/Latino ethnicity.

Apart from these, other signs of a paradigm shift in the discussion of race in the United States were also available during this time. An increasing number of philosophers of race paid attention to the situation of Hispanics/Latinos, and the same applies to the number of Hispanics/Latinos who began addressing questions in the philosophy of race. Black philosophers, such as Robert Gooding-Williams, Howard McGary, and George Yancy, for example, had publications relevant to Hispanics/Latinos. Some feminists, such as Alcoff, who works also on race, integrated concerns about Hispanics/Latinos in their discussions. And historians of Latin American philosophy were being increasingly attracted to the philosophical problems of Latinos in the United States, as happened with Susana Nuccetelli, Gregory Pappas, and Renzo Llorente. Indeed, Gracia and Nuccetelli integrated concerns about race in the National Endowment for the Humanities Summer Institute they organized in 2005, the first one ever on Latin American philosophy. Even philosophers in Latin America, such as María Cristina González and Nora Stigol, who engage in dialogue with Gracia in this volume, followed suit. More recently Wiley-Blackwell brought out *A Companion to Latin American Philosophy* (2010), which also includes chapters on race and ethnicity.

For his part, Gracia continued to help the development of the new direction with the publication of *Race or Ethnicity? On Black and Latino Identity*

(2007b). This volume, for the first time in the United States, gathered contributions from African, Hispanic/Latino, and Anglo-American philosophers under two general topics: "Racial and Ethnic Identity" and "Racism, Justice, and Public Policy." The contributors were black, white, colored, Hispanic/Latino, and Anglo-American.

The shift in direction in the philosophy of race did not concern only the questions of race that had been asked in the United States going back to the nineteenth century. It also signaled a move away from the historical approach commonly used by scholars interested in Hispanic/Latino philosophy and toward a systematic one of which Gracia was a leader. Earlier historiographical work by Hispanic/Latino scholars did sometimes address issues of Latin American identity, but seldom of race and ethnicity. Even when it did, moreover, the emphasis was historical in that it sought an understanding of what Latin Americans in Latin America had thought about their identity. The work of Alcoff, Corlett, Gracia, Eduardo Mendieta, and Nuccetelli in particular is different. These authors function as Hispanic/Latino philosophers who formulate and address philosophical problems arising from their particular condition as Hispanics/Latinos, although some of them, as well as other philosophers, have continued to do purely historical work in addition to their philosophical studies.

This brings me to an important issue that should not be overlooked. These changes have not only affected the work on race, ethnicity, and Hispanic/Latino identity in the United States but they have also begun to affect such work in Latin America. The discussion of these topics south of the border began at the very beginning of the colonial period in the controversy in which Bartolomé de Las Casas (1484–1566) and Juan Ginés de Sepúlveda (1489–1573) engaged in the sixteenth century concerning the humanity of Amerindians and their rights. Later, after independence from Spain was achieved, the leaders of the newly formed countries were not only aware of but also keenly concerned with the racial and cultural mix of the populations that they were supposed to govern as well as with the need to forge new nations out of heterogeneous and mixed populations. This is evident, for example, in works by Simón Bolívar (1783–1830) and José Martí (1853–1895), two of the leaders of independence from Spain. Still, the discussion of race and ethnicity by philosophers was rather scant.

The definitive change in direction in the philosophical discussion of race in the United States was achieved in Gracia's three books *Hispanic/Latino Identity: A Philosophical Perspective* (2000c), *Surviving Race, Ethnicity, and*

Nationality: A Challenge for the Twenty-First Century (2005b), and *Latinos in America: Philosophy and Social Identity* (2008b). The topics and approach used in these monographs exemplify the three developments that mark the beginning of a new direction in the philosophy of race: the exploration of the notions of race and ethnicity and not just of race, the metaphysical analysis of these phenomena, and the integration of topics related to Hispanics/Latinos into the discussion.

As significant as the publication of these three monographs was the response that they elicited in the American philosophical community, as the dialogues included in this volume demonstrate. The fact that all three were the subject of discussions at professional meetings and the participants in the discussions were African American, Anglo-American, and Hispanic/Latino philosophers of high standing in the profession is particularly significant. It indicates that the topics and approach characteristic of the new directions were accepted and amenable to philosophers beyond the boundaries of the Hispanic/Latino community.

The remainder of this volume includes the exchanges between Gracia and the philosophers who have engaged his views and arguments. The volume begins with *Surviving Race* because, although published after *Hispanic/Latino Identity*, it was completed shortly after it and contains a more general and systematic treatment of race and ethnicity, which together form the core of the new direction in race theory and of Gracia's philosophy of race. This is followed by the more pointed dialogues about Hispanic and Latino issues in *Hispanic/Latino Identity* and *Latinos in America*. The rest of this introduction contains a general conceptual map of the exchanges divided into three parts that correspond to Gracia's three books. The dialogues are full of arguments, back and forth, between Gracia and his critics, too many to take up in the space I have at my disposal. My focus, then, is on the details and topics that seem more significant and representative.

RACE, ETHNICITY, NATIONALITY, AND PHILOSOPHY

At the center of discussions of race, ethnicity, and nationality stand four topics. First, whether the notions and terminology used to think about and refer to these phenomena should be preserved at all. Second, the role that philosophy should play in their understanding. Third, the way in which these phenomena should be conceived. And fourth, the relation among them. All four of these topics have been the subject of continued and heated debate among philosophers, but Gracia's *Surviving Race* is the first attempt to address them in a systematic and comprehensive analysis.

The main thesis that Gracia defends is that the concepts of race, ethnicity, and nationality are distinct, coherent, and necessary in order to understand society. Accordingly, he rejects racial and ethnic notions of nations, ethnic notions of race, and racial notions of ethnicity. This goes against many mainstream views that argue that they are incoherent and pernicious and therefore should be abandoned or, alternatively, that they are so closely tied that they cannot be separated, even logically.

Gracia argues against Appiah's (1992, 1996) rejection of race both as a reality and a coherent concept and his adoption of a notion of racial identity in their place. Instead, Gracia proposes a social view of race conceived in terms of descent and genetically transmittable physical features, which he calls the Genetic Common-Bundle View. For him, race involves both descent and a set of socially determined phenotypical properties.

Gracia also argues against Corlett's (2003) rejection of the notion of race and his genetic view of ethnicity and instead defends a position, inspired by Du Bois, that he calls the Familial-Historical View. According to Gracia, ethne function as extended families that result from historical contingent events. Members of ethnic groups do not share fixed sets of properties throughout the histories of the groups, although each member of each group shares some properties with some other member, or members, of the group. Because of the historical and contingent conditions that cause the formation of ethnic groups, the conditions of identity for each group may, and usually do, vary from group to group.

Gracia's political view of nationality goes back to the French Enlightenment. It is presented as an alternative to David Miller's (1995) conception based on territoriality, a history, and a common public culture. For Gracia, nationality is not about territory, history, or culture but rather about political organization on the basis of the common will exercised in accordance with the good of the people. Although race, ethnicity, and nationality are distinct phenomena, their membership may overlap or coincide in particular cases and circumstances, leading frequently to the confusions that surround them. Finally, Gracia understands them to be social constructs, although the constructs integrate realities and, therefore, cannot be dismissed as imaginary.

In the preface to *Surviving Race*, Gracia presents an extended argument in favor of the role that philosophy should play in the inquiry about race and ethnicity. Philosophy aims to produce a comprehensive conceptual understanding that takes into account the results achieved by other disciplines while being unhampered by the limitations imposed on them by their specialized methods. Philosophy asks certain questions—logical, metaphysical, ethical, and aesthetic, among others—that are not explored in other disciplines. And philosophy functions as a watchdog of other branches of human knowledge making sure their conclusions are supported by sound arguments and backed by proper evidence.

In the first chapter, Gracia turns to the main arguments—political, moral, factual, epistemic, and pragmatic—that have been voiced in favor of doing away with the terminology and concepts of race, ethnicity, and nationality. He responds to these challenges by arguing that there are strong reasons in favor of keeping their terminology and concepts. However, their effective "survival" is contingent on the proper understanding of each of them and of their relations. Indeed, the very arguments that militate against their "conservation," to use Du Bois's term, arise from repeated confusions about them, hence the need for clarification.

The task of clarification begins, in the second chapter, with a discussion of some methodological distinctions that Gracia holds are required to understand the nature of the inquiry, avoid ambiguities, and have a clear sense of the object pursued. He distinguishes among two questions (dealing with, respectively, definition and metaphysical categorization), three approaches (metaphysical, epistemic, and linguistic), and three kinds of evidence (facts, views, and value judgments). For Gracia, keeping these distinctions in mind in the inquiry is essential to achieving credible results.

The three chapters that follow are devoted to ethnicity, race, and nationality, respectively. In them, Gracia elaborates the conceptions mentioned earlier. The last chapter of the book summarizes the overall view presented and warns against the conceptual, political, and social dangers of understanding ethnicity as race or nationality, race as ethnicity or nationality, and nationality as ethnicity or race.

In short, Gracia's answers to the four problems posed earlier are as follows:

1. The survival of the terminology and concepts of race, ethnicity, and nationality are essential.
2. Philosophy has a unique and fundamental role to play in the understanding of these phenomena.

3. Race, ethnicity, and nationality should be understood as social constructs that are nonetheless real—race in terms of descent and a bundle of variable phenotypical properties, ethnicity on the basis of properties caused by historically contingent phenomena, and nationality founded on the common will to unite in a political organization for the overall good.
4. Race, ethnicity, and nationality are distinguishable, although their membership may overlap or even coincide.

All four answers are disputed by the commentators in this volume.

Outlaw's general philosophical position about philosophy and race is inspired by a pragmatic approach in which social and political concerns are of the essence. Accordingly, he disputes Gracia's views because of both what he considers an unwarranted and excessive emphasis on philosophy and an insufficient attention to social and political considerations. His main objection concerns the role of philosophy in the understanding of race, ethnicity, and nationality. He argues that there is no such thing as philosophy conceived in the way Gracia does, nor has there ever been. There are, and have been, philosophers and philosophies, but the history of the discipline does not vouch for anything like what Gracia has in mind. Besides, what could there be in philosophy that would make it play the powerful role that Gracia assigns to it? Outlaw is quite sympathetic to Gracia's arguments in favor of keeping the terminology and notions of race, ethnicity, and nationality alive, but he rejects Gracia's claims concerning philosophy's role in the inquiry. He also asks for greater attention to social and political matters. This last point ties his criticism to one of Alcoff's objections to Gracia's views.

In answer to Outlaw, Gracia argues that he shares with him a view of philosophy as incomplete and always in a process of change and revision. Still, we need a discipline, call it philosophy or what you will, that tries to integrate the information we gather from all other disciplines into an overall view. We also need a discipline that is not so specialized as the sciences are. Finally, we need a discipline that fills gaps existing among other disciplines—logical, ethical, political, aesthetic, metaphysical, and so on—and the only candidate for this is philosophy. So, although philosophy is a work in progress, it is the only alternative we have. We also need philosophy because only it can be the critic of other disciplinary enterprises.

Alcoff (2005b, 2005c) consistently argues in her publications for the importance of taking into account the political dimension of phenomena.

Indeed, she has engaged in a dispute with Gracia (2005a, 2008a) about the benefits of using the label 'Latino' versus 'Hispanic' and has defended the use of the first on the basis of political considerations. Her view is that values affect racial and ethnic facts such as identity and, therefore, are essential when articulating arguments for positions that may not appear to be political. Another factor that needs to be considered in order to understand Alcoff's criticism of Gracia is that she has defended the position that race and ethnicity are not separable, because ethnicity is always racialized. Along this line, she has proposed to replace the notions of race and ethnicity with the notion of ethnorace, a concept she borrowed from David Theo Goldberg (1993).

In answer, Gracia repeats and defends his stated view that, particularly in the contested notions of race, ethnicity, and nationality, it is essential that one should not mix fact and value. This does not mean that values should not be considered in argumentation, but rather that these categories should not be confused or conflated if one wishes to understand the phenomena in question and how fact and value play roles in them. Value judgments and facts should be kept distinct in argumentation so that one can understand the claims being made and the proper force of the arguments being used.

With respect to the relation between race and ethnicity in particular, again Gracia defends a view contrary to that of Alcoff. For him, ethnicity and race are conceptually distinct and their conceptual analysis should be kept independent of each other, even if in fact race and ethnicity are frequently tied. Their confusion is not only unfortunate for the clarity of their understanding but it also carries social dangers, such as the oppression of certain citizens because of their ethnicity or race.

Appiah's position on the role of metaphysics in the understanding of race and ethnicity is quite concordant with that of Gracia and contrasts with the views of Outlaw and Alcoff. Like Gracia, he holds that metaphysics is, in P. F. Strawson's language, "revisionary" rather than "descriptive," but he disputes Gracia's views of race and ethnicity.

Appiah's own view on race and ethnicity is that they are not realities. Both science and history show that these are not facts in the world and thus he argues for their elimination and replacement with the notions of racial and ethnic identities. This leads him to question Gracia's conceptions of both race and ethnicity. His strategy is to show that both conceptions are inadequate in that they would require the addition of certain conditions for them to do what Gracia wants them to do, but when those conditions are added, race and ethnicity cease to be what Gracia first thought they were. The two most important issues in question are the need to add the notion of an ancestral people to conditions of both ethnicity and race, and the fact that Gracia's formulation about race does not account for the difference between "Aborigines" and "Negroes." He thinks that the notion of an ancestral people would help in the resolution of these two issues, although it would collapse the notions of race and ethnicity, contrary to Gracia's attempts to keep them separate.

Gracia responds by pointing out that his own view of race concerns conditions of a racial group, not conditions of the distinction between particular races, and thus that, although Appiah is right in noting that Gracia's view does not account for differences among races, this is irrelevant as a criticism of his position insofar as his theory is not intended to account for that but only for race. With respect to the criticism concerning the lack of reference to ancestry, Gracia responds by referring to a point he often reiterates and believes is supported by empirical evidence, namely, that the conditions of particular ethne are not uniform throughout ethne but result from particular and contingent historical conditions. It makes no sense, then, to insist that all ethne, or races for that matter, should be conceived in terms of ancestry.

Blum's criticisms of Gracia's views have been influenced by the importance that he gives to society and social perspectives, what might be called social facts. His main philosophical interests are in social and political issues and more recently in matters that have to do with race. He argues that Gracia's view of race is inconsistent in that it is presented as descriptive, but in fact it is prescriptive and does not match the ordinary conception of race prevalent in the United States. Like Appiah, Blum voices concerns about Gracia's familial views of race and ethnicity. He also brings up the counterexample of "blacks" and "Aborigines" mentioned by Appiah and points out, for example, differences between ethne and families, such as rules of membership, geographic dispersion, and organization. Moreover, he argues that Gracia does not provide proper empirical criteria to identify ethne.

Gracia responds to Blum by pointing out that metaphysics is always prescriptive insofar as it proposes particular understandings of facts but that, as in science, it has to begin by taking facts into account. In the case of race and ethnicity, it is important to consider the attitudes and views people have, but a proper theory should go beyond the views available if these are inconsistent or inaccurate and propose positions that are not. He responds to Blum's objections against the familial conception of race and ethnicity by noting that Blum assumes both that Gracia understands ethne as nuclear families, which he does not, and that the organization of ethne is similar throughout different groups, which Gracia disputes. To the charge that Gracia omits particular empirical criteria of ethnic identification, Gracia responds by recalling that, as he has argued, there are no such criteria across the board, a reason why they cannot be identified.

HISPANIC/LATINO IDENTITY

A different set of problems are raised in part II of this volume, which contain exchanges between Gracia and his critics in the context of Hispanic/Latino identity. The first question that can be raised regarding the topics involved is whether it makes sense to talk about ethnic identity at all. The second, which has elicited considerable controversy and even resentment in certain quarters, is whether Hispanics/Latinos constitute a legitimate and identifiable ethnic group. The third concerns the relative value of using the labels 'Hispanic' and 'Latino,' or any label at all for that matter, to refer to a social group. The fourth involves the proper way to understand Hispanic/Latino identity. The fifth refers to the historical origin and development of the Hispanic/Latino ethnos. And the sixth raises the issue of how Hispanics/Latinos are perceived in the United States, especially in a philosophical context.

Gracia's *Hispanic/Latino Identity* is the first attempt to address these topics in a systematic and comprehensive analysis of fundamental questions dealing with race, ethnicity, and Hispanic/Latino identity. The book defends several significant and novel theses. First, Hispanics/Latinos constitute an ethnic group that is functioning, identifiable, and distinguishable in context from other ethnic groups, over and above the various nationalities that are frequently identified as Hispanic/Latino, such as Mexican or Chilean. Second, although both terms, 'Hispanic' and 'Latino,' have advantages and disadvantages, in a philosophical context the first is more advantageous because it brings attention to cultural aspects and historical relations that otherwise would be missed. Third, in spite of some serious disadvantages, ethnic labels are useful for the constitution of an ethnic group and help with the identification and development of an ethnic identity. Fourth, the Hispanic/Latino ethnos, just as other ethne, is best understood in familial-historical terms and its origin is to be found in a historical period marked by encounters between Iberians and Amerindians that begins in 1492 and the subsequent process of cultural and population mixing (*mestizaje*). Finally, Gracia argues that Hispanics/Latinos are perceived as foreigners in the United States and this leads to exclusions and discrimination as illustrated in their situation in American philosophy.

García, the first critic of Gracia's views in part II, has explored questions of ethics and racism in particular and generally favors a deflationary approach. A lean and realistic ontology has led him to oppose Appiah's move from race and ethnicity to racial and ethnic identities. Likewise, from García's perspective, Gracia's acceptance of the notion of a Hispanic/Latino identity makes no sense insofar as talking about what a person is should be sufficient for purposes of dealing effectively with racial discrimination and similar phenomena. In his view, Gracia does not need to have recourse to the notion of an ethnic identity, which García finds problematic and dubious. Identity always needs two points of comparison because it is always relational. García grants the need to speak of and identify Hispanics for purposes of affirmative action, for example, but he rejects the need for the notion of a Hispanic identity. Although he commends Gracia for his realistic ontology and his methodology, he goes on to formulate other objections, to which I shall turn later.

Gracia responds to García's criticisms of his view of identity by pointing out that García begs the question, assuming that identity has to be relational and cannot be extended to groups. Both assumptions are unwarranted, having reputable opponents throughout the history of philosophy and operating contrary to ordinary linguistic use. In Gracia's view, it is only because García is still thinking about ethnic identity in essentialistic terms that he adopts such controversial assumptions.

Not everyone in the group of critics agrees with García's objection to Gracia's position. However, although they are willing to accept Gracia's talking of a Hispanic or Latino identity, they reject other aspects of his view. For example, Richard Bernstein, Ilan Stavans, and Pappas disagree with Gracia in the constitutive mark of such an identity.

Bernstein works within the Continental philosophical tradition and has a distaste for strong realism. Unlike Gracia's preference for talking about what people are, he underscores the importance of what people think they are. He finds fault with Gracia's position because it does not take into account what really matters for identity, which is the view people have about themselves. Although Bernstein agrees with Gracia that history is important for identity, he argues that history needs to be individuated in order to function effectively in the formation and identification of an ethnic group. The factor that is missing in Gracia's position is the self-identification and awareness of one's history. In Bernstein's view, self-identification and self-awareness are the only effective ways to establish clear boundaries to Hispanic identity.

One of Stavans's criticisms of Gracia's position is related to Bernstein's objection. Stavans is a cultural commentator and essayist who has written extensively on the situation of Hispanics/Latinos in the United States. Contrary to Gracia's rejection of any attempt to regard any particular property or set of properties as necessary and sufficient conditions for the Hispanic/Latino ethnos, he identifies the history of self-reflection by Hispanics/Latinos as essential for it.

Gracia does not agree for several reasons that the history an ethnic group regards as particular to it is necessarily essential to the group's identity. Among them are that ethnic groups often lack a sense of themselves and knowledge of their history but nonetheless effectively function as groups, and that people may be taught to think of themselves in ways contrary to the facts. Latent in the position that the history of a group's views about itself is essential for its identity, Gracia claims, is the confusion between opinion and fact, to which he points in chapter 2 of *Surviving Race*. Moreover, he claims that proponents of this position do not take into account another important distinction, between history and philosophy, which is pertinent because Gracia's account of Hispanic/Latino identity is philosophical, not historical.

Stavans brings up another objection to Gracia's position, one that is unique among Gracia's critics represented in this volume. According to him, Gracia does not give language the place it deserves in an account of identity and particularly Hispanic/Latino identity. Spanish, according to Stavans, is of the essence for Hispanics/Latinos. To this Gracia counters that Spanish is not the only native language of Hispanics/Latinos; therefore it makes no sense to say that Spanish, or even any particular language, is of the essence when it comes to Hispanic/Latino identity.

Pappas is among other critics of Gracia who disputes his view that there are no essential properties common to Hispanics/Latinos. He is a pragmatist with a strong interest in culture and context. His disagreements with Gracia are a matter of emphasis. His most clear and salient objection is that Gracia does not grant culture its due place in the constitution of Hispanic identity, for in his view culture is the most important factor in ethnic identity in general and in Hispanic identity in particular. To this objection, Gracia responds that history is responsible for culture and, therefore, the influence of culture in identity is included in his view that history is the source of the properties that accrue to members of an ethnos. Culture is implicitly taken for granted in Gracia's position, and this makes Pappas's criticism irrelevant.

Several of Gracia's critics raise social and political concerns. For example, Mendieta focuses on the controversy concerning the proper label to use to refer to Hispanics/Latinos. His position is that adopting a term such as 'Hispanics' globally to refer to what are, in fact, different groups of people is not only inaccurate but "disastrous." The groups of people Gracia refers to as Hispanics are so different from one another, in Mendieta's view, that the use of any term globally to label them homogenizes them in ways that fail to do justice to their struggles and reality. Latin Americans and Spaniards, in particular, are very different peoples but so are Mexicans and Colombians.

Gracia responds by noting that, although Mendieta is right in pointing out the differences among different groups of Hispanics, he fails to note the historical ties that unite them. These historical ties, considered in the places and times in which they occur, account for the various properties that unite subgroups of them. Taking note of these ties is essential for an understanding of those groups and their complex historical relations. In addition, Mendieta's criticism is inconsistent because it is applied discriminately. Consistency would require that it be applied also to labels such as 'Mexican,' because this group also is constituted of many other ethnic groups that live within the Mexican national territory. But then, Gracia asks, where do we stop if we follow Mendieta's rejection of more general terms in favor of particular ones? Mendieta does not only use his argument inconsistently but also fails to see the need for labels that are more general and labels that are less general. Gracia explores this point in more detail in chapter 1 of *Latinos in America.*

Gooding-Williams raises a historical point that also has political implications. He is a political philosopher whose work has focused on issues related to the politics and social dimensions of race in particular. Thus, he would be sympathetic to the perspectives of Alcoff and Bernstein discussed earlier. His objections to Gracia's position are related to history. Indeed, he questions the choice of 1492 as the starting point from which, and in time, it makes sense to speak of a Hispanic identity. The reason is that the political and social structures related to slavery that were to be so important for Hispanics go back to a time before 1492, when the Portuguese began the slave trade on the coast of Africa. Instead of 1492, he favors 1441.

Gracia's answer to Gooding-Williams is that the earlier date he proposes is not accurate insofar as slavery was in place in Europe before the Portuguese established the slave trade on the coast of Africa around 1441. Besides, the impact of the first encounters between the Americas and Iberia is quite notable in our part of the world, whereas other encounters and events lack the same level of significance.

Gracia's *Hispanic/Latino Identity* ends with reflections about the character and current situation of Hispanic/Latino philosophy in the United States, a topic that also generates disagreement. García disagrees with the view that Hispanics/Latinos should be encouraged to know the history of Hispanic/Latino philosophy in particular. He takes a position according to which the only philosophy whose study should be encouraged is a philosophy that has been proven to be universally applicable. No consideration of ethnic or national factors should be used to justify the study of particular philosophies. And Gooding-Williams doubts that Hispanics/Latinos are perceived as foreign, as Gracia holds, insofar as English, French, and German philosophers are not perceived as foreign, as they should be if Gracia were right. Moreover, he questions Gracia's view that this explains the marginalization of Hispanics/Latinos in American philosophy. In his view, Gracia misses the real culprit: race.

Against García, Gracia contends that his view does not involve the claim that Hispanic/Latino philosophy has no distinguishing characteristics in particular historical periods and thus this criticism is unjustified. Moreover, the large body of philosophical work in Hispanic/Latino philosophy and its differences with American philosophy are good reasons to study it, insofar as searching for the causes of the differences presumably will reveal something about philosophy itself. In addition, the marginal situation of Hispanic/Latino philosophy should reveal important aspects of the sociology of philosophy, since marginalization is by itself an important factor in the understanding of marginalized phenomena.

Against Gooding-Williams, Gracia points out that his view is not that the marginalization of Hispanics/Latinos is due only to their perception as foreigners. Race can also be a cause of it. Moreover, the perception of Hispanics/Latinos as foreign contrasts with the perception of the groups Gooding-Williams mentions, because these groups are considered the roots of American culture in general and the philosophical culture in particular.

HISPANICS/LATINOS AND PHILOSOPHY

Part III of this volume addresses some of the same questions addressed in part II, but it focuses on the particular topics that Gracia emphasizes in

Latinos in America. The primary context in *Latinos in America* is "Latino philosophy," which leads us to revisit the question of the use of the labels 'Hispanic' and 'Latino.' Do they pick out the same items or not, and apart from this question, which is the best label to use in a Latino philosophical context? This in turn leads to various questions concerning Latino philosophy and problems that may arise in this context. Finally, questions concerning linguistic rights and affirmative action for Latinos are given attention.

Gracia's *Latinos in America* is the first systematic and comprehensive discussion of issues related to Latino philosophy published in the United States. It proposes several novel and provocative theses integrated into an overall view that not only challenges prevalent views but also establishes the parameters of future discussions of these issues.

Philosophy is highly self-reflective, so it is not surprising that it has been a field where the issues of Hispanic/Latino identity have played out. In Latin America, the question of a pan-ethnic identity has been, in various garbs, part of philosophical discussions going back to the 1500s. The issues were raised first in the context of the Spanish conquest and colonization. As mentioned, questions about how to consider Amerindians and their rights in a newly established Spanish political order were raised by the likes of Las Casas and others during the colonial period. And not only the status of Amerindians, and later of the Africans who were brought to the region as slaves, but also that of the descendants of Europeans who had been born in the colonies was a source of concern and controversy.

After independence, when the former colonies were trying to organize into nations, questions of racial, national, and Latin American and Hispanic American identity became paramount. Efforts were made to manipulate the character of the populations. In some cases this was attempted by encouraging white immigration from Europe, and in others by trying to blend different groups into homogeneous populations and promoting identification with pre-Columbian cultures. These issues were addressed in the political and social arenas but also entered the more rarefied atmosphere of philosophy. Indeed, in the twentieth century, they became particularly popular among philosophers, who frequently explored the way to conceive national identities and beyond these, in the 1940s and later, an overall Latin American and Hispanic identity. Authors such as Samuel Ramos (1897–1959) sought to define what is truly characteristic of the Mexican, and others, such as José Vasconcelos (1882–1959), were more ambitious, speaking of what is or will become a Latin

American people, which he conceived in biological terms as a kind of mestizo race.

The interest in the identity of the peoples of Latin America was eventually transferred, in the forties, to the question of whether the philosophy produced in Latin America itself had idiosyncratic characteristics, either nationally or in Latin America as a whole. Does it make sense to talk about a Latin American philosophy? Does such a thing exist at all? These questions became central topics of debate among Latin American philosophers and continue to be so to this day.

As in Latin America, the interest in an overall American identity became a subject of discussion, particularly among political philosophers, in the United States. Moreover, toward the end of the nineteenth century and the early twentieth century, black thinkers such as Locke and Du Bois raised questions about the black population. Similar questions were raised about immigrant groups, such as the Irish, but they tended to be asked by sociologists and anthropologists rather than philosophers. As we have seen, it was much later, beginning in the nineteen eighties, that black philosophers appropriated the discussion and tried to address issues of identity in a strictly philosophical context and manner. And the question of Hispanic/Latino identity was not raised by American philosophers until even more recently. It is not surprising, then, that as in the case of blacks, who were the first to address the question of black identity, Hispanics/Latinos have been the first to raise the question of Hispanic/Latino identity in the United States.

The attention to American identity and the identity of social groups was bound to be transferred to philosophy itself, as happened in Latin America. Thus we find discussions of the existence and character of not only American philosophy but also black philosophy and Hispanic/Latino philosophy in recent years in the United States. In this development there is some symmetry with that in American and Latin American philosophy, although an important difference between them stands out. Questions about the identity of American philosophy, and of the philosophy produced by various social groups in the United States, have been generally marginal to the philosophy establishment. These topics have not constituted part of the mainstream core in philosophical discussions, and the philosophers who have been involved in them are generally parochial in this sense: the interest in the question of the identity of American philosophy has been generally restricted to historians of that field; the question of the identity of black philosophy has usually been undertaken by black philosophers; and the discussion of the identity of

Hispanic/Latino identity until recently has been carried out by Hispanic/ Latino philosophers. There have been exceptions, but they have not been many. Now, the situation in Latin America concerning the discussion of the identity of ethnic and national groups, as well as their philosophies, has likewise been carried out by members of those groups, but the discussions of a pan–Latin American identity and the identity of a pan–Latin American philosophy have been, unlike that of American philosophy in the United States, part of the philosophical mainstream. Very few philosophers of note in Latin America have not participated in them.

This is where Gracia's main contribution is evident. First, in the books he has edited, Gracia has drawn Anglo-Americans and black Americans into the discussion of Latino issues, and of Latinos into the discussion of topics that before had been generally the province of Anglo-American and black Americans. Second, because he has developed a comprehensive framework of concepts and novel ideas about such topics as race, ethnicity, and Hispanic/Latino identity that have challenged the status quo, he has elicited a response from both Latinos and non-Latinos.

In *Latinos in America*, Gracia addresses questions around these topics. Some of them are closely related to issues he discussed in *Surviving Race* and *Hispanic/Latino Identity*, but he develops his position further and makes additional claims that round up the views he had presented before. The motivation for writing the book was that the growing population of Latinos in the United States had attracted attention and generated fear in both the Latino and the non-Latino communities. Latinos began to be perceived as posing various threats to the non-Latino population, and Latinos themselves felt threatened by both how they were perceived and the consequences of having a Latino identity. These perceptions were revealed in the interaction of Latinos in American society, particularly the marketplace, affirmative action, and linguistic rights.

Gracia's response to this situation is to argue that an important, and generally neglected, contributing factor to the generation of these perceptions is a misconception of Latino identity. It is common to think of Latinos as having a common essence and as being essentially different from non-Latinos. This is a source of the fear that the growing numbers of Latinos will result in the elimination of values that are considered to be distinctive of the American way of life. Yet the reality is very different, according to Gracia, for there is nothing common to all Latinos. Latinos are not homogeneous but diverse, even though they are united by historical relations and contingent and contextual properties that draw them together. Going back to the position he defended in *Hispanic/Latino Identity*, Gracia argues that Latinos constitute a kind of family, and it is familial-historical connections that tie them and allow for the effective use of the term 'Latino' when they are taken in the particular contexts in which they find themselves.

Chapter 1 of *Latinos in America* is devoted to the presentation and defense of the application of Gracia's Familial-Historical View of ethnicity to the Latino ethnos. He claims that his view avoids two dilemmas that are a source of misunderstandings: globalism versus particularism and essentialism versus eliminativism. The first precludes the possibility of the coexistence in the same group of both general identities, such as Latino, and particular ones, such as Mexican. The second forces a choice between conceiving Latinos in essentialistic terms as sharing a set of fixed and unchanging properties and rejecting a shared identity.

In chapter 2, Gracia defends his view against two objections based on circularity and demarcation, and in chapter 3 he shows how the use of ethnic names have political implications that need to be taken into account. It is for this reason that he favors 'Latino,' rather than 'Hispanic,' in *Latinos in America*. He also claims that 'Latino' and similar ethnic labels function as proper names, and as such they are established through a kind of baptism and have as their primary function to refer, not to describe. Still, we learn to employ these terms through contingent descriptions that reflect the historical and familial nature of their identity.

The second part of the book turns to the situation of Latinos in the marketplace, affirmative action, and linguistic rights, three areas where Latinos are at the center of controversy and that affect their place in American society. Using the philosophy marketplace as an illustration, Gracia argues that Latinos become marginalized because of the structures of power along which the philosophy profession is organized. Unless Latinos become de-Latinized in the sense that they are alienated from their Latino communities and intellectual roots, they have difficulty finding philosophy jobs and becoming public voices in America. The existence of these difficulties justifies the establishment of affirmative procedures that ensure the full participation of Latinos in the life of our democratic nation. He also claims that the English First argument in the context of the education of Latino children is unsound and may be inspired by mistaken conceptions of American nationality as an ethnos, and of ethnicity as necessarily involving a set of properties, views contrary to the position on identity Gracia has proposed.

The third part of the book moves to the way Latinos think of themselves and of their intellectual heritage. Gracia begins with the question of how to conceive Latino philosophy in view of the controversies that have surrounded it. Instead of following the well-known universalist, culturalist, and criticalist views proposed in one of the books we coedited (Gracia and Jaksić 1988), he advocates a new conception of it as ethnic. Understanding Latino philosophy in this way, he argues, creates a framework in which problems of historiographical inclusion and exclusion can be more easily understood and resolved. It also facilitates a better understanding of the relations between Latino philosophy on one side and American philosophy on the other.

This leads to the consideration of the canon of philosophy and the exclusion of Latino philosophy from it. Gracia claims that one important, but commonly neglected, factor in the explanation of this phenomenon is the key role that tradition plays in the development of a philosophy canon, and particularly in that used in the United States. Tradition, conceived as a web of practices adopted by a community that designates some of its members as philosophical authorities, accounts for the absence of Latino philosophy in both the American and world canons of philosophy.

The last chapter argues that a contributing factor to the neglect of Latino philosophy in the United States and the world is the negative attitude that Latinos themselves have concerning Latino philosophy. Gracia maintains that this negative attitude is the result of many factors. In part it has to do with a well-known colonial mentality in which what comes from outside, from a dominator, is regarded as good, and what comes from inside, what is native, is regarded as bad. But an important element frequently neglected is that the history of Latino philosophy is generally studied and taught using a wrong approach that emphasizes history rather than philosophy. In order for Latino philosophy to be regarded as valuable, it must be taught philosophically, using what Gracia calls the Framework Approach.

The views Gracia proposes in *Latinos in America* are intended to make it easier for both Latinos and non-Latinos to grasp that they are not inexorably estranged from each other in the United States. These groups are not homogeneous and should not be regarded as foreign to each other. Nor are Latinos and non-Latinos like nations, political units separated by legal and territorial boundaries. They are rather like families, and as families, they may be related in some important respects and unrelated in others. Some Latinos and some non-Latinos share important things in common, just as some do not. This view separates Gracia's contribution from the contributions of other philosophers both in the United States and in Latin America who have addressed similar issues.

Gracia's critics in this volume focus on six topics: Latino versus Hispanic philosophy; the use of 'Latino' versus 'Hispanic' in general; Latino philosophy as ethnic; global Latino philosophy versus Latino philosophy in the United States; Latino linguistic rights; and affirmative action for Latinos.

Llorente is a specialist in social and political philosophy and in Latin American philosophy, particularly the history of Marxism. He voices several objections that go to the heart of some of Gracia's views. Given that Gracia changes the terminology from 'Hispanics' that he favored in *Hispanic/Latino Identity* to 'Latinos' in *Latinos in America*, Llorente begins by arguing that Gracia's position with respect to the use of these labels in the two books is inconsistent. He also claims that Gracia does not provide sufficient evidence for the political connotations of 'Latino,' thus undermining its usefulness, nor for the introduction of the label 'Latino philosophy' to refer to a philosophy that combines Latin American philosophy and the philosophy of Latinos in the United States.

Gracia responds that there is no inconsistency in the use of the labels in the two books, because their differences have to do with different aims. Labels send messages and their appropriate character depends on their aims. In the first book, the aim was the understanding of Hispanic/Latino ethnicity and the history of philosophy, and in the second, the social and political situation of Latinos in the United States. 'Hispanics' is appropriate in the first book because of its strong cultural and historical connotations; 'Latinos' is appropriate in the second book because of its strong political and social connotations. As to the lack of substantiation of the political connotations of 'Latino,' Gracia does not offer much because others, such as Alcoff elsewhere and Mendieta in this volume, have done so extensively.

Nuccetelli is a well-established analytic philosopher working on issues in the philosophy of language, logic, epistemology, and ethics, but she also has contributed substantially to the historiography of Latin American philosophy and has engaged topics related to Latinos in the United States. One of these has to do with the function of ethnic names, arguing for a position that Gracia (2008b:chap. 3) rejects. Her criticism here, however, refers to Gracia's notion of ethnic philosophy. She claims that this notion fails to do justice to both philosophy and Latin American philosophy insofar as it fails (1) to present an effective criterion of inclusion and (2) to apply the criterion it uses.

In Gracia's view, Nuccetelli misunderstands the criterion he offers insofar as she believes it applies generally to *works that belong to an ethnos*, rather than to what Gracia identifies, namely, *works that are judged to satisfy certain criteria of belonging to the philosophy of the ethnos.* Moreover, he argues that he does not apply this criterion to any particular work from Latin America because in this book he does not see his role as doing historiography of Latino philosophy but rather as providing a theory that will allow us to do effective historiography. If he were doing historiography, he would, in accordance with his theory, begin by establishing what constitutes philosophy according to the Latino ethnos, and then apply the implied criteria to particular works.

González and Stigol are Argentinean philosophers who work in Buenos Aires. They are closely associated with the Sociedad Argentina de Análisis Filosófico and the journal *Análisis filosófico.* They work in mainstream analytic topics but recently have been interested in issues related to the philosophical canon and the historiography of philosophy. These topics have led them to Latin American philosophy. Like Llorente, they voice concerns about Gracia's views of a Latino philosophy as well as of Latino philosophers. They argue that he does not take into account the important differences between the philosophy of, and the philosophers who work in, Latin America and the philosophy of, and philosophers who work in, the United States. As substantiation for this claim they point to differences in history, community vigor, engagement in dialogue, discrimination, eagerness for novelty, marginality, and authenticity.

Gracia answers that this criticism is still based on the misguided essentialist view that both ethnicity and philosophical identity have to do with certain shared properties, whereas Gracia's view is that ethnicity has to do with history, and properties come into the picture only through it. It is a mistake, then, to judge his position by focusing on particular properties. Moreover, Latino history reveals ties that unite all Latinos, separate them from Anglo-Americans, and implicitly take into account such differences as gender, nationality, and contexts.

McGary is an analytic philosopher who works in the areas of social and political philosophy. His criticism focuses on Gracia's particular defense of affirmative action. In his view there are two forward-looking strategies for affirmative action—one based on utility and one based on justice—and one backward-looking strategy, the rectification of past wrongs. He questions

Gracia's proposal insofar as it dismisses the backward-looking strategy in favor of the two forward-looking ones. The reason is that the forward-looking strategies do not provide proper justification for favoring one social group rather than another, something that is necessary in affirmative action.

Gracia responds by questioning the clarity of the distinction between backward- and forward-looking strategies insofar as the aim of the backward-looking strategy is to correct in the present, *and for the future*, whatever abuses were committed in the past: the strategy looks backward and forward, not just backward. The important difference between these two types of strategies is not the temporal direction but the fact that the backward-looking strategy is concerned with addressing past transgressions, whereas the forward-looking strategy is not.

In closing, let me recapitulate that these dialogues between Gracia and his critics show his presence and influence in the profession and particularly in the philosophy of race. His impact has been felt not only in the original ideas he has proposed and the method he has employed but also in the way he has affected the direction of the philosophy of race in this country. He has been a key figure in all three developments that mark a change of direction in the discussion of race in the United States in the recent past: the increasing attention to ethnicity in discussions of race, the application of a metaphysical conceptual analysis of the pertinent problems, and, perhaps most significant, the consideration of topics related to Hispanics/Latinos. Although the fifteen authors who challenge Gracia's views do not agree among themselves and vary in their perspectives and approaches, their responses indicate the extent to which all of them have participated in, and contributed to, these three developments. The fact that Gracia has brought together topics that before were rarely, if ever, discussed together and has facilitated through his publications the discussion of these topics by African, Hispanic/Latino, and Anglo-Americans has broken barriers in the profession. Indeed, every one of Gracia's books has played a significant role in the topics discussed here and the way philosophers have engaged them.

Gracia's influence has gone even further in that he has proposed novel views of race, ethnicity, and Hispanic/Latino identity that have transcended the parameters within which their treatment was confined. His most significant contribution is the Familial-Historical View of ethnicity and Hispanic/Latino identity. This position has made it possible to move beyond the essentialist/eliminativist binary that so frequently has dominated such discussions. It has helped to supersede the widespread view that general identities conflict and preclude more particular ones. It has provided a way to conceive race and ethnicity that keeps them conceptually separate but allows us to understand why they are frequently confused or mixed. It has created a way to fight the fears that some non-Hispanics/Latinos feel when they are confronted with Hispanic/Latino demographics and the prospect of losing their own identity as well as the fear that Hispanics/Latinos feel when they are confronted with the possibility of assimilation into American society. It serves in understanding the importance of linguistic Hispanic/Latino rights and the fact that they do not endanger the linguistic mainstream in the United States. And it justifies affirmative efforts to integrate the Hispanic/Latino population in the country.

Along with the Familial-Historical View, Gracia has also provided an understanding of how the Hispanic/Latino ethnos came to be and how its various racial and cultural components have shaped it. Gracia's general theory of how ethnic names are developed and function further supports his position, making clear how the language of ethnicity both impacts and reveals the way we think and act. The clear distinction Gracia establishes between race, ethnicity, and nationality does not just serve to understand these phenomena but also explains why they are misunderstood, resulting in all kinds of bad consequences, such as the discrimination and oppression of racial and ethnic groups.

Concerning the contested issue of the proper label to use for Hispanics/Latinos, Gracia goes beyond the standard position that chooses one over the other in order to understand that, as happens with all labels, context and aim are important for the choice. His view allows him to argue that in certain contexts 'Hispanic' is more appropriate, whereas in others it is 'Latino.'

Finally, with respect to the controversial topic of the identity of Latino/Hispanic American philosophy, Gracia proposes, first, that we adopt the general label 'Latino philosophy' and that through it we conceive it as ethnic, that is, as the philosophy of the Latino ethnos. In this way, he argues, we get away from the unproductive discussion of whether this philosophy is authentic or not, universal or not, or what its idiosyncratic properties are, topics that have dominated the discussion until today. As the philosophy of an ethnos, Latino philosophy should be conceived, as the ethnos, in familial-historical terms. This view also allows us to understand why certain works should be considered part of it and others should not.

All this reveals how far Gracia has moved the discussion of issues having to do with race, ethnicity, Hispanic/Latino identity, and Hispanic/Latino philosophy beyond the boundaries within which it was confined. He has offered an original and comprehensive theory that helps us sort through, and understand, the major topics that have been the subject of controversy.

NOTES

1. We still see this emphasis in the work of Lawrence Blum, J. L. A. García, Robert Gooding-Williams, and Howard McGary, among others.
2. Among pertinent authors are Robin O. Andreasen, K. Anthony Appiah, Daniel Blackburn, Joshua Glasgow, Sally Haslanger, Berel Lang, Ron Mallon, Charles Mills, Susana Nuccetelli, and Naomi Zack.
3. Among important books are Harris (1999), Bernasconi and Lott (2000), Bernasconi (2001a), Boxill (2001), Blum (2002), Corlett (2003), Appiah (2004), Gracia (2005b), and Stubblefield (2005).

PART I

RACE, ETHNICITY, NATIONALITY, AND PHILOSOPHY

1. WRITING A CHECK THAT

PHILOSOPHY CAN'T CASH

LUCIUS T. OUTLAW JR.

The real issue . . . is to find a political solution to the survival of humankind that takes into account the variety of ethnic and racial groups of which it is composed.

> Jorge J. E. Gracia, *Surviving Race, Ethnicity, and Nationality*

It was while absorbing this declaration, set out near the end of his *Surviving Race, Ethnicity, and Nationality* (2005b), that Jorge J. E. Gracia's agenda came together for me in a forceful way such that I appreciated, much more fully than I had before during my reading, his passionate concern with the task of working out a clarified *philosophical* understanding of race, ethnicity, and nationality. At issue for Gracia is the very survival of humankind in light of the long and bloody histories of conflict, domination, fratricide, and genocide motivated by valorized investments in notions of race, ethnicity, and nationality. In particular, what was so moving about Gracia's declaration was my realization of our agreement: that he, too—as am I—is convinced that these vexed notions, while we take full cognizance of the still more vexing invidious valorizing investments of various kinds in them that have been the motivations and rationalizations for oppression and bloodshed, are nonetheless important resource-concepts for shaping and guiding and enriching the formation and maintenance of human identity and sociality. I came to see, that is, that I have in Gracia an intellectual fellow traveler who, while carefully critical of these resource-notions, embraces race, ethnicity, and nationality.

I've known since I was a child that it's not wise to try to judge a book by its cover. This wisdom must be taken up and applied by us knowledge workers who labor on and through books: namely, that one shouldn't attempt to determine what's up with a book by its title. Now, it's not that I tried to do so—or not do completely, if truth be told. However, I did (as I suspect most of us do when approaching a new book) try to get some sense of what Gracia was up to from his title. But, I couldn't quite figure out from his title what he was offering. So, I began my reading without either the assistance or the prejudice of heuristic expectation. I was, though, a bit guarded just in case I encountered a strong argument in favor of discarding or moving "beyond" race, ethnicity, and nationality in order to enhance the prospects that humankind would, indeed, survive. Such an argument would have been a case against my position on raciality and races, hence my nervousness.

However, what I gained through my reading and consideration of this book by Gracia is the comfort of good intellectual companionship: a fellow traveler whose capabilities and contributions improve one's understandings and, thereby, one's capabilities for continuing the journey toward even more critical and cogent understandings that, if shared and taken up by significant others, will, hopefully, enhance living by providing the basis for recipes for praxes through which to make progress. And this, for Gracia, is the compelling need that must be met if we are to survive the vexing challenges involving race, ethnicity, and nationality: namely, that we *adapt through learning*—for the issues at hand by way of clarified notions that he offers of race, ethnicity, and nationality—so as to improve the prospects for survival. In other words, the need is to produce clarified understandings, then mediate the understandings to significant numbers of significant others who take them up as guides to praxis (though these mediations are matters that Gracia does not address) of the notions of race, ethnicity, and nationality given their centrality to the construction and living of the realities of individual and shared life in the ontologically foundational contexts of sociality that are meaningfully ordered and valorized around and through the species-specific, spatially and temporally conditioned, contingent groupings of races, ethnie, and nations.

I

Now, that there *are* such groupings seems a settled matter for Gracia. Problems arise when these groupings are misunderstood—or, perhaps better put, when investments in conceptualizations and valorizations of these social groupings are understood inadequately and then applied to social groupings that, thereby, are misconstrued. The consequences are misunderstandings and distorted and distorting valorizations that motivate and/or rationalize misguided or pernicious behaviors.

In *Surviving Race*, Gracia devotes his efforts to rescuing us from these misunderstandings and related practices by working out what he offers as clarified and coherent concepts of ethnicity, race, and nationality (chapters 3, 4, and 5, respectively) such that the concept of each is distinct in its own right and in relation to the other two. I will recapitulate his clarified formulations for each. First, ethnicity:

Ethnicity: ". . . the *relational property of belonging* that characterizes the members of an ethnos." (Gracia 2005b:54; emphasis added)

Ethnos: ". . . a subgroup of individual humans who satisfy the following conditions: (1) they belong to many generations; (2) they are organized as a family and break down into extended families; and (3) they are united through historical relations that produce features that, in context, serve (i) to identify the members of the group and (ii) to distinguish them from members of other groups." (54)

Gracia terms his formulation the Familial-Historical View of an ethnos: such a group is like a family in terms of the *relations* among the members; those relations are historically contingent, not fixed essences; and the group is not constituted by "features common to all the members"; rather, the features are "based on a series of changing relations that tie the members throughout history and generate features common to at least some members of the group in particular contexts. . . . The basic principle of the Familial-Historical View is that there is no necessarily identifiable feature, or set of features, that is shared by members of an ethnic group throughout its history" (49).

Now for race:

Raciality or *race*: ". . . the *relation of belonging* that characterizes members of a race." (Gracia 2005b:85; emphasis added)

A *race*: ". . . a subgroup of individual human beings who satisfy the following two conditions: (1) each member of the group is linked by descent to another member of the group, who is in turn also linked by descent to at least some third member of the group; and (2) each member of the group has one or more physical features that are (i) genetically

transmittable, (ii) generally associated with the group, and (iii) perspicuous." (85)

Of particular note here is the important factor that the relationality definitive of raciality is determined by descent: "Membership in a race can result
only from birth" (84). Still, on Gracia's view, races are *not* characterized by
features common to all members; rather, "there are features shared in certain circumstances." And while these definitive features are physical, and
"perspicuous," they are, nonetheless, matters of historical contingency, not
immutable essences bound by necessity. On what he terms this Common-
Bundle View, races, like ethnie, are like family groups: "They all share that
the members of these groups are individual human beings tied through
historical, contingent relations . . . , but they differ in the specific conditions
that apply to them" (88).

Finally, nationality and nation:

Nationality: ". . . the *relational property* of *belonging* to a nation that characterizes its members." (Gracia 2005b:130; emphasis added)

A *nation*: ". . . a subgroup of individual humans who satisfy the following conditions: they (1) reside in a territory, (2) are free and informed,
and (3) have *the common political will* to live under a system of laws that
(i) aims to ensure justice and the common good, regulating their organization, interrelations, and governance, and (ii) is not subordinated
to any other system of laws within the territory in question." (130; emphasis added)

On this "Political View," as Gracia characterizes it, the relations through
which nations are constituted, as for ethnie and races, are *not* bound by
necessity, thus are "neither necessarily permanent nor closed communities . . . are not trapped in their history" (129). Further, nations are distinct
from states, in his view, and should neither be ethnicized nor racialized,
though it is easy to conceive of conditions under which a nation could produce an ethnos or race, or a race or ethnos could become a nation, even a
state—but he recommends against these developments. Nations, as communities formed by *political will* and devoted to ensuring justice and the *common*
good, become distorted if co-opted by a particular race or ethnos; so, too,

states. Hence the many centuries of troubles in which such co-optations have occurred.

II

There is a great deal more work accomplished by Gracia in developing his concepts of ethnicity, race, and nation. For example, he takes care to set out and respond to other views and prominent objections that have to be answered if his view is to pass muster. In other words, he has not developed his views in isolation from other thinkers. Quite the contrary. He engages a substantial number of scholars, across a variety of fields or disciplines of discourse, in crafting his positions. The first chapter of the book is a rehearsal of arguments against grouping persons by race, ethnicity, and nationality. He sorts these arguments into "five main classes: epistemic, factual, moral, political, and pragmatic" and then discusses the "general formulations" of each class and concludes that none manages to thwart the persistence or render unintelligible the concepts of race, ethnicity, or nationality. Instead, the vexing challenges wrought by way of these heavily laden notions must be met and resolved by rehabilitating them. And for this crucial work, there is one enterprise, one discipline, and one alone, that is up to the task: "philosophy."

It is at this point in the book I have the urge to grab my fellow traveler's arm and urge him, in the vernacular language of certain " 'hoods": "Hold up, Dawg! Don't write checks with your mouth that your ass can't cash!" My concern is with Gracia's *grossly* inflated job description for what he refers to as "philosophy." To the question he poses "Where can we turn for a reasoned response to the issues raised by race, ethnicity, and nationality?" he offers the following:

One possibility is philosophy. Unlike other disciplines, which are narrower in scope and have developed specialized methodologies, philosophy aims to be comprehensive and lacks a single set of methodological norms. Philosophy tries to produce a comprehensive view that integrates all the knowledge we have, whereas other disciplines attempt to be less inclusive insofar as they are circumscribed by their methodological boundaries and limited subject matter. . . . Philosophy is essentially interdisciplinary . . . philosophy's history vouches for its breadth. Philosophy is comprehensive in a way no other discipline is . . . philosophy tries to integrate the conclusions of all these [psychology, sociology,

mathematics, physics, anatomy, botany, astronomy, literary criticism . . .
"and so on"] into an overall conceptual framework that makes sense, is
faithful to our experience, has support in sound arguments and evidence, and satisfies our various needs. . . . Finally, philosophy functions
as a critic of other disciplines, *imposing on them* the requirement that
they meet the most general criteria of understanding. This is a task resulting from both its comprehensive reach and the areas of inquiry that
are uniquely philosophical. By addressing issues that have to do with
the overall requirements of understanding and the very foundations of
knowledge, philosophy *stands guard over* other disciplines. And philosophy not only *sits in judgment over them*, but also relates their
claims and methods, seeking to integrate all we know into a coherent conceptual schema. (Gracia 2005b:xv–xvii; emphasis added)

Now, does Gracia *really* believe that he can cash this check drawn against the
account of philosophy? Isn't this a decidedly medieval and early-modern notion of philosophy as the "queen of the sciences," a decidedly antiquated
view that can't possibly be cashed out? In my humble opinion, there is no
viable referent for his notion of "philosophy" as some singular, unified disciplinary something, as suggested by his noun usage, that can fulfill the mis-
sion he set out in terms of integrating the knowledge of all other disciplines.
Was this not the wish of the Encyclopedists? Did they succeed? Better
put: Didn't they fail? And given the continuing intensive and expansive developments in knowledge production of the nineteenth and twentieth centuries, accelerating as we move along in the twenty-first century, what sense
does it make to speak of philosophy as the *one* discipline that can serve, will
serve, as the authoritative critic of and guide to knowledge production and
knowledge verification in all other disciplines while setting the criteria for
understanding them all, and while integrating the conclusions of all disciplines into a coherent and comprehensive understanding? And is there to be
one person, or some group of persons, who, as "philosophers," shall achieve
this near-godlike comprehensive, integrative, regulating understanding?

I say "No!" No person, no collection of persons, not the variegated, unco-
ordinated discipline of academic philosophy today, in the United States of
America and elsewhere, can cash this check. The breadth and depth of knowl-
edges are too great for mastery by one or even a few philosophical minds,
and for mastery by the discipline of academic philosophy. Furthermore, I beg
to differ with Gracia (2005b) on his claim that "philosophy's history vouches

for its breadth" (xvi). On my (limited) understanding, what has been produced and mediated by a great many academic philosophers, historians among them in particular, as "the History of Philosophy" or of "Western Philosophy" has been distorted by numerous omissions, distortions, and so forth. In this regard I'm disappointed that Gracia doesn't apply as strenuously to philosophy the same critical cast of understanding informed by historicity that he applies to notions of raciality, ethnicity, and nationality: namely, that they are all conditioned by circumstances of socialized times and places, as it were. So, too, what we professionals regard as academic philosophy: affected by blind spots, distorting prejudices of sexism and racism, invidious ethnocentrism, by ignorance combined with arrogance that virtually always results in instances of stupidity. Gracia does note, though, that "from the very beginning of philosophy until the present, there seems to have been a steady stream of philosophers whose views about race, ethnicity, and nationality can only be described in the most negative terms" (xix). Why else, as Gracia notes, have professional philosophers taken so long, been so reluctant, to attend to matters of racism especially, as well as to ethnicity and nationality, in ways that would contribute to reductions of the confusions and misunderstandings that have fueled the pain and bloodshed produced at their behest?

Gracia's highly inflated, near hyperbolic mischaracterization of whatever he intends to refer to by 'philosophy' is, I propose, *entirely* unnecessary for the good work that he takes up and attends to in very fine fashion in *Surviving Race*. He does not need these claims for philosophy as bona fides for his work. As a venture in conceptual clarification, it will stand or fall on the cogency and persuasiveness of his arguments, including the passionate call he makes on us all to be mindful that what is at stake is the survival and wellbeing of humankind. Philosophy will not save us. I do believe, though, with him, that our chances for survival are directly linked, to a significant degree, to our success in "getting our concepts clear," to paraphrase Peirce. And it is to this important work that Gracia's book is a notable contribution worth the attention of all concerned with working to resolve the challenges to our wellbeing, even our survival as a species, that have to do with our investments in race, ethnicity, and nationality.

As a contribution to that work, a challenge to my fellow traveler Jorge Gracia: Assuming that we get our concepts clarified, along the lines that he proposes in *Surviving Race* even, then what? How are we to have our clarified concepts become effective socially? How are we to "cash them out"? Gracia has all but declared that philosophy is our last resort, and to "it" falls the responsibility of clarifying our concepts and integrating all knowledge such that we "know" best how to survive, and why. I've made clear, I hope, my disagreement with this agenda for philosophy, though I do believe that important contributions can be made by persons involved in various forms of *philosophizing*—that is, thinking carefully and clearly about concepts and related practices. However, I do not believe such thinking—"philosophizing"—is done, and done well, *only* by those of us with formal training, degrees, and appointments in academic philosophy, though more than a few such persons, "philosophers," have and can make important contributions to the work. He is among them. Philosopher that he is, then, can he at least sketch out for us what is to follow from the work completed in *Surviving Race* in terms of how it is we might have our clarified understandings become more effective socially and thus beneficial to our survival?

III

I urge readers not to take my rejection of my colleague's check written on behalf of philosophy because of insufficient disciplinary resources as a rejection of his efforts regarding clarification of notions of raciality, ethnicity, and nationality. In reading *Surviving Race* I was treated to a stellar case of disciplined reasoning (except regarding philosophy) characteristic of the accomplished Scholastics: theses are stated clearly and defended; objections are stated with equal care and answered. In fact, Gracia characterizes his efforts as an endeavor in metaphysics. However, his efforts in metaphysics are decidedly not of the kind that seek to set forth the nature of "being qua being," or of governing transcendental realities, nor of the transcendental conditions of possibility of our concepts that determine their propriety. Rather, his efforts are devoted to developing clarified and coherent general concepts of important terms of ordinary language, concepts by which to understand social realities critical to our well-being. In this regard his position is straightforward: "The main thesis I defend is that race, ethnicity, and nationality are distinct and coherent concepts necessary in order to understand society" (Gracia 2005b:xxiv). And in defending his thesis by way of metaphysical analysis his aim has not been "to present definitions that include the complete set of necessary and sufficient conditions" of the terms but "merely to establish some parameters on the basis of which these [concepts] can be distinguished" and kept separate from one another (130). And this Gracia does particularly well and to the benefit of those who take the time to engage him in a close and careful reading of this book.

IV

It is in the close and careful reading that one encounters and comes to appreciate the devoted labors of a thinker; such reading is an important way by which to come to know, and know better, a person. This has been my unexpected pleasure on the occasion of reading *Surviving Race* in order to prepare and offer this commentary. I have gained much from the time and effort I invested and urge readers of this commentary who have a serious interest in the issues, and in serious philosophizing, to take up this work and give it the time and attention required to reap the benefits prompted by Gracia's challenge. For while we academic philosophers, as a group of disciplinary professionals, are neither a race, ethnos, or nation, we are willfully tied by collegial norms that, if honored, can produce mutual growth. We can model the sociality Gracia offers up for our consideration: that is, we can retain our senses of ourselves as engendered—and much more—persons of races, ethnie, and nations, as well as citizens of the United States of America or other nation-states, while enjoying coming together as embodied, encultured minds.

The stakes are high; the potential rewards stunning even to consider. Catch a glimpse through Gracia's (2005b) closing words in *Surviving Race*: "It is essential . . . that we understand them [race, ethnicity, and nationality] better. In order for humanity to meet this challenge effectively and survive, the notions of race, ethnicity, and nationality must also survive, but they must do so in conceptions that are appropriate to resolve the many problems that they pose and we need to address" (168).

I wish to hear more from my colleague and fellow traveler Gracia just why he is convinced these notions must survive, why they are crucial to our survival, thus why we must work harder to rehabilitate them with clarified understanding. I am already convinced but would benefit from having him make a fuller case. Meanwhile, I offer my very sincere thanks to Gracia for his concern for and contribution of efforts to the clarified understanding of the important and vexing concepts of race, ethnicity, and nationality, and by way of those clarified concepts, for his contributions to our survival.

2. MAPPING THE BOUNDARIES OF RACE, ETHNICITY, AND NATIONALITY

LINDA M. ALCOFF

Jorge J. E. Gracia's *Surviving Race, Ethnicity, and Nationality* (2005b) makes a major contribution to the debates over the meaning and political implications of race, ethnicity, and nationality. He strives to bring clarity and even precision to muddied concepts that are used inconsistently, and that are subject to a confused plethora of cross-disciplinary treatments. The book is helpfully detailed in its arguments and in its scholarly overview of the existing debates, though I found myself wishing that he had been at times more explicit about whom he is arguing against. Gracia suggests that part of the reason why there is so much muddleheadedness in the public discourse as well as the philosophical discourse about these forms of identity is because people are muddled in their methodological approaches to the question. Thus he helpfully distinguishes the epistemological questions (i.e., how we can know what a race is) from the metaphysical questions (i.e., what is it that a race really is), from the linguistic questions (i.e., what is the proper usage of the term 'race'), and then distinguishes further questions within each of these groupings.

Gracia's attempt to carve out a middle ground between essentialism and eliminativism on all three of these concepts is a laudable project, and the definitions that he develops for each term have a lot of merits. The book's title is a bit misleading, because it sounds as if he sees race, ethnicity, and nationality as, essentially (and I use that word purposefully), problems that human beings must find a way to contain or transcend. But this turns out not to be his view at all. Rather, he believes that many if not most of the problems, the political violence, enmity, and so on that are related to these forms of identity are actually based on confusions about what they truly are, such as ethnic conflict mistakenly taken as national conflict, or race taken as the sign of innate biological traits. Thus, he hopes, a slim work of metaphysics might make some positive difference.

Here is where I find myself disagreeing most with Gracia. He states that the main goal of this book is to address the metaphysical questions rather than the epistemological or linguistic questions that arise in regard to these concepts. And his aim is to base his metaphysical definitions on history and science, not ideology. This is laudable, but sometimes the way in which he characterizes this approach makes it sound pre-Quinean in its formulation of objectivity as the separation of fact from value and description from prescription, with an emphasis on intentional acts. Gracia seems to assume that philosophers can and should mandate the proper use of terms and concepts, invoking the imagery of Adam naming the animals in a virgin forest.

Gracia aims at ideational accounts of meaning, and he wants meaning stabilized across both physical contexts and temporal ones. But how can an ideational sense of meaning operate in a dynamic and polyvalent hermeneutic? That is, how can we stabilize meanings in a world where there exists an irreducible plurality of diverse contexts, where the diversity cannot all be translated into one minimalist conceptual language and where what the concepts are referring to is constantly changing, both in place and in time? Philosophers can play an important clarificatory role, without doubt, showing, for example, when reference is occurring with a term and when it is not. Yet I find it implausible to assume that what is being referred to across this diversity and complexity of contexts is the same thing. Such criticisms might well originate from methodological or metaphilosophical differences and thus constitute more of a disagreement than a faultfinding.

As stated earlier, this book offers an essentially metaphysical approach (and a particular form of metaphysical approach) to defining race, ethnicity, and nationality. One of Gracia's most important aims here is to carefully and clearly distinguish the three forms of identity from one another.

In regard to ethnicity, Gracia defends what he calls a Familial-Historical View, expanding on the idea that he developed in his previous book *Hispanic/ Latino Identity* (2000c), in which ethnic groups are understood to be formed through contingent historical relations in somewhat the same manner as families are formed through contingent relations. For ethnic groups, however, the relations are initially developed through a historical event or a set of historical events, such as the *encuentro*. Such events inaugurate a complex set of relationships—reproductive, cultural, economic, political, and otherwise— out of which begin to emerge shared features that then constitute the ethnic group. There is no one feature all members must share (except, presumably, their ethnic genealogical relation to the principal historical event). But because there is no shared feature in terms of behavior, belief, or appearance, Gracia counts his view as nonessentialist.

In regard to race, Gracia defends a Common-Bundle View, in which genetically heritable physical traits and open sets of perspicuous characteristics form races. All those persons who are of the same race must be linked by descent to some other member of the group, who themselves must be linked by descent to some third member of the group. Furthermore, and here is where race differs from ethnos, races must also have one or more inherited, visible physical feature that is associated with this group. By this definition, Gracia hopes to provide a rejoinder to eliminativists such as K. Anthony Appiah and Naomi Zack but without embroiling the concept of race in any specious biological claim.

In regard to nationality, Gracia defends what he calls a Political View, which understands nationality as the product of a group's will to live within a given territory under a shared set of laws. Nationality is voluntary in a way that neither race nor ethnicity are voluntary, and nations, unlike either racial or ethnic groups, have explicitly normative goals. Nations are constituted, Gracia believes, somewhat hopefully, or imaginatively, in order to ensure "justice and the good of all members."

Ultimately Gracia's account of all three forms of identity succeeds at his goal of marking out a middle position between eliminativism on the one hand and essentialism on the other. He rejects eliminativism (a position especially popular in regard to race), because it seriously undercuts our ability to describe the social world. I really appreciated Gracia's contributions to the effort to show that the problems with essentialism do not lead to eliminativism, and that there are coherent ways to define these three concepts without the problems that eliminativists think are indefeasible. His account allows for (and even explains) heterogeneity and the existence of ambiguous cases without losing its capacity to refer.

But Gracia is just as strong in his arguments against essentialism. In his view, ethnicity, race, and nationality are all socially constructed, though in different senses of social construction—nations are more volitional, race is dependent on the human meanings we attribute to physical characteristics, and ethnicity is dependent on human history. All are thus historically contingent, and none can be characterized as having any essence that confers uniformity or homogeneity across individual members of the group. Gracia aims to demonstrate that the politically attractive middle position between eliminativism and essentialism can be grounded in a rather hardheaded metaphysics achieved through an apolitical methodology. In this way, somewhat paradoxically, he hopes that the political advantages of his middle position—advantages that he details throughout the book—can be secured without a political argument.

Many of the participants in the current debates, especially over race and ethnicity, will find Gracia's account a welcome addition to the discussion, since it methodically lays out the issues of debate and develops plausible accounts that are far better than most of those definitions previously put forward. Though Gracia is a universal humanist and a rationalist and avowedly modern (as opposed to postmodern), he does not, like many other liberals, support a facile cosmopolitanism or assume that ethnic and racial and national identities will, or should, simply wither away. Ultimately, I understand Gracia to be arguing that if we take *history* seriously, then we must take the social categories of race and ethnicity seriously as well, and understand them as the somewhat organic outputs of macrohistorical forces that will only change and evolve and perhaps wither away as historical events unfold further. The caricatured "typical American view" that history is irrelevant, a caricature based on some measure of reality, is a view Gracia healthily rejects. Related to this, Gracia rejects the view that affective attachments or loyalties to one's race, ethnic group, or nationality do not constitute an inherent moral failing, as many modern rationalists would have it, that inevitably leads to violent conflicts. This refusal to see the conflict as an inherent result follows, I believe, from taking a nonessentialist view about what these identities are.

It is undoubtedly helpful to separate out the epistemic, metaphysical, and linguistic formulations of the questions about what race, ethnicity, and nationality are. It is helpful to distinguish them so that if someone argues that we should answer the metaphysical question via a linguistic approach, then, given Gracia's distinctions, they will need to defend the crossover of approaches rather than taking it as a priori legitimate (and in making such a requirement, obviously Gracia is taking on some pretty entrenched analytic dispositions). Against some of the postmoderns, I also share Gracia's view that we should not approach these matters as reductively strategic, that is, as if we can simply give a strategic argument about the best way to conceptualize race based on an antiracist goal. Gracia suggests, to read between the lines a bit, that we must give a plausible description of how these things operate in the social world and how they make up a part of human lives. The aim of description cannot be reduced to or conflated with a political intervention (again, this would disagree with some Continental dispositions). All of this is eminently plausible. Nonetheless, Gracia's sharp separation of fact and value in his portrayal of objective philosophical argument is too simplistic. Thus, although I largely have agreement with Gracia's substantive definitions, I disagree with his metaphilosophical characterization of these definitions. Gracia stresses the importance for philosophers to consider history, sociology, and anthropology in order to address the topics of this book, yet he still sets out the philosopher's role as master of the domain of meaning. This picture of philosopher-kings is in conflict, I would suggest, with the idea that philosophers are of the societies of which we analyze, within the political domains of meaning and interests rather than standing apart from them. We do have helpful tools of clarity and analysis, but these tools are wielded by human beings, limited in our ability to imaginatively and constructively use them by our own time, place, and personal identity.

Now let me turn to the specific definitions that he develops for each term, showing in each case how the metaphilosophical disagreements come up.

ETHNICITY

One of the virtues of the Familial-Historical View that Gracia develops for ethnicity is its emphasis on the *familial* itself. Members of an ethnic group have a complex, historical set of relations with one another, often manifested in shared language, religion, and other cultural practices but also in historical and geographical ties. The analogy with family suggests that there is no necessary shared agreement, political or otherwise, just as there generally is no uniformity of belief shared by all members of a family, and yet the relationality helps to explain the affective preference we often feel for, and our sense of obligation to, our ethnic compatriots. It can also explain why we feel more anger toward those we share an ethnicity with when they act stupid politically than we do with other bad political actors. It is painful to see one's group act oppressively or irresponsibly. Liberal cosmopolitanism can only explain such feelings as the product of false consciousness or inaccurate understandings of our truly universal moral connections to all human beings. The Familial-Historical View, by contrast, borrows from intuitions about family relations and puts them to use to explain these common experiences: the way in which compassion is naturally triggered by close material relations and physical similarity within families is transposed to ethnic groups. I consider this a materialist account, one that accepts the materiality of human existence without contempt or disdain.

However, Gracia portrays his definition of ethnicity—as forming through historical events that produce ongoing relations—as if it describes an entirely objective phenomenon. But how is it decided which historical relations are significant enough to determine the origin of an ethnic group? Assessments of comparative significance involve interpretative and qualitative judgments of history and political context, among other things, that generally presume a given location or perspective. For Jewish Spaniards, 1492 represents the point of their demise as Spaniards, not the start of a new identity. Privileging 1492 as the originary point is under dispute by scholars who wish to bring in the growing ideology of blood purity in Spain before this point, the colonization of the Canary Islands, and the persecution of Jews, all of which played a role in subsequent Spanish actions taken in the New World, the institutions they founded, and so on. In other words, the colonization and enslavement of the New World that began in 1492 was prefigured in race-based visions of empire begun much earlier. Gracia and I have already had a vigorous debate over the historical significance of 1492 versus 1898 on the formation of U.S. Latinos. So the question of historical points of origin is not politically neutral, or objective, in quite the sense Gracia seems to put forward. This does not make it an arbitrary question reducible to strategic considerations, but I believe we need a hermeneutic reflexivity to make visible the pragmatic projects and particular historical locatedness that contribute to articulations of historical points of origin. In other words, which historical point of origin we privilege will be connected in important ways to what we are trying to explain, such as affective relations among U.S. Latinos across national differences or the economic situation of Latin American countries today or the lived experience of Africans in the diaspora across the Americas. (For more on my debate with Gracia's account of the objective nature of ethnic names, see Alcoff 2005b, 2005c.)

A pragmatic approach would also foreground the fact that what has historical significance can change over time and across perspectives. Feminist historians have pointed out that the Renaissance was not a Renaissance for women, who lost their ability to belong to guilds, to operate as merchants, to have social standing of any sort, and were also being tortured and burned as witches throughout this period. The epochs by which history is marked always have a present-day relevance, in terms of which the divisions explain, resonate, or justify something or other. This means that the finality and stability Gracia seeks is just not possible. As Hilary Putnam (2002) puts it in his essay "The Entanglement of Fact and Value," "recognizing that our judgments claim objective validity and recognizing that they are shaped by a particular culture and by a particular problematic situation are not incompatible" (45). Within a given explanatory project and context, we can attain objectivity, but not finality.

Gracia further solidifies the familial aspect of his account by highlighting the importance of surnames as visible ties of relationality. I have some concern here that this will privilege paternity over maternity, this despite the common Latino practice of including both mother's and father's surnames for children. When the girl grows up and marries, only her father's name is included in the new hyphenated name, thus privileging the patriarchal line (and the difficulty North Americans often have in including two surnames often means that even that is dropped in favor of her husband's surname). On the one hand, we could argue that in male-dominant societies, the paternal line does have more social significance, so if we are aiming for an accurate description of identity, then our account must reflect this fact. On the other hand, we should be wary of reinforcing male dominance by supporting the normativity of paternal significance over maternal significance in a child's identity formation. This is an example of the way in which normative considerations must necessarily enter even in the endeavor to provide accurate descriptions. If Gracia's definition of Latinos privileges the paternal line over the maternal line, this has normative consequences that need to be reflected on, since such privileging is not clearly mandated by genealogical considerations.

Part of the way in which Gracia aims to distinguish race from ethnicity is with the criterion of descent: he takes descent to be necessary for race but superfluous for ethnicity. I remain unconvinced, however, that descent or genealogy plays as negligible a role as Gracia thinks it does. He argues against Angelo Corlett's (2003:chap. 3) genealogical account of Latino ethnicity, in which Latinos are defined as having been formed by genealogical ties to a geographical location. This is descent but does not carry the further stipulation that Gracia adds to race that there be some visible physical feature associated with that racial group. For ethnicity, Gracia holds that descent is neither necessary nor sufficient and that relations within an ethnic group can be entirely extrabiological. Corlett's account, however, has virtues that Gracia does not address, in particular in making it possible to account for a wide range of diversity within the group despite the fact that he includes descent (Alcoff 2005a). If Chinese immigrants to Peru have grandchildren that move to Los Angeles, those children can be ethnic Latinos by Corlett's account. I am not clear why Gracia rejects the idea of genealogical ties to a geographical location that has its own specific cultural/historical/political character as a feature of ethnicity. Such an account even allows that adopted children would be Latinos. So it seems to accord with Gracia's quest for an antiessentialist and contingent account.

RACE

This brings up the question of the relationship between ethnicity and race. Can we make these as clearly and rigidly distinct as both Gracia and Corlett want to make them? Race and ethnicity often mingle in ordinary language, both formal and informal, for example in the way in which 'African American' is an ethnic term with racial connotations, and the way that institutions like the Educational Testing Service report SAT scores by race as including Puerto Ricans and Mexicans (for more examples, see Alcoff 2006:chap. 10). For Gracia, this is just a sign of more muddled thinking, but I question whether philosophers can mandate clarity. If the use of ethnic terms invokes associations with racial concepts, at least in some cases, then we need to be aware of what connotations we are mobilizing in the given use of a term in public discourse. Philosophers cannot control unbidden connotations.

Contrast Gracia's account of race with Appiah's early account, for example. Appiah argued that the concept of race entails biological assumptions that do not obtain; therefore the concept is specious; therefore all who use it are at fault. Appiah's mistake was to assume that there is only one originary meaning of the concept of race, only one thing it might refer to. He did not take into account permutations that the concept has undergone, various meanings it has in different communities of discourse, or the very real possibility that its referent might change. Gracia insightfully criticizes Appiah's account for making the mistake of reducing the question of race to the question of science, as if science holds hegemony over the domain of meaning. Gracia also argues that one cannot get all that one needs out of the concept of ethnicity, as Appiah tries to do after he rejects the concept of race. What one cannot get are precisely the visible features of physical identity, the phenomenology of race, and thus Gracia proposes a distinct definition of race that can account for these phenomena. In other words, Gracia's approach, which I far prefer, takes *lived social* reality as the test for reference and tries to define concepts that will make sense of that reality. That is what Appiah did not do early on (he is now in his more recent work), but it suggests a very different methodological approach to the assignments of meaning, that is, an approach that would be so naive as to think that one rather small sphere of discourse—no matter what it is, biology, or even philosophy—might hold hegemony over all the ways in which language can be used and can impart meanings.

But note that if we adopt this different methodology, which I see Gracia doing against Appiah, then the merged realities of race and ethnicity cannot be so easily dismissed. Perhaps we do need a hybrid term, like ethnorace, to conceptually capture the specific meanings operating in regard to some specific cases. Such terms would respond to the pragmatic project of trying to make sense of how Puerto Ricans or Mexicans or African Americans are actually understood in broad public discourses today. Gracia might say here that they are understood wrongly! No doubt, but do we correct this with a set of concepts that are clear and distinct and irrelevant, or by correcting the factual and historical claims being made?

My point here is that if reference is what we are after, then ethnorace is a concept we need because it is a concept that refers, not just by a mistake but because of real historical relations that have been associated with visible features.

NATIONALITY

Finally, and briefly, let me turn to nationality, which Gracia defines as a voluntary association based on the rule of law and with the normative aim of ensuring justice and fairness for all its members. I would contest this representation of the normative aim. Which nation has ever aimed for justice for women? Nations aim for stability and security, protecting the interests of the elite, and just enough justice to keep revolutions from happening.

But I do share Gracia's goal of defending the idea of nations. He allows that they sometimes lead or contribute to war but argues that this result is not inherent to the form, and in this he is surely right. But in what sense is one's nationality voluntary, except for those who willfully immigrate, and willfully change their citizenship (a minority of immigrants). We don't control where we are born, nor where we grow up, and yet the place of our birth and of our childhood inevitably creates a powerful sense of familiarity and usually some affection for the place and its customs to which we are arbitrarily assigned by the laws of chance. These ties of familiarity and affection arise organically in an unchosen way yet have an impact on our way of being in the world, our way of inhabiting space, our sense of entitlements, and our set of initial beliefs. If this begins to sound like an ethnicity, it is intentional. I want to suggest that Gracia's aim of being purely descriptive and factual comes at odds with his hope for clarity and distinctness in our conceptual language. If we are to describe what it means to have a national identity, it shares a great deal with what it means to have an ethnic identity: Europeans can spot most North Americans a mile away by their attitude in comportment, their dress, before they open their mouths to speak the inevitable English. This also makes sense of the old joke about heaven and hell in Europe. Heaven in Europe would be where the cooks are French, the police are English, the engineers are German, the lovers are Italian, and everything is run by the Swiss. Hell in Europe, in contrast, would be where the cooks are English, the police are German, the engineers are French, the lovers are Swiss, and everything is run by the Italians. We find this joke funny because the nationality designations in it operate as ethnicities, with shared recognizable features. Thus, nationality and ethnicity are not distinct concepts.

So I would suggest that our concepts are, perhaps, not as muddled as they appear. They overlap because the designations, the experiences, and the institutions overlap. Gracia works hard against the overlap between ethnicity and nationality in particular because he thinks that ethnic conflicts would be more contained if carried out against a backdrop of shared nationality. Perhaps he is right, but that shared backdrop might better be understood as in some sense a shared way of being in the world, despite our obvious differences. For those of us in the United States, it means a shared background of some new hybrid national-ethnic identity that is becoming more Latino by the minute. All to the good.

3. RACE, ETHNICITY, AND PHILOSOPHY

K. ANTHONY APPIAH

I am not a big fan of attempts to define philosophy (or, as you will see, anything else at all interesting), but if you asked me for a definition, I would probably send you to something that Wilfred Sellars (1963) wrote in *Science, Perception and Reality* fifty years ago: "The aim of philosophy, abstractly formulated," he said, "is to understand how things in the broadest possible sense of the term hang together in the broadest possible sense of the term" (1). And if there is anyone I know who has had a career in philosophy and lives up to this definition, it is Jorge J. E. Gracia. He began his career with a dissertation on the fourteenth-century Catalan Franciscan friar Francesc Eiximenis, exploring the third volume of his great uncompleted encyclopedia of Christianity, *Lo Crestià*, which deals, in 1060 chapters, with the question of sin and evil. But that didn't stop him publishing work on Eiximenis's slightly older contemporary, Thomas Bradwardine (Gracia 1970), who was Archbishop of Canterbury for a little more than a month in 1349, a man who said thoughtful things about the liar paradox but also, as we learn from reading Gracia, about the theory of proportions, which turns out to be an early approach to the theory of exponential growth developed by Daniel Bernouilli and Leonard Euler. Then there's his first published paper on "Gonsalvus Hispanus's [ca. 1255–1313] Question XIII" (Gracia 1969) and a discussion of the convertibility of *unum*—that would be the One—and *ens*—that would be Being—in the work of the Catalan Carmelite Guido Terrena (ca. 1270–1342). That was his eighth published paper, by the way, and we are in 1973. Two years had not yet elapsed since he received his doctoral degree.

In the very same year Gracia branched out in a new direction, publishing a paper titled "Medio siglo de antropología filosófica en la América Latina," which I am going to guess is about half a century of philosophical anthropology in Latin America, an article that is undoubtedly *not* about medieval Franciscans and Carmelites in Catalonia. And he has since become one of our leading experts on the history and practice of philosophy in the southern part of this continent.

In between these earliest articles and the 246th article in his CV, not yet published, he wrote *Francis Suarez on Individuation*, a translation and commentary (Suárez 1982); *Introduction to the Problem of Individuation in the Early Middle Ages* (1984), for which the work on Suárez must have been useful preparation; and a 1988 book that addresses questions of individuality not as a historical question but as a central question of metaphysics. Not surprisingly, then, perhaps, in 1992, he published a major discussion of *Philosophy and Its History: Issues in Philosophical Historiography*. There are book-length works, among other things, on the logic and epistemology of textuality (Gracia 1995), on tradition (Gracia 2003), on philosophical theology (Gracia 2001a), on Hispanic/Latino identity (Gracia 2000c), and on *Painting Borges* (Gracia 2012). (Some of these works, by the way, are available in Serbo-Croatian and Chinese, and, of course, Spanish.) He has edited nearly a score of books on an incredible range of topics, too, written for art catalogues, and he has produced special editions of journals. I think you will see why one is driven to an encyclopedia in approaching his work—for most of us do not know even a little about many of the things he has written about and no one I know knows about all of them.

I confess I have not read all these works. But the ones that I have read, I should mention, are written with clarity and care and very often bring philosophical distinction—between metaphysics and epistemology and ethics, for example—and philosophical modes of argumentation usefully to bear in addressing questions that have often been addressed unphilosophically and with less care or clarity.

So I think we can fairly say that Gracia writes about "things in the broadest possible sense of the term," abstract and concrete, universal and particular. (Item 246 on the list of his articles, by the way, just to underline the point, is on "Immigrant Identity in Art." I don't think it's out yet.) And, to complete Sellars's thought, he has done a great deal to contribute to our understanding of how those things hang together.

You will excuse me therefore if I focus my remarks on Gracia's contribution to the philosophy of race and ethnicity, about which I know a little. I am extremely grateful for his work in this field, especially for its willingness to connect the philosophical literature on race with the literature on ethnicity and to throw nationality into what turns out, as a result, to be a very rich brew. I'm grateful, too, because he has paid me the greatest compliment one philosopher can pay another: he has taken the time, in print, to explain, in some detail, why my own views are wrong.

I will try to repay this great compliment, all too briefly, here; not by defending my own views but by offering some suggestions for developing his own. To do so fairly, though, requires giving you a sketch of the theoretical treatment of race and ethnicity that he developed in his book *Surviving Race, Ethnicity, and Nationality: A Challenge for the Twenty-First Century* (2005b). Now this is a subtle and detailed treatment and, as I say, I can offer you only a sketch, but I hope it will be enough to recommend the book itself to those of you who have not yet read it. Enough, too, to make clear my own criticisms of it.

The central idea of his treatment of race and ethnicity is one that, as he points out, has some affinities with a proposal made by W. E. B. Du Bois in the essay "The Conservation of Races," delivered to the newly formed American Negro Academy in 1897. Du Bois (1897) wrote, "What then is a race? It is a vast family of human beings, generally of common blood and language, always of common history, traditions and impulses, who are both voluntarily and involuntarily striving together for the accomplishment of certain more or less vividly conceived ideals of life" (75–76; 1970:73–85). I would add that we have reason to think that this idea was in circulation in Du Bois's milieu, since Alexander Crummell (1966), one of his few mentors, his predecessor as president of the academy, also wrote, in 1888, in a discussion of "the race problem in America": "Indeed, a race *is* a family" (184).

But Gracia's proposal is worked out more rigorously than this idea that Du Bois and Crummell shared. Here, then, is his own summary of what he calls the Familial-Historical View of ethnic groups:

> An ethnos is a subgroup of individual humans who satisfy the following conditions: (1) they belong to many generations; (2) they are organized as a family and break down into extended families; and (3) they are united through historical relations that produce features that, in context, serve (i) to identify the members of the group and (ii) to distinguish them from members of other groups. (Gracia 2005b:54)

Now as anyone who has studied philosophy knows, appreciating a thesis, such as this one, involves engaging with the arguments for it. And I don't have space to do much of that here.

There are obvious things to commend this view beyond the fact that the basic thought—that races are a kind of family—was proposed by the man who can lay some claim to having been the greatest theorist of race in the twentieth century. Both races and ethnic groups do follow a kind of family logic: all three standardly go, as we say, by descent. One thing that all three have in common, more precisely, is that which ethne or races or families you belong to is normally determined by who your parents are. Indeed, you might think that just as a nuclear family can be part of a wider extended family, so extended families can be part of ethnic groups.

On the other hand—and here I begin with some worries about the view— the logic of the extended family and the ethnos and the race do not run precisely in parallel. People standardly belong to a number of extended families, for example. (For anthropologists, I should say that I am aware that there are patrilineal and matrilineal and bilateral systems of kinship, so that how you think about family depends to some extent on where you come from. I know this in part because my father's family was matrilineal and my mother's patrilineal, which meant that their two families were ones that thought I didn't belong to them.) Whereas, while you can, in principle, belong to more than one race or more than one ethnic group, most people probably don't. Or, at least, when they do, it is often because the group is thought of as nested within a broader group: the Bantu race might be thought to be a subgroup of the Negro race; the Catalans might be thought to be a kind of Iberian. If you had a one-drop rule (whose historical reality I know has been questioned a good deal recently), you wouldn't expect there to be overlapping races: the distinction between black and white would be binary. Whereas the reason people belong to more than one family is that they belong to their mother's family and their father's family, their maternal-grandfather's family and their paternal-grandfather's family, and so on, and these groups are overlapping but not nested.

Furthermore, there is a pretty strong rule of descent in races and ethnic groups that says that if your parents belong to the same race or ethnos, you are of the same race or ethnos as they are (though I am not sure this rule always works in Brazil, where a race, or a *raça*, to be precise, seems to be much more phenotypic than here). One difference between races and ethnic groups, at least as conceived in North America, is that *parent* here covers adopted parents for ethnicity but often not for race. The contrast with families here is fairly strong: for the way in which new families begin is by the union of one family with another. Races and ethnic groups are often endogamous, they marry their own: families can't be, without running into the risk of incest. I do not therefore think I agree that ethne are "organized as a family."

So while I think the thought that the notion of ethnicity ought to connect with family is clearly right, I think the idea that an ethnic group is a kind of family has problems. I'm not sure that it's too hard to put it right, though. We need three steps. First we have to identify an ancestral group. Then we can define the current ethnic group as consisting of those who join the group by marriage or by being born to members of it or who are included by some form of assimilation or adoption, these being the main elements in the formation of families. (Call these the descendants.) We then need some way of identifying those descendants who leave the group. (Call these the defectors.) So there are three mechanisms that need to be understood in defining an ethnic group. It's initial formation, the addition of members by marriage and descent or adoption, and the loss of members. An account shaped in this way will maintain the thought that there is an important connection between ethnicity and families, because the addition of members in each generation occurs through the *very same mechanisms* that generate families.

I want to underline the requirement for some reference back to an ancestral population, whose initial formation cannot be explained by the mechanisms that account for its persistence through time, a fact that Gracia underlined in his discussion of the "historical origin and location" of ethnic groups but which is not explicit in the definition I just quoted. The theory does not require that anyone in the present should know much about the originating population, save that it must have existed. Look at a society at any time and you will be able to find the ethnic groups by way of the features mentioned under item (3) in the definition. The group in the next generation will consist of its descendants minus its defectors.

I think of this all as a friendly amendment to the first part of Gracia's Familial-Historical theory (though those of you who follow *Robert's Rules of Order* will know that they do not recognize friendly amendments). But the second part strikes me as, broadly speaking, fine as it is. Once you have identified the familial mechanisms through which membership in ethnic groups is transmitted through the generations, the members of the groups will be likely to develop features—accents, ways of dress, cuisines, religious convictions, tattoos, styles of beard, preferences for professions, or what you will—that will allow people of their own ethnicity and others in the society to identify them. That is how I read item (3) in his proposal. It seems to me right, if I have understood it right. I would only add to this that one reason why such differentiating features develop is that ethnicities within societies develop behaviors that are intended to maintain their boundaries, so that the differentiability of ethnic groups is not an anthropological accident but a response to facts of the social psychology of Self and Other (Barth 1969).

Now many people have suggested that races are just a specific kind of ethnic group, one in which the "features that, in context, serve . . . to identify the members of the group and to distinguish them from members of other groups" are heritable bodily features, features of the phenotype like skin color and hair type and the gross morphology of the skull. And others have suggested that there is a bundle of phenotypic characteristics such that possession of enough of them is necessary and sufficient to make one a member of the group. I will call this view disjunctive essentialism: the essence of a race, the condition that defines it, in this view, comes from a list of properties some or all of which you must have to be a member. (I would accept as a version of this view one that gives different weights to different things on the list, so that some features may be sufficient for membership on their own, though there need be no single feature that is necessary for membership.)

These views—disjunctive essentialism, on the one hand, and the view that races are ethnic groups whose differentiating features are discernible phenotypic characteristics—have often been seen as alternatives. And indeed they are, because disjunctive essentialism doesn't require that there be any specific relations of descent among members of the group and thus would probably count, say, Aboriginal Australians as Negroes, because they have dark skin and curly hair, even though they are probably closer cousins to some Chinese than to any Africans.

So disjunctive essentialism is not a historical view, since the way in which the features on the list were acquired by the members of the group plays no role in defining membership. I call this view disjunctive essentialism even though it fits Gracia's (2005b:66) definition of what he calls the Common-Bundle View, because he endorses the Common-Bundle View for races (86) while insisting as well, as we shall see, that membership in races is historical, which, as I say, in the disjunctive essentialist view it is not. So I don't think I can have correctly understood his view.

What I think I do understand is that Gracia's view of races seeks to accommodate the intuitions behind both these views. Here, then, is his proposal for defining race:

> A race is a subgroup of individual human beings who satisfy the following two conditions: (1) each member of the group is linked by descent to another member of the group, who is in turn also linked by descent to at least some third member of the group; and (2) each member of the group has one or more physical features that are (i) genetically transmitted, (ii) generally associated with the group, and (iii) perspicuous. (Gracia 2005b:85)

Now item (1) here serves the function of making a race a group defined by descent and thus like a family, whereas that is achieved in the definition of an ethnos in a slightly different way, as we have seen. This way of connecting race and descent is meant, as Gracia makes clear, to exclude the idea that Aborigines belong to the Negro race. I don't see that it does that. Every Aborigine is presumably linked by descent to another Aborigine who is linked by descent to a third. And every non-Aboriginal Negro is, ex hypothesi, linked by descent to another non-Aboriginal Negro who is linked by descent to a third. Create a set consisting of all Negroes and all Aborigines. Call this the group. Then every member of the group meets the first condition that Gracia offers. But they also all meet the second condition. So it follows that they are one race.

Now, so far as I can see, Gracia can avoid this problem by simply accepting as a substitute for his (1) the account of the connection between ethnos and family that I suggested as a friendly amendment earlier. But that amounts to accepting the proposal that a race is a kind of ethnic group where the defining features are easily detectable heritable physical characteristics on a list defined by what is widely associated with the group in the society. (The latter idea, captured in his clause [ii], makes race socially constructed, since it makes essential reference to the beliefs of a social group. This seems to me a virtue of the account.) Since Gracia clearly believes it's important to distinguish race and ethnicity, I suspect he may reject this suggestion. I am interested to hear what he has to say about it.

I myself think that clause (2) here means that something like the Common-Bundle View will be true of races, as he argues. But, unlike him, I think this is a disadvantage of the view. For the conception of race in our country allows that persons may be "passing" for white, because they are members of a family with African American members while failing to have any or, at any rate, enough of the visible heritable characteristics associated with the black common bundle. Now Gracia expressed skepticism about the idea of passing, so he is consistent on this. But if we are engaged in descriptive metaphysics, that is, trying to understand the conception of the nature of race that we currently have, and if 'we' means most people in the United States, I think it is descriptively inadequate in ruling this out.

On the other hand—and this will be my final observation—I think, as I said at the start, that most interesting concepts are not susceptible of a simple and illuminating definition to which one cannot provide counterexamples. (I offer in evidence the history of attempts to define "knowledge" in epistemology.) What a philosophical proposal like the two proposals of Gracia's I have considered can do is provide an illuminating model, a schematic simplification of the way a concept works, one that helps us to think about possible problems in the way we mobilize it. Such a proposal is never descriptive metaphysics, I want to suggest, it is always revisionary. And his proposals are guided by a humane intelligence and reveal some of the difficulties with the way we ordinarily think about race and ethnicity. They do, in other words, the only job I suspect a philosophical definition can do.

4. RACE, ETHNICITY, NATIONALITY, AND PHILOSOPHY

LAWRENCE BLUM

Jorge J. E. Gracia develops his metaphysical accounts of race and ethnicity (i.e., accounts of racial and ethnic membership) against a background in which both notions have been challenged on several distinct grounds—conceptual, metaphysical, epistemic, moral, and political. He takes up these challenges systematically and argues that race and ethnicity are coherent and consistent concepts that apply to the world and reveal features of the world that would be invisible without these concepts. The accounts are meant to "be descriptive in that they reflect the most fundamental principles that underlie the ways in which we think about race, ethnicity, and nationality because these ways are based on a common, collective experience of the way the world is" (Gracia 2005b:37). His book *Surviving Race, Ethnicity, and Nationality* (2005b) is the main locus of this philosophical account, but his earlier work *Hispanic/Latino Identity* (2000c) is relevant as well.

Gracia (2005b) notes that philosophers have only recently come to pay attention to these notions, especially ethnicity, and he suggests that a philosophical approach is superior to that of the disciplines most commonly associated with them (e.g., sociology) in aspiring to "put together as complete a picture of the world as possible" and thus necessarily being interdisciplinary and so lacking "a specific methodology" (xvi). But Gracia's philosophical approach to race and ethnicity does draw on his background in metaphysics, philosophy of language, and history of philosophy, as well as involving great care in constructing arguments for the claims he makes and in seriously addressing important challenges to his views.

Gracia is particularly concerned to distinguish between race and ethnicity and thinks they are often confused with each other, with deleterious con-

ceptual and moral consequences, such as confusing cultural and genetic characteristics and not recognizing that ethnic groups can change over time. At
the same time, once he has clarified the conceptual distinction, he believes
that race and ethnicity can overlap, both in the sense that the same group, or
portions of the same group, can be both racial and ethnic (as are African
Americans), and that race can itself be one marker of ethnicity for particular ethnic groups at particular historical periods.

Gracia also regards certain general but false views of both race and ethnicity as obstructing the possibility of a coherent account of them. One is
what he calls essentialism—the assumption that all the individual members
of a racial or ethnic group possess *individual* properties (such as psychological
characteristics of temperament and character, or the sort of characteristic
J. Angelo Corlett [2003] adverts to in his account, such as speaking a particular language) that are necessary and sufficient for membership in that
group. But, Gracia argues, members of a given ethnic group do not share such
features with all other comembers. Gracia argues, however, that certain *relational* properties characterize both race and ethnicity (different ones for
each), so that he is proposing what he takes to be a nonessentialist account
of race and ethnicity.

A second false assumption is that races and ethnicities have clear boundaries so that it is always clear whether a given individual is or is not a member of the race or ethnicity in question. Gracia points out that many of our
most important human concepts do not have clear boundaries in that sense;
for example, it is often not clear if someone should be thought of as "dead"
or "healthy." We should be able to accept the same indeterminacy with
respect to both race and ethnicity.

The third assumption is that racial and ethnic groups are internally
homogeneous. This assumption leads to inappropriate and harmful stereo-
typing of such groups and has led some to reject the possibility of a coherent
and socially useful account of race and ethnicity entirely. Gracia's accounts of
both concepts explain why neither racial nor ethnic groups are generally internally homogeneous in this sense.

ETHNICITY

Gracia calls his account of ethnicity the Familial-Historical View. He gives
much more attention to the familial than the historical aspect. But by the
latter he appears to mean that an ethnic group is a group that exists over
time, and that it has a history and a changing membership over time as some

members die and others are incorporated through birth and other ways (that will be discussed later). Members of the same ethnic group stand in "historical relationships" to one another.

Hispanics/Latinos, the group to which Gracia devotes most of this attention, began to exist as a result of the encounter of the Iberians and the indigenous peoples of the Americas and, slightly later, African slaves, beginning in 1492. Prior to this point there were no "Hispanics," only groups that came to be Hispanic subsequent to 1492, such as Castilians and Aztecs (not that they necessarily or typically lost these prior identities).

One meaning of 'historical' that Gracia definitively rejects is that descent or ancestry is a necessary feature of ethnic membership. He rejects descent because, in his view, people who have no descent relationship to other Hispanics can come to be Hispanic; for example, if they are Welsh immigrants to Argentina, and then their offspring migrate to the United States, the latter are Hispanic, though none of their ancestors are (in his view). He rejects descent as sufficient because someone definitively descended from Hispanics but "who has not lived in a Latino country, has not associated with other Latinos, and does not share with them any perceptible traits" is not Latino (Gracia 2005b:41). This view contrasts with that of Corlett (2003), who would employ such facts as indicating "degree of Latinoness" but not membership itself.

So Corlett's and Gracia's ethnic groups have different membership, not merely different accounts of the same membership. For Latinos, Corlett accepts anyone descended from certain Latin Americans, but Gracia excludes those of this group who have given up their cultural or identity ties to Latin America. But Gracia includes any Latin American national, or at least her descendants, while Corlett excludes some of them, for example "pure" descendants of more recent European immigrants (and descendants of Asians as well). Corlett's criterion has the effect of excluding a fair number of Latin Americans and their descendants since parts of Latin America are major immigration ports for Europeans and Asians. But Corlett's account makes sense (at least with respect to Europeans) in terms of his focus on Latinos as a victimized or discriminated-against group in the United States, since it is plausible to think that the people of Latin American origin who are perceived to be "European" are less likely to be discriminated against as Latin Americans than those not so perceived.

FAMILY AND ETHNICITY

Gracia gives a good deal of attention to the "familial" dimension of ethnicity, which he draws from W. E. B. Du Bois (1897), who predicated it of races, although at that time Du Bois thought of races as possessing what we would think of as ethnic characteristics. The idea of "family" is put to several distinct, if related, uses by Gracia that he does not clearly distinguish. One is to invoke Wittgenstein's notion of "family resemblance" to say how different persons can be members of the same ethnic group (like the same family) without sharing a common property, but different ones sharing different properties. A second is to illustrate the idea that ethnic membership can come about through more than one relationship. That is, membership in families can come through a diverse set of relationships—marriage, birth, adoption. Similarly, Gracia wants to say, membership in ethnic groups comes about through differing sorts of relationship. There is no one relationship that constitutes ethnicity, as there is no one relationship that constitutes family.

Gracia never attempts to spell out in a systematic way what those ethnicity-making relationships are. Some of them are (some of) the same ones as familial relationships, and this is the third use of 'family' in relation to ethnicity. That is, Gracia thinks that birth is one way of acquiring ethnicity, as is adoption. Some would question, however, whether a Vietnamese adoptee of a Russian American couple becomes "ethnically Russian" by being brought up in a Russian American cultural environment, as Gracia's view asserts, although perhaps fewer would deny that she is "culturally Russian (American)."

Gracia (2005b) believes that he has a principled reason for not spelling out the relationships that constitute ethnicity—namely, that they can be spelled out only for particular ethnicities in particular historical contexts: "Practically any feature can count toward uniting an ethnos, including racial and national ones" (55). For example, Gracia says, in a particular region, say of the United States, Mexican Americans may be the only Catholics and also the only people with a certain skin color and so could be distinguished by those features (64). But without giving us some idea of the relationships that constitute ethnicity, we have no basis for differentiating empirical *correlates* with ethnicity in a particular context from characteristics that actually *constitute* ethnicity in that context. Suppose, for example, Mexican Americans in a particular city are confined to one particular neighborhood, so that residing in that neighborhood becomes a way to pick out Mexican Americans in that context. This would not make "residing in X neighborhood" a feature of Mexican American ethnicity. Gracia's stated view provides no basis for seeing the Spanish language but not residential patterns as internally related to Mexican ethnicity (as Corlett [2003] holds), although neither one is actually *required* for ethnic membership (a Mexican American need not speak Spanish), and both allow us to pick out particular groups in certain particular contexts.

Returning to the issue of "family" in his account, Gracia wants family to be more than an analogy to ethnicity. He says that ethne are themselves a *kind* of family, and this is a different use than the two so far mentioned. But what kind of family? Gracia (2005b) gives this summary of his position:

> An ethnos is a subgroup of individual humans who satisfy the following conditions: (1) they belong to many generations; (2) they are organized as a family and break down into extended families; and (3) they are united through historical relations that produce features that, in context, serve (i) to identify the members of the group and (ii) to distinguish them from members of other groups. (54)

The idea that ethnicities are made up of extended families is questionable; people who marry a member of an ethnic group are not generally thought of as becoming members themselves, even if they embrace its ethnoculture. Moreover, most ethnic groups are large and range over a wide, often dispersed, geographic area and are not "organized" in any overall sense at all, though there may be ethnicity-based organizations. An ethnic group is not really like an actual family, no matter how extended.

ETHNICITY, NATIONALITY, AND SUBNATIONALITY

Gracia regards it as arbitrary to confine ethnic membership to national borders. Indians in the United Kingdom have historical relationships to Indians in India, so why confine Indian ethnicity to groups that are a minority in a non-Indian nation, and Polish ethnicity to Poles not in Poland? And his account of Hispanic/Latino ethnicity embraces Salvadorans in El Salvador as well as in the United States.

Gracia uses the expressions 'Hispanic,' 'Latino,' and, more rarely, 'Hispanic/Latino' but says in a footnote that he prefers 'Hispanic' because he regards it, as do many but not all commentators on this terminological issue, as being more inclusive in including residents of the Iberian Peninsula as well as Latin Americans (and their descendants). But it is not clear why inclusiveness is a virtue in this context. Others (e.g., Corlett) favor 'Latino' precisely on the grounds that it captures the European colonial status that unites Latin America and distinguishes it from the colonial powers. The fact that one term includes more people than another does not clinch the issue as to whether it is preferable to the less-inclusive term.

Gracia's open-ended and expansive conception of ethnicity does not comport with one aspect of his rationale for his accounts of ethnicity and race, namely that the concepts of ethnicity and race are meant to help us to see aspects of reality that we would not see were we not in possession of these concepts. This point is a useful antidote to a profligate "social constructionism" that Gracia rightly rejects; ethnic groups might be historical accidents and human constructs that might even disappear, but they are nevertheless real features of our social world, real human groups that are meaningful to people in and outside of them, and that affect social well-being in various ways. But in light of this, the usual notion of ethnicity that distinguishes between Mexican Americans and Mexicans, with the latter being a *national* and the former an *ethnic* group, is pointing to precisely this feature of our social world. Being an ethnocultural subnational group (i.e., what Gracia recognizes is ordinarily meant by an "ethnic group") is a distinct and significant social location; it is not the same as the national identity from which the original immigrant group arose, even if there are cultural connections between the two. Gracia himself provides a striking example of this very point in *Hispanic/Latino Identity* (2000c). A Mexican author is speaking to a group of Mexican Americans and making clear to them the difference between being Mexican and being Mexican American, when the audience was hoping she would connect them more closely. In this sense, ethnicity understood as an ethnocultural minority is something quite different from nationality, even when the latter is understood culturally rather than politically. This familiar (in the United States at least) view of ethnicity, in contrast to Gracia's, seems to satisfy Gracia's (2005b) overarching criterion of adequacy for a view of ethnicity, that it "reflect the most fundamental principles that underlie the ways in which we think about . . . ethnicity, and nationality" (37).

GENETIC COMMON-BUNDLE VIEW OF RACE

Gracia also sees races as a type of family. He recognizes the scientific challenge to the idea of race that many philosophers, including Corlett (2003), have also accepted as showing that there are no races. Gracia gives special attention to K. Anthony Appiah's (1996) attempt to retain a notion of racial identity while jettisoning the notion of race, and Gracia rightly sees this as a confused and unacceptable view. But Gracia also thinks, in contrast to Corlett, that a coherent and scientifically respectable view of race can be resurrected that abandons the implication of large genetic differences between "races" implied in the discredited scientific view.

Gracia's account of race has two necessary conditions for membership. The first is descent; each member of a race is linked by descent to another member of the group, who is in turn also linked by descent to at least some third member of the group. The second is phenotype; each member of the group has one or more physical features that are (1) genetically transmittable, (2) generally associated with the group, and (3) manifest to the senses (what Gracia calls perspicuous).

Gracia's phenotypic condition is characterized as "the Common-Bundle View," that there exists a bundle of phenotypic characteristics, the possession of some of which render someone a member of the race in question. For blacks, for example, it involves a certain skin shade, hair texture, facial features, and so on.

The descent condition for race is meant to contrast with Gracia's rejection of that condition for ethnicity. It may seem that Gracia is not vulnerable to the circularity problem regarding race of which he accuses Corlett regarding ethnicity, since the phenotypic criterion can provide a nondescent condition to save descent from circularity or infinite regress. But this will not work, since, for example, some Australian Aborigines have the same phenotypic characteristics as blacks but are not generally regarded as being of the same race as they. Gracia may ultimately have to rely on a continental origin criterion to replace or at least supplement the phenotype one—Africa for blacks, Australia for (Australian) Aborigines, Europe for whites—to allow the descent dimension to do the work he wants it to.

Gracia treats his phenotypic and descent criteria as equally operative, thus explicitly rejecting the prioritizing of ancestry over phenotype that characterizes the U.S. view of race, captured in the notion of the "one-drop rule"—that is, that any degree of African ancestry renders someone black, independent of phenotype. Gracia rejects this rule because he sees it as inconsistent; it cannot be applied equally to all races. It is inherently asymmetrical; black ancestry trumps white, but not vice versa. In Gracia's view, no ancestry is privileged over any other; the degree of ancestry generates a comparable degree of membership in the given race, independently of the phenotype condition. But if a person with half-African and half-European ancestry looks like what most people take to be white, in Gracia's view he is white because of the phenotypic criterion.

Gracia describes a view of race, or at least of phenotype and ancestry, common in Latin America that contrasts with that in the United States; in the former, there are many terms describing varying combinations and degrees of mixture (of both phenotype and ancestry), such as mestizo and mulatto. All parts of the phenotypic and ancestral heritage are recognized in this terminology. This Latin American view is much closer to Gracia's own conception of race than is the U.S. view, for it jettisons the one-drop rule and is symmetrical across races. However, it is not quite the same as Gracia's, since his retains a small number of racial group terms; racially mixed persons are not seen as falling in a classificatory group of those with that particular racial mixture (as in the Latin American conception) but rather as falling within multiple but a small number of standard racial groups corresponding to the distinct elements of their mixture.

There is an inconsistency between Gracia's account of race and what we saw that he wants his accounts of race and ethnicity to do, namely track the sociohistorical, experiential reality of race. He imposes a purely intellectual requirement of symmetry across races, which is independent of the shared historical experience of race. But in the United States race was, historically and experientially, never a symmetrical concept. Its purpose was to validate the superiority of whites and the inferiority of all other races. This asymmetry is part of the meaning of race in the United States. The one-drop rule reflects how U.S. Americans understood both the concept and the social reality of race. The rule had an intelligible, if complex, rationale, viewed historically. First, by declaring the offspring of slave masters and slave women "black," these offspring were deprived of a claim to the superior status of whites, or at least nonblacks. The rule increased the number of slaves and facilitated slave masters' not acknowledging their liaisons with slave women. The rule also helped to preserve, in the eyes of whites, a social correlate for the view of race that Gracia recognizes as under attack by recent scientific developments, that of a permanent and unalterable biological subdivision of the human species. And after Emancipation in 1865, the one-drop rule also had certain advantages for blacks and was explicitly discussed and contested within the black community. It prevented divisiveness between mixed and unmixed blacks (that there could not in reality be a clear phenotypic distinction between these two groups only supports this point); made it more difficult for whites to use mixed blacks as an intermediate group to discipline blacks; and forged ties of solidarity based on the experience of discrimination shared (even if to different extents) by mixed and unmixed blacks. Abandoning the one-drop feature of the U.S. idea of race means abandoning something Gracia says he seeks—to reveal aspects of reality that would be hidden were we to lose or abandon those concepts and to capture the principles underlying the way (non-Latino/a) Americans think about race.

5. RACE, ETHNICITY, NATIONALITY, AND PHILOSOPHY

a response

JORGE J. E. GRACIA

The issues raised in part I of this volume have for some time been a central concern of those interested in philosophical discussions of race and ethnicity. At the outset, the question that looms large is the role that philosophy can play in these discussions. Some philosophers question this role, whereas others find it essential to their understanding. Given the significance of race and ethnicity in the contemporary world, it is not surprising that they have been the subject of discussion in most disciplines. The social sciences have taken a leading role in the investigation of their social dimensions. The natural sciences, such as biology, have not been left behind, to the extent that race in particular has often been claimed to be a biological reality. History has explored the historical trajectories of these phenomena. And literature and art have presented engaging portraits of them and their impact in human lives. But what can philosophy add to the conclusions reached in these disciplines? Does not the abstract nature of philosophy, and its often touted irrelevance, stand in the way of any significant contribution to the elucidation of these, evidently practical, topics?

The question becomes particularly poignant because, in *Surviving Race, Ethnicity, and Nationality* (2005b), I have claimed that philosophy's role not only contributes substantially to the understanding of race and ethnicity but also is in many ways essential to it. Am I right? Is philosophy's role indispensable for an understanding of race and ethnicity? And if so, what is it that philosophy provides that other disciplines do not, and what are the assumptions that govern the discussion?

A second question that looms large in contemporary philosophical treatments of race and ethnicity is the very understanding of these phenomena. What is race? What is ethnicity? And what are the boundaries between them and between them on one side and other closely related phenomena, such as nationality, on the other? Answers to these questions seem fundamental to resolve difficulties that surface concerning racism, ethnic prejudice, nationalism, and various forms of discrimination and social oppression that are critical in contemporary society. Race has been frequently understood ethnically or even as a kind of nationality, whereas ethnicity and nationality have been understood in terms of race and each other. Efforts have been undertaken to eliminate one or more of these notions from our thought and the corresponding terms from our vocabulary, whereas the contrary claims have also been put forth. The answers I have proposed serve to prompt those participating in this project both to criticize those parts of my views with which they disagree and to explore what they consider to be the correct answers and approaches to them.

I am reassured that the philosophers included in this part of the volume—Lucius T. Outlaw Jr., Linda M. Alcoff, K. Anthony Appiah, and Lawrence Blum—found much to agree with in my views on the role of philosophy in the understanding of race and ethnicity as well as a proper conception of these and related notions. However, the purpose of this exchange is not to call attention to agreements but, rather, to think about the topics at hand and see whether we can advance the discussion in the context of their questions. Hence, my response will concentrate on working through some of the issues that the commentators bring up, although in some cases it will point out misunderstandings and ways in which I can support my views against the criticisms expressed.

I begin with the question, raised by Alcoff, concerning the objectivity of philosophical theories in general and how that affects the notions of race and ethnicity, as well as the related notion of nationality. Next I turn to the challenge, voiced by Outlaw, that philosophy is limited and cannot carry out a constructive task that goes beyond that of other disciplines of learning. From this I move briefly to the question of whether a metaphysics of race and ethnicity in particular is a descriptive or prescriptive enterprise, a matter briefly raised by Appiah and developed by Blum as a criticism of inconsistency of my theory. Finally, I turn to the consideration of an effective set of conditions for race, ethnicity, and nationality, explored by Appiah and Blum.

OBJECTIVITY OF PHILOSOPHICAL THEORIES

The issues raised by Alcoff can be divided into two kinds: first, the metaphilosophical issues that she is right to bring up because of both their importance and currency as bones of contention among philosophers, and second, various criticisms having to do with particular claims I make in *Surviving Race*. The metaphilosophical issues concern the objectivity that can be achieved in a philosophical theory of race, ethnicity, and nationality. In Alcoff's view, I go astray in that I assume a sharp distinction between fact and value and the possibility of philosophers functioning independently from society and politics. But is she right or wrong in this criticism?

Before this question can be effectively answered, we need to make a distinction between the following three questions. First, whether a philosopher can achieve objectivity in philosophical theorizing, be it in general or in the particular context of social issues that have to do with race, ethnicity, and nationality. Second, whether I claim that a philosopher is capable of achieving such objectivity. And third, whether I claim that I have achieved such objectivity in *Surviving Race*.

The first point has been discussed by philosophers from the very beginning of the discipline and the disagreements among them are notorious. Just consider Plato and Gorgias. This issue is at the heart of philosophy and it is so far unresolved. I do not think I can resolve it here, but nonetheless I will have something to say about it presently that I hope will suffice to assuage Alcoff's discomfort concerning my approach. The other two points are historical. One concerns the question: Does what I say in the book entail that I believe philosophers can achieve objectivity? The other, although also historical, is more parochial, having to do with whether I hold that I, in particular, have achieved the kind of objectivity in my theory for which Alcoff claims I seem to be searching.

Obviously the question concerned with the possibility of achieving philosophical objectivity is the most interesting of the three mentioned from a general philosophical standpoint. The other two are of interest primarily historically and for an understanding of my views. I think I can show with textual references that I have not made claims to support the criticism that I hold either that philosophers in general can achieve the kind of objectivity Alcoff questions or that I in particular have done so. Although *Surviving Race* is not about this metaphilosophical topic, I tried to make clear throughout, and particularly in the concluding chapter, that, as I repeat in the closing thoughts with which this book ends, philosophy is an unfinished business. It is unfinished for a variety of reasons. A claim to finality in any sense, complete objectivity if you will, is really incompatible with the views I have presented. Still, Alcoff may be right to the extent that I may not have made this point as clear as I should have, or that perhaps in certain parts of the book I give the impression that I hold the contrary. Rather than quote chapter and verse, however, let me address the first, more general question to open a space for further discussion.

Is complete objectivity possible in philosophical discussions, can fact and value be separated in philosophy? Given the history of this issue and what appears to be an unresolvable state of affairs, perhaps the best way to approach it is to change the question. In my experience, what appear to be unresolvable philosophical problems are often the result of attempts to answer questions that are too complex or even muddled—in this I agree with much that mainstream analytic philosophy has claimed in the twentieth century. So, rather than asking whether fact and value can be separated, or whether objectivity can be achieved independently of any subjective factors, I would like to think instead about the genesis and function of philosophical theories and the criteria philosophers use to determine their value. How do philosophical theories get formulated, what do philosophers who formulate them aim to do with them, and how do philosophers judge whether they have a good or a bad theory? Then I would like also to ask about how I think philosophical theories *should* be generated, the aim that they *should* have, and the criteria that *should* be used to judge their value.

The question of how philosophical theories are generated, the aims that philosophers have when they formulate them, and how philosophers judge whether they are good or bad is again a historical enterprise, and one that yields many different results because philosophers strongly disagree on these matters, both in theory and in practice. A brief excursion into the history of philosophy should convince anyone of the truth of this claim. For this reason, I do not find it profitable for us to engage this matter here. I would rather tell you something about what I think *should* be the case. So, first, how should philosophical theories get formulated; second, what do I think their aim should be? And third, on what bases should the value of philosophical theories be judged? And let's keep in mind that, although these are metaphilosophical questions, the context is the philosophy of race, ethnicity, and nationality.

Let's begin with the first: How do I think a philosophical theory should be generated? First let me tell you the wrong way to begin. I think most modern philosophy is wrong about philosophy's point of departure, and this goes for Descartes, Locke, Hume, Husserl, and many others. Descartes was wrong in thinking that one ought to begin with a methodological doubt arising in a kind of introspective process. Locke was wrong in thinking that one ought to begin with a blank slate of narrowly empirical experiences. Hume was wrong in thinking that we must begin from an atomistic analysis of our perceptions and sensations. And Husserl was wrong in thinking that we should begin by bracketing our fundamental ontological commitments and intuitions. In opposition to these views, I believe that Aristotle was right in that he identified the point of departure of our philosophical theories as our experience broadly understood, and this should be taken to include our most ordinary beliefs.

We are persons in context and it is we who begin to philosophize, and we philosophize from our point of view, which is pregnant with beliefs, some true and some false, and most rather unclear. When I begin to think philosophically, I do so as who I am and where I am, or as José Ortega y Gasset was fond of putting it, "myself and my circumstances." How else and where else could I begin? To think that I could start this process in any other way would be a delusion. In my case I begin as a Hispanic/Latino, with three nationalities, a particular racial mix, and a bag full of past experiences, beliefs, and prejudices. Can I abandon this context? Can I ignore it? Of course not. My perspective, the experiences that have given it shape, and the beliefs I have formed as a result constitute the raw data from which I must begin to philosophize if I want to move forward. I cannot start to think from a blank slate because there is no such thing. And I believe that in this Alcoff and I are not far apart. Humans are not disembodied wraiths—we are people of flesh and blood. We are not individuals isolated from other persons—we are members of societies and groups. And we are immersed in particular cultures. This is where we must begin, and how fast we progress in our quest for understanding will depend to a certain extent on the richness of the pool of experiences we have.

Why? Because our philosophical theories ought to make sense of our lives and of the very experiences that give rise to them. This does not mean that the aim of philosophy, as some philosophers believe, is necessarily "pragmatic" or that philosophy necessarily has to have a "use." Again, Aristotle was right about this. Some philosophy has a practical application, but some philosophy has no immediate application—its aim being merely to make sense, to satisfy the curiosity of seeing how things hang together, as Appiah indicated. This is the answer to the second question raised earlier, concerned with the aim of philosophical theories. Their aim is to give us a picture of how things are related and how it makes sense to think of them, even if in fact part of the theory we develop is that things do not make sense or at least some things do not.

But what makes a theory good or bad? The tendency of philosophers is to think in terms of one overall criterion. Consider the project of the logical positivists, for example. They had a very narrow understanding of what gives value to philosophical views. But any narrow view of this matter seems wrongheaded. Philosophical theories are of different sorts and therefore different value criteria apply to them—consider that some of them are descriptive, whereas others are prescriptive. (More on this ahead.) Still, if the aim of philosophical theories is to make sense, then the requirements of sense apply to them. And here there are a few things that are clearly involved. For example, it does not make sense to hold a view that we know to be false. So philosophical theories must be such that those who propose them think they are not false, or their parts are not false. Likewise, it does not make sense to hold contradictory beliefs. So it does not make sense to hold theories that are internally contradictory or that lead to contradictions, provided that we know they are or do so. Finally, it makes no sense to hold views that are contrary to known facts, and so philosophical theories that go contrary to them are not good ones.

Now let us go back to my theory of race, ethnicity, and nationality. In it, I tried to propose a view that satisfies these conditions. I began with my experiences as a human being, a member of a particular society, and a philosopher. The aim I pursued was to develop a theory that makes sense of my experiences as a human being, a Hispanic/Latino, and so on. I began with who I am and where I am, and then proceeded to test various ways of thinking about race, ethnicity, and nationality, discarding views that did not fit, or did not make sense. Some of the views that had to be discarded were personal views, others were culturally shared views, others were views proposed by other philosophers (including some that I had previously held myself), and so on. Finally, I got to a view that seems to meet the criteria that any good theory should satisfy. But even at this point, I believe the theory should be held *provisionally* precisely because its very grounds are limited and contextual, and these limitations and conditions are in a constant process of change and expansion. Indeed, this very discussion will probably show that the theory needs changes in response to the arguments voiced against it by Alcoff, Outlaw, Appiah, and Blum.

My response to Alcoff's metaphilosophical concerns, then, is that I agree with her that we cannot ignore the context from which we philosophize, and we certainly should not think that we are beginning with a tabula rasa, or that we can ensure that our reasoning and conclusions are completely objective and insulated from social and political presuppositions. But it is important *to aim* for objectivity, and to do so requires that we adopt procedures that should help. For example, one methodological principle we should follow is to try to make explicit the very assumptions that we have. Not that we should necessarily abandon them, or even that we can actually identify all of them. But we should try to make these assumptions explicit, both with a view to understanding where we are philosophically at the beginning of, and during, our quest and also to inform our audiences and interlocutors of our points of departure. We should also try hard to formulate clearly the problems that we address, and we should be open and frank about what we hold and the conclusions that we reach. Finally, our goals should also be clear. This is crucial and I have in fact integrated this requirement into a historiographical method I proposed in *Philosophy and Its History* (1992) and have followed in most of my historical work, of which *Introduction to the Problem of Individuation in the Early Middle Ages* (1984) is a good early example. I call this method the Framework Approach. The key to it is to develop a conceptual framework that meets the mentioned criteria and, therefore, helps us to reveal the assumptions operative in our philosophy.

In *Surviving Race*, I tried hard to do this as well, although I was not involved in a historical project. For example, I did not try to hide that some of my main concerns in addressing issues of race, ethnicity, and nationality have to do with ethical and political worries, or even that they arise from personal experiences. Indeed, in the last chapter of the book I point out how some views about these topics seem to me to be pernicious. So I tried, and tried hard, to follow this procedure because I agree with Alcoff about the dangers of ignoring context and thinking that philosophers work in an ivory tower of objectivity. I also tried hard because when I appear to be dictating and prescribing, I wanted it to be clear that I do so as a proposal and not because I have any kind of authority on this matter. (More on this in my response to Outlaw.)

So much, then, for the metaphilosophical issues that Alcoff raises. She also raises some important issues that have to do with my particular claims about race, ethnicity, and nationality. I discuss them after I deal with other metaphilosophical questions raised by Outlaw, Appiah, and Bloom. I turn first to

Outlaw. He makes one main criticism of my position and issues a challenge. The criticism, although different from Alcoff's, is like hers a metaphilosophical one. He is concerned with what he thinks is my unnecessary and inflated conception of philosophy and its role. The challenge is a request for an elaboration of how the theory I have proposed can be used to satisfy the goal that motivated it, our social and political well-being.

LIMITS OF PHILOSOPHY

Outlaw's critical remarks can be divided into two parts: one concerns the discipline of philosophy; the other concerns philosophers. The first part claims that the task I have set out for philosophy is not possible for at least two reasons: one, there is no such a thing as a discipline of philosophy that can carry out the task I have in mind; two, knowledge is too variegated for any single discipline to do so. The second part of Outlaw's criticism claims that no single person or group of persons can carry out the task.

In spite of appearances to the contrary, Outlaw and I, just as Alcoff and I, share much in our views of philosophy. Certainly we share our disappointment about what philosophy has thus far accomplished and will probably continue to accomplish, particularly when it comes to race, ethnicity, and nationality. The very prejudices that philosophers have shown to have in their views of race and ethnicity, for example, support this disappointment. Consider the views about race voiced by Hume and Kant, and the anti-Semitism of Heidegger. We also share a view that philosophy is in the making, that there do not seem to be any philosophical positions that have been shown to be true beyond doubt, and that the discipline, like everything else human, is a historical and contextual enterprise. There is no godlike view here, only more or less comprehensive perspectives, and its development, based on human experience, is always limited and partial. We can see only as far as our horizon, and everyone's horizon goes only so far. We also share a distrust of any kind of individual or group authority in matters philosophical. No person or group of persons has this kind of legitimacy or should have this kind of power. Indeed, as Outlaw knows, I have been a critic of any kind of philosophical establishment (Gracia 2000c, 2008b). So where do we differ, when we agree on so much?

I would like to think that Outlaw and I agree in substance, but that he has been misled by my rhetoric. Maybe I got carried away and said some things that sound inflated, when in fact I have a very deflationary view of almost everything, including philosophy and what it can accomplish. So, is there something that we can call philosophy that can do the things that I claim need to be done? Frankly, I do not care about the name of the enterprise or discipline in question. We could call it X, if you will. Nor do I think it is unified in any rigid and well-defined way. Disciplinary boundaries are porous. Still, we need to engage in activities that aim to do the things I say philosophy should do. We need to examine the very bases of scientific views, because the sciences themselves do not do it, and this goes by the name of philosophy of science and epistemology. We need to examine good and bad ways of reasoning, and this is what we call logic. We need to develop conceptual groupings from the less general to the most general, so that we understand how different categories depend on one another, and this is metaphysics. We need to think about the way we act and what is right and wrong about it, which we call ethics. We want to find out what makes something beautiful, and this is done in aesthetics. And so on with other branches of philosophy. Moreover, there is a history, contrary to what Outlaw seems to think, that helps me here. Because in many ways Socrates and Aristotle were doing many of these things and so is Outlaw, so they must have something in common.

To repeat, knowledge is not compartmentalized. All knowledge is continuous, although the methods used to gather it differ from discipline to discipline. The sciences are ahead of the humanities in their attempt to break down barriers between disciplines insofar as most sciences rely heavily on mathematics and many of them depend on one another to advance their investigations. Does not biology work closely with chemistry and sociology with statistics, for example? Yet when it comes to the humanities, we see that they tend to be separated not only from the sciences but also from one another. Philosophy and literature seem to share a mutual aversion to each other. I remember the gibes one of my philosophy teachers at Chicago took against "the literati," who in his view did not know the difference between a premise and a conclusion. But the same situation is true of other humanities, such as classics and American studies.

Contrary to Outlaw's view, philosophy is essential in the effort to transcend disciplinary boundaries for two reasons. First, philosophy is the only discipline that defies specialization in both method and subject matter. This discipline does not have a method of its own but uses the most basic tools available to the human mind: reason and observation. This allows it to be methodologically promiscuous, insofar as it is open to the use of any specialized procedure in order to achieve its aim of greater understanding of the world and ourselves. Second, philosophy covers ground that is not covered in other disciplines, thus completing our picture of human knowledge. Philosophy's aim is to produce an overall framework of understanding rather than to develop the specialized understandings that other disciplines seek. Consider the subfields of philosophy mentioned earlier. No discipline other than philosophy discusses the laws of good reasoning, the morality of human actions, the canons of beauty, or the criteria for knowledge, for example. This makes possible for philosophy to investigate these fields in the contexts of other disciplines, leading to enterprises such as the philosophy of art or the epistemology of physics. This in turn functions as a kind of glue that ties the pieces of knowledge produced by various disciplines into a fuller picture than the one given to us by particular disciplines.

Naturally, this process is both difficult and inconclusive. It is difficult because each discipline wants to defend its turf and complains when it is forced to take into account the results of other disciplinary studies. Interdisciplinary work encounters considerable resistance, as is evident in the fact that departmental colloquia are rarely attended by anyone from other departments. Moreover, it is difficult because philosophers cannot pay the kind of attention to each disciplinary method that the specialist demands. How could they? Indeed, if they were to do it, their work would surely not be different from that of specialists; philosophers would de facto become literary critics, or historians, or some such "experts."

Achieving this overall integration from the standpoint of philosophy remains inconclusive because human knowledge is constantly shifting and growing, so that there is no moment at which we can rest in the integration that philosophy seeks to achieve. And its inconclusiveness works against it, becoming a source of criticism. It is not surprising, then, that Outlaw finds that my claims do not do justice to the reality.

Keep in mind also that we must distinguish between the history of philosophy understood as the philosophical past and the discipline of philosophy. The past is frozen, but the discipline of philosophy is what we make of it, and it is always in the making. There has to be something like it—whether we call it philosophy or something else—because we do need to think about the matters mentioned. And here I must bring back Alcoff's criticism that I appear to be searching for a kind of finality and stability that are impossible to achieve. Again, my language probably misled Alcoff, as it may have misled Outlaw, and for that I am sorry, because my aim was not at all to reach, or even prescribe, any kind of finality. I do not believe any such thing is possible in philosophy. My theory about race, ethnicity, and nationality is meant merely as a model, and a work in progress, a point of departure rather than an end. But, of course, I present it as something of which I am convinced, and whose virtues I praise, which may suggest that I regard it as much more than it is or was intended to be. (More on this in my response to Appiah.)

Now for the second part of the criticism voiced by Outlaw: Is the task I laid down for philosophy to be delegated to someone in particular? No if by this one means a particular person or group of persons who can claim authority over others—there is no philosophy Pope or Council of Elders. But yes if what we mean is that each of us is engaged in it and that our limited success is contingent on dialogue and communication with others. Much of what I said earlier in response to Alcoff can be used here to answer Outlaw.

Apart from this criticism about the nature of philosophy and its role, Outlaw also issues a challenge, as follows: "Assuming that we get our concepts clarified along the lines Gracia proposes in *Surviving Race,* then what? How are we to become socially effective . . . ? How are we to 'cash them out'?"

There is nothing that I would like to do more than to answer Outlaw's challenge and question, but this is a tall order and must be left for another occasion, for what Outlaw asks is for the ethical and political theories that should accompany the metaphysical view of race, ethnicity, and nationality I have presented in *Surviving Race.* Still, I can illustrate the sorts of things that I have in mind with an example. One of the things that I have claimed is that the notions of ethnicity and nationality are frequently mixed, confused, or purposefully conflated. People in different paths of life treat ethne and nations as one and the same. Some believe that to be an American is to have a certain set of values and culture, to speak a certain language, to have a certain religion, and so on. Thus the notion of an American nation is understood ethnically. This has some serious consequences, because those who do not fit the ethnic profile are deemed to be less American, or not true Americans, even though they hold American citizenship (see Llorente, III:13; Gracia, III:17). The situation becomes even more serious when phenotypes identified with particular races play a role in the equation. People with dark skin cannot be truly American, or German, when the American or German nations are identified with groups of people that share particular physical phenotypes, including lighter skin.

Our first step as philosophers to address this situation, then, is to understand that ethnicity and nationality can be construed in ways that would allow us to distinguish nations and ethne and see how they are related. This in turn would make it possible for us to build a political theory that avoids the kinds of discrimination that become unavoidable when nations are conceived in ethnic terms.

I saw my task in *Surviving Race* as preparing the way, setting a foundation, not as achieving a result that is final but rather as a starting point of discussion. The next step is to engage in further dialogue, as we are doing here, with a view toward achieving further refinements in proper conceptions of race, ethnicity, and nationality and the development of both the ethical and political dimensions of the theory. But, even before that can be effectively done, we need to take a look at a question raised by Appiah and Blum in their commentaries. This is the question of whether the task of a metaphysics of race, as I undertook in *Surviving Race*, is descriptive or prescriptive.

DESCRIPTION, PRESCRIPTION, AND THE UNDERSTANDING OF RACE AND ETHNICITY

Appiah is known for his subtlety in addition to the elegance of his writing, and the fact that he suggests amendments to my views of race and ethnicity, and indicates areas where further work is necessary, is both friendly—malgré the *Robert's Rules of Order* to which he refers—and useful. Besides, it is eminently philosophical in that good philosophy begins and proceeds in dialogue. Presently it is particularly appropriate because he and I share a common understanding of the limits of what philosophers can do and what the purpose of philosophical theories is, which at least in my case goes back to one of the two philosophers who have influenced me the most, Ludwig Wittgenstein. (The other for those readers who do not know and are curious to know is Aristotle.)

Toward the end of his commentary, and echoing a distinction made famous by P. F. Strawson (1959), Appiah notes that there is no such a thing as descriptive metaphysics—all metaphysics, and indeed all philosophy, is revisionary. I agree for two reasons (see also Gracia 1999b). One is that the purpose of any theory, and this extends to science, literary analysis, and art, is not merely to canvas what we think about something or other but to redirect our views so that we take into account something that we had missed, and to offer a new perspective in order to prompt us to rethink a matter that perhaps we regarded as settled. The other reason is that it is quite naive to think that any view one may propose about any topic whatsoever is the final word on the topic. As I already suggested in my responses to Alcoff and Outlaw, it is particularly clear to me that there is no such a thing when it comes to a theory about such complicated matters as race or ethnicity. But this does not entail that one should refrain from offering the best possible defense of a view one thinks is good, or from pointing out the shortcomings of views one considers to be misguided. It is also essential that one try to stick to the facts as much as possible, that is, that one try to offer a theory that relies on observation and careful description, including linguistic description. This is indeed the spirit in which I have always offered my views about the topics on which I have written.

Thus, when I identify a set of conditions that apply to race or ethnicity, for example, I am taking into account usage, but I am going beyond description to suggest that the usage is not quite right and something I believe important is missing. This leads me to a point that Appiah raises concerning my rejection of the very important notion of "passing." His point is that "if we are . . . trying to understand the conception of the nature of race that we currently have, and if 'we' means most people in the United States, I think it [Gracia's view] is descriptively inadequate in ruling this [the phenomenon of passing] out." Of course he is right if we restrict our domain of discourse and investigation to the United States and we aim at a purely descriptive account. After all, people pass all the time. But if we go by what he says at the very end of his commentary and to which I referred earlier, namely that to do metaphysics involves not only description but also revision, and thus prescription, then my proposal makes sense to that extent and for that reason.

Indeed, the motivation behind my proposal concerning race, and consequently passing, is that the conception of race is not uniform throughout the world and therefore we need a better understanding of it. As I have noted elsewhere, in Cuba to belong to a race means something different in significant ways from what it means in the United States (e.g., Gracia 2005b, 2008b). Moreover, the American folk conception of race in terms of the one-drop rule when it applies to blacks but not to whites is inconsistent and as such does not serve us well to deal with this phenomenon globally, even if it expresses some widespread intuitions about it in this country. This is the reason why I do not stick to description. I go beyond it by proposing a view that I tried to make consistent and I hope serves to account for race not just in the United States, resolving the inconsistencies of the American view and accounting for race in places like Cuba, where it is conceived differently. In short, I suggest that, if measured by the criteria that I use to develop my view, my conception of passing is not inadequate, although it may not exactly reflect the folk understanding of race in the United States.

This response should also suffice to answer Blum's charge that there is "an inconsistency between Gracia's account of race and what . . . he wants his accounts of race and ethnicity to do, namely track the sociohistorical, experiential reality of race." The problem, in Blum's view, is that I seem to endorse, using the language of Strawson, a descriptive view of the method that I employ in the philosophy of race, whereas in fact I end up using a prescriptive method in which I lay down conditions that a proper view of race and ethnicity need to satisfy. If I were merely to describe, I would not impose a criterion of consistency in the appropriate view of race but merely accept the inconsistencies of the American (or any other) folk view of it.

As I mentioned in my discussion of Outlaw, my view of metaphysics, and it is a metaphysics of race in which I am engaged in *Surviving Race*, is that it involves both descriptive and prescriptive phases. Metaphysicians need to begin by describing what they experience, particularly as reflected in language. But our experiences and linguistic usage are full of inconsistencies and inaccuracies. This means that metaphysicians need to go beyond these and formulate consistent theories that take into account as much as possible the information they get from experience and language in order to get to the core of the concepts in question. Indeed, one may even question whether any description is completely objective, and here what I responded to Alcoff should also help. Any theory worth its salt is prescriptive to some extent, as is the case in science.

So far I have been referring to metaphilosophical issues raised by Alcoff, Outlaw, Appiah, and Blum. These issues are important if one is to understand what philosophers try to do and may accomplish with a philosophy of race, ethnicity, and related phenomena, such as nationality. The matter involves not just particular phenomena; it also concerns how philosophers proceed, the purpose of philosophical accounts, and the way to judge philosophical theories. Now let me turn to the questions they raise concerning my understanding of these particular phenomena.

CONDITIONS OF RACE, ETHNICITY, AND NATIONALITY

One of the claims I make concerning race, ethnicity, and nationality refers to the importance that historical relations have for them. Alcoff, echoing the metaphilosophical criticism discussed earlier, asks whether history is enough to determine ethnicity, since it is not clear which historical relations are significant for it. Consider Hispanics/Latinos, for example: Which historical events and relations are relevant for the individuation of the group? And can we identify a set of conditions that is uniform for all members of the group? What if one is Jewish, for example?

The point that Alcoff brings up is crucial, but I did answer it in the book, although perhaps not as clearly as I should have. (Bernstein [II:7] raises a similar objection, although in a different way.) The issue involves two kinds of facts. The first are facts that are, as it were, independent of human opinion. Examples would be hurricanes, death, diseases, geographic location, famine, genotypes, evolutionary processes, external invasions, and wars. The second are facts that consist of opinions that people hold: views about the first facts mentioned, feelings of solidarity and antagonism, views about how to do certain things, religious commitments, and so on. All of these potentially play roles in the formation and dissolution of ethnic groups—and if I understand Alcoff correctly, her concern is precisely with ethnicity.

Now, philosophers who work on ethnicity usually have three views about this matter. Some are *externalists*—they think that the factors that determine ethnicity are exclusively of the first sort, namely, external. Some philosophers are *internalists*; they hold that the factors that determine ethnicity are purely of the second sort, that is, internal. Within the internalist camp there are those who emphasize factors common to all members of the group (e.g., an opinion shared by all members of the group, call them *group internalists*), whereas others emphasize factors common to only some members of the group (e.g., an opinion that only some members of the group share, call them *group member internalists*). Moreover, some externalists pick as the sole external factor the opinion of a group or groups who are not the group whose ethnicity is in question, such as the opinion of Anglo-Americans about Hispanics/Latinos. Last, most of these philosophers hold that their views, whether externalist or internalist, apply to all ethnic groups.

I differ from these philosophers in the following ways: First, I do not believe that the factors that determine ethnicity are exclusively internal or external. Both internal and external factors play roles in the determination of most ethne. That I am ethnically Cuban involves not only the fact that I was born in Cuba but also that Cubans have developed a sense of themselves, that I have embraced that sense in some ways, and that there are non-Cuban groups who think about Cubans as an ethnic group (Gracia 2008b:chap. 1).

This distinguishes my position from those who adopt an exclusivist view, whether externalist or internalist.

Another important element of disagreement I have with most philosophers who write about ethnicity is that they seem to think that their theories about ethnic determinations apply to every ethnic group (call them *universal ethnicists*). My view, however, is different. I argue that it is precisely an important feature of ethnicity, in contrast to race and nationality, that the facts that determine a particular ethnos are not always the same or of the same kind (call them *particular ethnicists*). Why? Because history is variegated and what goes into the ethnic determination of a particular group is contingent on that history. Whether external or internal factors predominate, or a mixture of the two, whether the views of other groups or individuals play a role, and if it is internal factors, whether these involve the view of individuals or the group, are all contingent matters that depend on context and therefore must be determined through an investigation. Now, this kind of investigation is not philosophical, it belongs to history, anthropology, and sociology, because it involves empirical research. The province of philosophy is the development of a conceptual framework within which this empirical research can fit.

This should be sufficient to answer Alcoff's concerns voiced earlier but not a different concern also expressed by her. This is that the Familial-Historical View of ethnicity I propose does not give enough importance to descent or genealogy. She questions why a genealogical tie to a geographical location that has its own specific/cultural/political character would not be a feature of ethnicity. The answer to this concern follows from what I said earlier. As in families, where genealogy plays a role but not a necessary one—spouses are not generally tied genealogically—genealogy does play a role in ethnicity, but not a necessary one. But there is more to it than this, for it is altogether possible, and indeed it is a fact concerning certain ethnic groups, as some research has shown, that genealogy does function as a necessary condition in certain ethne. This does not mean, however, that genealogy applies to all ethnic groups. Whether it does or not depends on the conditions that have become historically determining factors for the particular ethnos in question. In short, I do not reject the role of genealogy in ethnicity, what I reject is the stipulation that this role is necessary for *all* ethne or that it has the same function in *all* ethne. Alcoff's criticism of my view rests on a disputable assumption, namely, that all ethne share the same conditions of membership.

This leads to a third concern voiced by Alcoff, namely, that the Familial-Historical View of ethnicity may privilege surnames and therefore paternity in certain societies. My answer to this is, first, that a familial model need not privilege a certain view of names or paternity insofar as issues of naming and paternity are parochial to particular conceptions of families in different societies. The concept of family does not entail any particular view about surnames or paternity. Surely there are matrilineal families! Moreover, the aspect of the family that the Familial-Historical View picks out has nothing to do with naming or paternity, so the view does not entail paternalism or male-centered lineage. Alcoff may have been misled here by my use of the Gracia family as an example of familial relations. I should have made clear, if I did not do so, that this was just an example, not a normative paradigm.

Finally, Alcoff questions how effective my attempt to separate race, ethnicity, and nationality is, bringing up the indisputable fact that race is often involved in ethnicity, so that the lines between the two appear blurred. This is a point that she frequently emphasizes and has led her to argue for the notion of an ethnorace to replace ethnicity (Alcoff 2000). Now, I grant that race often plays a role in ethnicity, but I give an explanation for why this is so that does not entail the result Alcoff suggests. One reason race often plays a role in ethnicity is that the latter is a very open, flexible phenomenon, so that race can often become part of ethnicity. This point seems to be missing in the literature. Some ethne include races, or, if you will, are racialized. But to distinguish the two notions and see why it is that they can be combined helps to understand this phenomenon. My view does not dogmatically assert that race and ethnicity are factually separate phenomena. Their factual separation depends on circumstances, as Ortega y Gasset would have said, but to understand when and if they do, it helps to have clear notions of their differences. (More later in this section and in parts II and III of this volume.)

The situations with nations, on the one hand, and ethne and races, on the other, is different, although it seems clear that in fact nations have often incorporated ethnic and racial elements, precisely because nations, like ethne and races, are historically developed entities and are therefore open to the contingencies of history. Yet one should (and this is a prescription) keep these notions separate and try to implement a conception of a nation that is largely insulated from ethne and races, for reasons that have to do primarily with morality.

The questions that Appiah raises can be divided into those that affect both race and ethnicity, ethnicity alone, and race alone. Let me take some of those that should help us think about race and ethnicity while setting aside others that would require a more extensive discussion and analysis. Keep in mind that the formulation of an objection is frequently more parsimonious than what its answer needs to be.

One of these questions has to do with my analysis of race and ethnicity in terms of the notion of family. The point, as Appiah puts it, is that "the logic of the extended family and the ethnos and the race do not run precisely in parallel." Although Appiah's argument is meant to apply to race in addition to ethnicity, in order to simplify matters and shorten the discussion, I address it only in the context of ethnicity, although some of what I say about ethnicity can be effectively applied, mutatis mutandis, to race.

Appiah's argument is based mainly on two considerations. First, "there is a pretty strong rule of descent . . . in ethnic groups that says that if your parents belong to the same race or ethnos, you are of the same race or ethnos as they are." And presumably this is not the case with families insofar as families do not require a descent connection, as marriage and adoption show. Second, he argues that ethnic groups are endogamous, that is, their members marry their own, whereas the case in families is precisely the opposite; members of families marry members of other families. This he thinks militates against the view that ethnic groups are kinds of families, as I propose.

The first of Appiah's objections does not carry sufficient weight insofar as, although in some ethnic groups descent is either a necessary or sufficient condition of belonging to the group, in others this is not so. It is true, for example, that in some Mongolian tribes descent is both a necessary and sufficient condition of ethnic belonging, so that even if a child is adopted from birth by a family from a tribe different from that of the child, the child remains a member of the original tribe and never becomes a member of the tribe in which he or she grows up. But the case of my friend Ignacio indicates that the ethne Latino, Hispanic, and even Argentinean function differently. Ignacio was born in Italy of Italian parents who moved to Argentina when he was three years old. His parents continued to be considered "Italian" while they lived, but he was Argentinean from the start and continues to be so, and also Hispanic and Latino. And his case is not a rare exception but a rather common occurrence.

To Appiah's second point, based on ethnic endogamy, one can also offer some counterexamples. Although perhaps endogamy is prevalent in many ethnic groups, it is certainly not a necessary condition for all ethne. Consider the very case of Latinos. Latinos did not exist before 1492. What we had were Catalans, Basques, Galicians, and so forth in Spain, and in what came to be called Latin America we had Maya, Aztec, Inca, and so on. The Latino ethnos came to be through a long process of mixing these various peoples with peoples outside their ethne. Nor does the Latino ethnos particularly favor endogamy. Latinos welcome ethnic mixing, a fact that is not rare among other ethne. It is common for some ethnic groups to look for mates outside their ethne through conquest, raids, or negotiation, including purchase. In addition, although family endogamy is frowned upon in certain societies, it is not universally proscribed. We need only look at the history of European royal families to see that endogamy was pursued with a vengeance by most of them. Considerations of wealth and blood purity, among others, often trump rules about endogamy.

These are very specific responses to specific objections. But here is a more general point: I never claim that the kind of family that ethne are is the same as the kind of family that Appiah seems to be talking about and where he finds grounds for his objections. My point is not that ethne are families exactly as nuclear families are, which seem to be the model Appiah has in mind. My point is that both ethnic groups and nuclear families have some features in common, such as a sense of kinship, that distinguish them from other kinds of social groups (e.g., religious groups, social clubs, professional societies, cities, nations, etc.), even if they do not share all the features that each of them has. Moreover, the very notion of a family varies from culture to culture, so we should not take the familial character of ethne to mean that these groups share a fixed set of properties.

Appiah also suggests that, in order to strengthen my theory, I need to elaborate on three mechanisms that we should understand if we are to understand ethnic groups: initial formation, addition of new members, and loss of members—call them origin, inclusion, and exclusion. Of course, he is entirely right about the fact that it would be enlightening to know more about these mechanisms. However, there are two reasons why I did not say much about them in my analysis. The first is that, as pointed out before, in my view ethne do not have a set of mechanisms that apply to every ethnos across the board, and this is also true when it comes to origin, inclusion, and exclusion. What applies to each of them depends on their particular histories. For some ethne, having a mother that belongs to the ethnos is both a necessary and sufficient condition of membership, for example, but for others cultural assimilation is sufficient. So I could not very well come up with a set of conditions—including conditions of origin, inclusion, or exclusion—for all ethne, since it is my considered opinion that, in contrast with race and some other social groups, ethne do not have uniformity in this.

The second reason I did not discuss these mechanisms is that their study in relation to particular ethne is not the business of metaphysics but rather of anthropology and other social sciences, whereas the analysis of ethnicity to which Appiah refers (Gracia 2005b) is metaphysical. Indeed, in *Hispanic/Latino Identity* (Gracia 2000c) I discuss the origin of this particular ethnic group and the way members are incorporated into it and leave the group. But I do this because in that book I consider a particular ethnic group and the inquiry extends beyond metaphysics and incorporates history and culture.

The first of these reasons also explains why in my discussion of ethnicity in general I did not refer, as Appiah would have liked me to have done, to an ancestral population. I just do not think that this is an essential element in all ethne, although it is certainly one in some, and perhaps many. Indeed, I do not think one can cogently argue that the Hispanic/Latino ethnos includes this reference to an ancestral group insofar as its roots are found in many and different groups and the ethnos does not require descent, and what applies to Hispanics/Latinos may also apply to other ethne.

Blum, like Appiah, is dissatisfied with my understanding of ethne as families, but not for quite the same reasons. Here is what he says: (1) "people who marry a member of an ethnic group are not generally thought of as becoming members themselves, even if they embrace its ethnoculture"; (2) "most ethnic groups are large and range over a wide, often dispersed, geographic area"; and (3) ethnic groups "are not 'organized' in any overall sense at all."

These reasons do not seem to me persuasive. The problem with the first is that the acceptance into an ethnic group depends very much on the rules of acceptance of the group, so even if it were true that most ethnic groups adhere to the rule proposed by Blum, this is not a universally accepted rule, and, therefore, such a rule cannot be regarded as constitutive across the board. In fact, Blum grants the point when he qualifies his claim by inserting "are not generally thought." There are plenty of cases in which marriage into an ethnic group makes the person a member of it.

The second reason assumes that only large groups are ethnic, whereas in fact only recently in human history do we have large ethne. Most ethnic groups originate in small numbers, as a family or conglomerate of families, and many of them are not geographically dispersed. Even today, some Amazonian tribes are quite small and live in restricted territories.

Something similar may be said in answer to reason (3). Blum is thinking of particular forms of organization prevalent in the groups he regards as paradigmatic. But a consideration of a larger pool of ethne shows strong organizing principles that go all the way from the political to the religious. Again, Blum's objections are based on a narrow understanding of ethne, similar to that of others who also object to my views. The problem is not only the narrow scope on which the objections are based but also the essentialist assumption that all ethne adhere to the same kind of membership criteria.

Blum questions my identification of ethne with families for still another reason. He points out that "without giving us some idea of the relationships that constitute ethnicity, we have no basis for differentiating empirical *correlates* with ethnicity in a particular context from characteristics that actually *constitute* ethnicity in that context."

The answer is "sure," Blum is right. Epistemic criteria in context do not tell us anything about ontological criteria out of context. But that is not the point, is it? Coincidental features in context may serve to identify members of an ethnic group in context, even if they do not reveal ontological constitution. What makes a Mexican such may not be the ability to speak Spanish, but in context speaking Spanish may tell us that someone is Mexican even though it does not tell us why the person is in fact Mexican. This fact may have to be established on some other basis.

Apart from these objections against my conception of ethnicity, Blum also voices concerns against my view of Hispanic/Latino identity. Since I discuss Hispanic/Latino identity in greater detail in my response in chapter 12, I address his objection there.

Now let me turn to what may be the main concern Appiah voices with respect to my view of race. The view I propose includes in it both a descent criterion together with a phenotypical, bundle-view criterion. Each of these functions as a necessary condition and together they function as a sufficient condition of a race. Someone who satisfies the descent criterion but not the phenotypical criterion is not a member of the race in question, and vice versa. Moreover, it is precisely these two conditions that separate race and ethnicity in general, although this does not preclude an ethnos from including descent and phenotypical features as conditions of membership.

Appiah's objection is that the descent criterion would not distinguish Aborigines from Negroes. The reason is that these two racial groups can be put together into a group whose members would satisfy the descent criterion (of being related to a member of the group by descent) and the phenotypical bundle criterion (of having some or all of a number of phenotypical features associated with the group), even though Aborigines would still be unrelated by descent to Negroes and not share with them a bundle of phenotypical features.

There are various, more or less, effective ways to answer this interesting objection (which, by the way, is also briefly raised by Blum), but let me refer to one that helps us see another side of the issue that perhaps I have not made sufficiently clear. This involves the distinction between two questions. One asks what makes a group racial, the other what distinguishes different racial groups. The answer to the first consists in the set of conditions I presented. A race or racial group involves both descent and a bundle of phenotypical properties of the sort mentioned. But this does not tell us how any two different racial groups or races are distinguished. So what? The purpose of the formula I propose is not to establish how different racial groups or races are distinguished from one another. That is the answer to the second question, and may involve a variety of conditions. For example, it may involve a different line of descent, or differences in the phenotypes associated with a particular race. This is not different from what we do, for example, with the notion of human. We have a formula (say, featherless biped) to encapsulate what is essential to humans, but then we make distinctions between subclasses of humans, such as male and female, on the bases of additional criteria.

Appiah saw that my formula does not answer that second question, as is clear in the counterexample that he provided. However, although I agree with him that my formula does not effectively distinguish between Aborigines and Negroes when these are put together in a group, I disagree with him in that I do not think this is a shortcoming of my formula insofar as it was not intended to establish such a distinction under those conditions. His counterexample does not, then, work against my conception of race, for Aborigines, Negroes, and the group of Aborigines and Negroes considered together constitute a racial group, although it brings attention to the fact that my formula does not contain criteria for distinguishing among different races. This is in line with the aim I explicitly identified for *Surviving Race*, namely, to establish a distinction between race, ethnicity, and nationality while leaving aside discussions of what distinguishes particular races, ethne, or nations.

Still, my position is concordant with the view that Aborigines would still not be Negroes insofar as none of them is related to a Negro by descent, if one were to adopt a theory of racial distinction based on descent, for even if they are put together into a group of people all of whom are related to some other member of the group by descent, they would be related by descent only to other Aborigines. And something similar could be said about the bundle of features that apply to Aborigines and to Negroes. The view I propose is intended to explain why a certain group of people are a racial group, not a particular race distinct from others, and it assumes that it constitutes a group distinct from nonracial groups.

Appiah's suggestion for solving the problem he believes his objection creates for my view is to recommend that I substitute a reference to an ancestral people for the reference to descent. Such a reference would separate Aborigines from Negroes, even when they are considered together into a group. But that, he acknowledges, would collapse the distinction between ethnicity and race, making race a kind of ethnic group.

My answer to Appiah's question, about whether I would accept this amendment, is, as he suspects, negative for two reasons. First, I do not need it for an effective conception of race, as I have already noted. Second, I would not want to put a reference to an ancestral people as a necessary condition of a race in general for the reason that I pointed out earlier, and which is rooted in turn in the very reason that race and ethnicity function differently: the conditions of ethnicity are not the same across the board. In some cases such a reference to an ancestral people would be appropriate, but in others not. This seems sufficiently significant to put ethnicity and race in two different categories rather than subsume race under ethnicity or vice versa, as some do. Nor do I want to put a reference to an ancestral people as a condition of race, although I would accept the view that a reference to a line of descent is one of the ways in which one might distinguish between one race and another. One reason is that the notion of an ancestral people, although involving descent, seems to be highly mythical, whereas what matters for race is something more factual. The lack of a reference to an ancestral people does not mean, however, that I give no role to history in any account of ethnicity, although this is precisely the point some of my critics raise in their commentaries in part II of this volume. I consider this objection more fully in my response there.

PART II

HISPANIC/LATINO IDENTITY

6. IS BEING HISPANIC AN IDENTITY?

J. L. A. GARCÍA

Jorge J. E. Gracia's book *Hispanic/Latino Identity* (2000c) is a rich and path-breaking exploration. It is a model of how to apply the methods and approaches of philosophy, especially contemporary conceptual analysis, to topics that philosophers usually ignore and social scientists often mishandle. The book is also a model of how to treat with an admirable calm, and with touches of humor, matters that sometimes touch on deeply personal feelings. Though suitably dispassionate, Gracia's analysis is not impersonal; it is frequently marked by personal anecdotes, observations, and reflections. We hope that Gracia's book marks the beginning of a fruitful new series of philosophically informed reflections on ethnicity and ethnic identity, whose discussion so badly needs the clear presentation, sharp thinking, and meticulous care that Gracia brings to his treatment. He has gotten this new subfield off to a superb start and set a high standard for its pursuit.

I cannot hope to meet that standard, but in the spirit of Gracia's (2000c:xvi, 189) own call for further discussion, let me make a few remarks voicing some concerns and questions whose consideration might form part of that discussion and perhaps advance it. Though hesitant to go toe-to-toe with Gracia on matters of metaphysics, where he is so learned (and I rather the opposite), I begin with a few questions about the very idea of ethnic identity, and whether we can explain it, moving on to some concerns about details of Gracia's own account of it, proceeding then to offer reasons to doubt ethnicity itself. I conclude with a summary of some points of intellectual engagement.

REASONS TO DOUBT THE VERY IDEA
OF ETHNIC IDENTITY

A question about what it is for someone to be a sovereign, or a citizen, or a saint, or other nouns, seems not to be a question about anyone's identity. Still less are any questions about which things are dishwashers or what it is for something to be a mouse. There are plenty of statements of the form 'S is P,' where P does not give the subject's identity. What makes it different here? Why think that being a Hispanic, a Latina/Latino, is having a special identity—a Hispanic one, especially when the discourse of any such "ethnic identity" differs so radically from central cases of identity-talk, as in discussion of identity over time or across possible worlds?[1] After all, logically perspicuous identity-talk (from the Latin *idem*, 'same') makes sense only when it naturally finds (or, at least, permits) two-term expression, as in talk of A's being identical with B (through qualitative changes, across time, in different possible situations).[2] Any inherently nonrelational identity-talk, which the discourse of "ethnic identity" seems to be, is therefore inherently suspect.[3] As the anthropologist Adam Kuper (1999) remarks, "The concept 'identity' is an oxymoron used in relation to an individual, since how can an individual not correspond to himself or herself? . . . The notion of Identity is connected rather to the idea that the self has certain essential properties and some contingent ones. There is a real me" (234ff.). Kuper's last remark, of course, opens the door for Gracia to construe identity as personal essence, what philosophers have called *haecceitas*. Unfortunately, any such move runs counter both to Gracia's antiessentialist approach to identity (see, especially, Gracia 2000c:48ff.) and to his claim that individuals have multiple identities.[4] For there is something odd in suggesting that a person could have a plurality of personal essences (Gracia 2000c:60).

Ethnic identity, then, is so dissimilar to identity in central and clear cases (as in the diachronic or transworld identity that philosophers discuss) that use of the term in the context of ethnicity is deeply misleading. Indeed, I suspect talk of "identity" here treads on illicit and misleading hypostatization (reification) insofar as it disallows the necessary question identical with whom, with what?

Gracia's concept of "achronic identity" is, as his text indicates, the one most pertinent to ethnic identity. For achronic identity, he tells us, we must "determine the necessary and sufficient conditions that make a thing identical irrespective of time. This is another way of saying one needs to establish what makes a thing to be the thing it is" (Gracia 2000c:30; cf. 53ff.). We need not pursue the ontological question of whether there is such a thing as what it is that makes something X to be what it is.[5] What concerns us is that this issue about essences is not really a matter of identity, for there is simply no such thing as something's "being identical irrespective of time." There can be no such thing as being identical simpliciter, only being identical with something. As I maintained in the foregoing, meaningful identity-talk must find natural expression in a relational idiom. Because talk of ethnic identity does not do so, its meaningfulness is at best dubious.

In addition, any talk, as we find in Gracia, of a kind of identity that can change over time is problematic.[6] First, any such view appears to reify identity, treating it as a temporal object. Moreover, in such a view, I will not merely be thought to be Hispanic in some places and times and not others but will actually be Hispanic in one time or place and also not Hispanic in another, without myself changing at all.[7] This, however, is highly counterintuitive, marginally intelligible, at best. For, if what it is to be (a) Hispanic is different at Time One from what it is at Time Two, then there really is no such thing as being (a) Hispanic, no such quality or essence—let alone identity. There are only what-it-is-to-be-Hispanic-at-Time-One, what-it-is-to-be-Hispanic-at-Time-Two, and so forth. Indeed, it would be preferable in careful (e.g., philosophical) discourse to talk simply of being-Hispanic-1, being-Hispanic-2, where the numbers help to identify these as different qualities, even if related ones. However, if the term 'Hispanic' is systematically ambiguous in this way, predicating different qualities in different uses and times, then there can be no such thing as what it is to be Hispanic. A fortiori, there could be no such thing as "Hispanic identity." That last conclusion—that there would be no such thing as "Hispanic identity"—seems right and accords well with what I have said about identity. So, I do not take that implication, though unwanted by Gracia, as reason to reject his account of what it is be a(n) Hispanic, but only to reject its use as an account of a supposed Hispanic "identity." The former implication—that there could be no such thing as even being Hispanic—is more troubling, however. There certainly does seem to be such a thing as being a Hispanic, and we should deny the possibility only with strong reason. Yet, if there is some such thing as being Hispanic, then what it is to be Hispanic cannot vary in the way that Gracia and others think it does. The problem here arises from Gracia's view that ethnicity is, in part, socially constructed. Constructionism necessarily relativizes ethnicity and therein subjects anyone's ethnicity to others' vagaries, and in making person X's ethnicity thus dependent on persons Y, Z, et al., it makes X's ethnicity largely inde-pendent of X herself.[8] That seems unacceptable even as an account of ethnicity, and it is still less acceptable as an account of anyone's identity. How can what it is to be someone depend so much on others' actions and beliefs? Must not her identity be something intrinsic, even if nothing else is?

Gracia (2000c) talks of people who, by their inattention to "Hispanic is-sues," "surrender [their] identity" (186). This requires more explanation than he gives it, I think. For his account of being Hispanic—and therein, in his view, possessing a Hispanic identity—says little about anyone's interests and seems to leave no room for renouncing identity by inattention. Moreover, an identity that can be lost in this way cannot go deep, calling into question its nature as an identity, if an identity is a matter of what makes someone to be what she or he is, as Gracia holds. He also talks anecdotally of encountering people who considered him not a Cuban once he informed them of his (Cu-ban) parents' ancestors, and of a wider perception among Euro-Americans that Hispanics are not really American (180). At one point he goes as far as to say that, because the former group thought he was not Cuban but some-thing else, "in the United States I became something I never thought I was." I doubt he means this last remark literally: he does not think he really stopped being Cuban just because these people thought he was non-Cuban. Nor does he think that Hispanics are non-American just because many Americans deny we are also Americans too. Yet notice that social constructionism does suggest these bigoted, narrow-minded people are correct. For it holds that people and things are what they are because society so "constructs" them, where this construction is a matter of collective conventions, conceptions, and intentions (Collin 1997:esp. chaps. 1, 8). So, eliding a few complications and qualifications that I do not think go to the heart of the matter, if, accord-ing to the standards internal to a social group's way of thinking, people such as Gracia count as neither Cubans nor Americans, then they are neither. That is the way this group "constructs" them. Nor will it avail for Gracia to insist that he must be Cuban for that is how he is seen in the Caribbean (and Amer-ican because he has lived in the United States so long and so mastered its ways). These facts cannot suffice to rebut the constructionist on her own terms, since her position's inherent relativism permits someone to be Cuban by one set of social standards but not Cuban by a second, American by one set yet non-American by another. In these ways, social constructionism threatens to disintegrate the self, which becomes all things to all men (and women) in such a fashion that it can itself be nothing. Gracia's flirtation with the idea that ethnicity and ethnic identity are socially constructed is, then, a dangerous game. It unleashes a virus that theorists are unlikely to be able to confine in quite the way they may want. In *The Eighteenth Brumaire of Louis Bonaparte*, Marx reminded us that we make history, but not always as we should like it. What makes us think that, if we insist that it is society that makes our ethnicity and even our identity, it will make them to our liking?

Note, in addition, that there may be a difficulty of circularity in the very ideas of ethnicity (let alone of ethnic identity) and of ethnic culture. For an ethnic group, an ethnie, is constituted and identified by its culture, while we feel some inclination to identify the group (and its members) by their living within the ethnic culture. (A Hispanic, we might want to say, is someone who likes salsa music, etc. But then what makes salsa music Hispanic if not the fact that it is the music developed by and popular among certain people who are already and independently Hispanic?) Moreover, cultures are most commonly thought of either as patterns of behavior or as systems of meaning (Kuper 1999). Any pattern, however, and still more any system, requires a high degree of internal unity, and a pattern of (conventional) behavior and any system of (conventional) meanings will require substantial stability, first, to come into being and then, second, to be recognized. Yet these requirements for unity and stability are in tension with the recent tendency of anthropologists to emphasize the internal disunity, the contestation, of societies and their tendency to constant evolution (Kuper 1999). All this suggests that the notion of culture and, with it, that of an ethnic group are more problematic than is often nowadays assumed. Despite these difficulties, which I think substantial, my claim here is not that there is no such thing as being Hispanic, say, or no such thing as belonging to any ethnic group. I make only the weaker claims that we should not think of being (a) Hispanic (or having other ethnic affiliation) as having a special identity.[9]

I also think that these difficulties offer one set of reasons why we should content ourselves with what we can call a deflationary understanding of ethnicity. Here I adapt language from philosophy of language and ontology, where some have suggested deflationary accounts of truth, accounts that allow us to retain our ordinary use of the truth-predicate but are thought to undermine or delegitimate the substantial ontological and axiological systems some think the concept of truth (or Truth) justifies.[10] Gracia also wants to dissociate ethnicity, and even ethnic identity, from robust ontologies of essence. I suggested that the latter effort may not succeed, because the very concept of identity of any clear sort must involve ontological commitments to shared qualities, and so on, that Gracia denies. The kind of deflation I have in mind, however, has less to do with ontology and more with evaluation. I think that we do well to de-emphasize ethnicity, take it less seriously, and recognize that someone's ethnicity may have little connection to how she ought normally to regard herself or others, may have little relation to what is sometimes thought of as her "moral identity," that is, to what she ought to be, or do, or prefer, or seek in life.

In his book's final chapter, Gracia appears to me to assign an undue importance to ethnicity, specifically, to being Hispanic. There he chastises those of Hispanic background without special interest in what he deems "Hispanic issues" for "divesting themselves of anything Hispanic," and invidiously contrasts their attitude with that of those, like Gracia (2000c) himself, whose special interest in these matters manifests a "wish to be true to ourselves" (187). Similarly, he offers a lengthy and speculative social psychology to explain Hispanic philosophers who do not study Hispanic culture (180–87). Unless Hispanic ethnicity, however, requires certain cultural preferences, a position Gracia's account precludes, such a lack of interest cannot make someone stop being Hispanic. It is only a Hispanic "identity" that could so depend and be so easily lost. And it is hard for me to find just where Gracia defends the needed claim that Hispanic identity requires such preference. Indeed, he does little to articulate or even acknowledge the distinction I have suggested here between someone's being (a) Hispanic and her having a Hispanic identity. What seems to be at work here is an assumption that any Hispanic ought, either normatively or probabilistically, and perhaps that anyone with a Hispanic identity logically must, have a special interest in things culturally Hispanic. This is a view widely held, to be sure, especially among those specializing in ethnic studies. However, neither its basis nor its truth is at all obvious. Alexander Pope famously maintained that the proper study of mankind is man, but even if that is correct, it does not follow that the proper study of Hispanics is Hispanics (and, of Frenchmen, Frenchmen, etc.). Philosophers, Gracia seems to hold, are people interested in the truth about certain topics. So, unless Hispanics have some reason to think that truth is especially likely to be found in Hispanic thinkers and culture, there seems no special reason for them, as philosophers at any rate, to study those thinkers or that culture. If they do have such reason, moreover, it would have to be a reason for any philosopher, Hispanic or not, to study them. I realize, of course, that some might think that ethnic culture is one of the best paths to the truths philosophers seek, and that it is best accessed through consideration of the culture in which one was reared and with which one is most familiar. Gracia does not offer this line of reasoning, nor any other defense that I find for his view that Hispanic philosophers ought, or ought especially, to study Hispanic philosophy.[11] His inattention to this argument may be well advised, since it has noticeable problems. Its initial thesis, that the relevant truths are best sought through study of ethnic culture, is not at all obvious and is open to objection both from those who model philosophical inquiry on the natural or mathematical sciences and perhaps also from those who model it on literary and artistic creation. Again, this sort of argument appears to presuppose that different cultural traditions are themselves equally helpful in the pursuit of the truths philosophers ought to seek, so that one does well to work within the tradition one knows best. This plainly runs contrary to the usual view in Western philosophy that there is a certain string of philosophers, beginning in ancient Greece and Rome and continuing through to some twentieth-century British, German, and American thinkers, whose thought is especially important for philosophical illumination. This view may be wrong, but even if it is, that hardly justifies the equality assumption on which the reasoning sketched in the preceding rests. Finally, note the fact that the claim that Hispanic philosophy may have been unjustly neglected and may hold unexpected riches does not at all show that it is, principally, Hispanic philosophers who should revive its study.

For these reasons, I have trouble seeing why we should follow Gracia in thinking that Hispanic philosophers ought, or ought especially, to study Hispanic philosophy. It is particularly difficult to see what such emphasis, which seems ethnocentric in an objectionable way, has to do with being "true to [oneself]," since Gracia generally recognizes that a participation in Hispanic culture is not necessary for someone to be Hispanic. I worry that this sort of phrase comes closer to rhetoric than to reason. Of course, various people have all sorts of expectations about what Hispanics are or should be like. Such claims about what Hispanics do, however, require empirical support. More important, the normative ones need defense through some articulated connection to moral or intellectual virtues, or to recognizable moral responsibilities. I do not find that in Gracia's brief treatment.

REASONS TO DOUBT GRACIA'S ACCOUNT
OF HISPANIC IDENTITY

Whether or not the concept of Hispanic (or other ethnic) identity is, as I have suggested, objectionable in principle, there are special difficulties in the account of it that Gracia offers. Gracia (2000c:60) insists that his Familial-Historical

View is not committed to Hispanics sharing any quality across all times and places, and he takes this as an advantage, maintaining that there is no such shared quality.[12] However, this creates difficulties for his view. Let us briefly treat a few of them.

1. If two persons, X and Y, share Hispanic identity, then it seems that they must share at least one quality, namely, that of having such an identity. (Moreover, no non-Hispanic will share this quality, making it, contrary to Gracia's claim, both necessary and sufficient.)

2. Again, if X is Hispanic in virtue of X's having quality Qx in society Sx at time Tx, and Y is Hispanic in virtue of Y's having quality Qy in society Sy at time Ty, and Z is Hispanic in virtue of Z's having quality Qz in society Sz at time Tz, then it seems that they must all share the disjunctive quality of having either Qx in Sx at Tx or Qy in Sy at Ty or Qz in Sz at Tz, pace Gracia. (Unless, of course, we disallow the very possibility of disjunctive qualities. There may be reasons to do that, but I do not recall them in Gracia's text, and it would be better to have an account without so esoteric a metaphysical commitment.)

3. Identity derives from sameness, as I said earlier, and makes no sense except in terms of it. However, Peter Geach maintains that X's and Y's being the same requires that they be the same F, for some F. Even if he is wrong in going that far, they must still be the same in some Q (color, size, shape, etc.). This suggests that, contra Gracia, identity without shared qualities is incoherent.[13]

Gracia (2000c:59) calls his a Familial-Historical View of Hispanic identity. Hispanics "must be understood as forming a unit which goes beyond political, territorial, linguistic, cultural, racial, or genetic frontiers. . . . A unique web of changing historical relations supplies their unity" (49). He elaborates, "We are speaking here of a people [Hispanics] who have no common elements considered as a whole. Their unity is . . . a historical unity founded on relations" (50).[14] He invokes Wittgenstein's (1953) famous discussions of the word 'game' and 'family resemblance' (paras. 75ff., 67ff.), saying the latter "metaphor" is "especially appropriate in this case, for the history of Hispanics is a history of a group of people, a community united by historical events." However, in an important qualification, Gracia complains that "the very notion of resemblance used by Wittgenstein is misleading insofar as it appears to require a genetic connection." In fact, Gracia (2000c) reminds us,

One does not need to be genetically tied to the other members of a family to be a member of the family. Indeed, the very foundation of a family, marriage, takes place between people who are added to a family through contract, not genesis. . . . Families are not coherent wholes. . . . Families are in a constant process of change and adaptation. My claim is that this is how we should understand ourselves as Hispanics. (50)

This creates trouble for Gracia's account. Without going into the details of Wittgenstein's discussion, his point is that the various practices all labeled "games" have little or nothing in common, and that the various members of a family likewise need have no property universally shared by them all. Rather, he reminds us that, say, Alicia, Bernardo, and Consuelo Acosta may all have similar eyes; and Bernardo, Consuelo, and Diego Acosta may all have similar noses; and also Consuelo, Diego, and Eduardo Acosta may all have similar mouths; and Diego, Eduardo, and Francisco Acosta may all have similar chins. So, no one characteristic is shared by all, but each is linked by similarity to some others who in turn link her or him to others. Games and, by extension, other things sharing the same common name may be similarly linked without their all sharing any one (nonlinguistic) feature. Note, however, that it is significant for genuine family resemblance that the persons be genetically linked.[15] For that is what explains the visually similar eyes, and so forth. By refusing to follow Wittgenstein on this last point, Gracia makes the analogy impossible to follow and apply. The notion of "family resemblance" simply has no literal application to spouses and in-laws, for example. The resemblance can only be illusory or aleatory.

More important, if there is no quality shared among all Hispanics, as Gracia sometimes maintains, then neither, as he also holds, can Hispanics all share a common identity nor can they all share a common history. It will not do to insist that what we have is "a common identity of a familial, historical sort" (Gracia 2000c:44). That common identity simply seems incapable of existing without shared qualities. Notice, too, that the history of Cubans appears to have been quite different from that of Mexicans, and still more from that of Spaniards or Portuguese. So it is doubtful there is one history that they all share, though there may be some common elements to the histories of these different groups.

Further, pace Gracia, Wittgensteinian "family resemblance" theory appears to preclude any shared identity. It uses the web of similarities to show how the various individuals are indirectly connected one to another in the absence of any universally shared identity. So, Gracia cannot properly invoke Wittgenstein's view to help explain such an identity. Gracia (2000c) insists that "Hispanics have a historical tie which unites them," that they "form a historical family," and that "there is a sense in which Hispanics all over the world belong together" (54, 55). Perhaps so, but each of these claims needs explication and defense. Gracia's Familial-Historical View of Hispanic identity, with its Wittgensteinian elucidation, only obstructs that project, as far as I can see. That is because Wittgenstein's project seems to be that of explaining why games—and why groups of individuals such as the Acostas—are called by the term, though, contrary to essentialism, they form no real unity metaphysically. It is difficult to see, then, how such a position can also advance a view such as that of Gracia's, which maintains that there is a real unity among the individuals classed as Hispanics.

Setting aside the special problems that arise from Gracia's talk of "identity," there appear to me to be serious problems in Gracia's account, even if conceived merely as an account of ethnic affiliation (membership): that is, as an account merely of being (a) Hispanic, as distinct from having Hispanic "identity." These are in addition to the difficulty, noted previously, that arises from Gracia's view that what it is to be a Hispanic varies from place to place, from time to time, and perhaps, too, from classificatory scheme to classificatory scheme.

Thus, Gracia's (2000c) account, in its most definitive statement, is that "Hispanics are the group of people comprised by the inhabitants of the countries of the Iberian peninsula after 1492 and what were to become [their] colonies . . . by descendants of these people who live in other countries (e.g., the United States) but preserve some link to those people" or, as he puts it a bit later, "preserve close ties to them" (48; see also 52). This final qualifying clause is troubling in its vagueness. We want to ask what sort(s) of ties are required, and how "close" must they be. More important, we want to know why these ties are needed. If Maria, a descendant of the Iberians, now loses all contact with them and their other descendants, does she at that point cease being Hispanic? (Would internal, affectional ties suffice to avert the change of ethnicity?) To think that seems to reintroduce a cultural element or something like it (behavioral? affectional?) to an ethnic category shaped by geography and ancestry. Maria is not culturally Hispanic, in that she does not participate in the ways of thinking, feeling, behaving, and so forth, that arose among the Iberians and their descendants and that characterize their group life. Yet she still seems to be of their lineage.[16] And what of Marisol, who was born and reared in Latin America but has no genetic ties to the Iberians? Or Marina, who now inhabits a former colony but has no other connection to what Gracia calls the Hispanic world?[17] Of course, we should expect there to be some difficult cases for any detailed account of ethnicity. That is the honorable price of precision, and I leave it to others to belabor the details.[18]

What concerns me more here is that, in this important qualification, Gracia seems to entangle himself in difficulties of the same sort on whose basis he rejects what he calls the Common-Bundle View of ethnic identity. That view conceives ethnic affiliation/membership as consisting in having any suitable subset from a certain bundle of defining features, so that someone is (a) Hispanic if she has enough of the features that, in appropriate combination, make someone (a) Hispanic. In his critical discussion, Gracia (2000c:58ff.) complains that those who advocate such a position face the burden, among others, of specifying just which features belong in the bundle, just how many features are needed, and whether all the features are equal or some can count for more than others. He seems to think no principled defense can be given any particular specification and, apparently for that reason, rejects the Common-Bundle View. Note, however, that it seems that a defender of Gracia's own account assumes a similar burden, in light of the qualification pointed out earlier. For the defender needs to specify just which kinds of "tie" someone must retain in order still to count as Hispanic, how many such ties she or he needs, and whether some ties count more (or less) than others. And the defender will need to explain and defend her or his chosen specifications as against others (or none). Given that, it is hard to see why Gracia's account has such an advantage over the rival Common-Bundle View, and how it escapes the difficulties he thinks suffice to sink that position.

WHY MAY WE NEED AN ACCOUNT OF HISPANIC IDENTITY?

Contrary to what Gracia (2000c:x) suggests, a "social ontology" that philosophically clarifies the concept of what it is to be a Hispanic is not needed for affirmative action and other political/legal policies. It may be helpful there, but we are familiar with the phenomenon of civil law artificially delineating by stipulation concepts unclear in ordinary discourse. Such stipulation is not without its drawbacks, but its possibility shows there are alternatives to "social ontology."

Even if we do need a philosophically sophisticated and defensible account of Hispanic ethnicity (i.e., of being [a] Hispanic), that still would not show that we need an account of being Hispanic as an "ethnic identity." Nor would it show that we need to or even should retain that idea. We do need (or, at least, reasonably want) to be able to identify Hispanics, as Gracia observes.[19] However, that no more requires a conception of Hispanic identity (in any contemporary social scientific sense of "identity") than does identifying, say, hassocks require a comparable concept of "hassock identity."

Gracia's learned work breaks new philosophical ground, is filled with provocative ideas and imaginative suggestions, and brings lapidary analysis to complicated topics often shrouded in social scientific jargon, emotional and intellectual confusion, and ideological bombast. With characteristic humility and understatement, he says that its aim is chiefly to stimulate thought and discussion. In that spirit, permit me to close with some quite tentative conclusions of the reflection that his work has so far stimulated in me.

1. The concept of ethnic identity needs to be distinguished from the weaker concept of ethnic affiliation/membership: simply being a Hispanic as distinct from having a(n) Hispanic identity. The former notion is unclear and problematic, but the latter is so dubious and rife with such difficulties as to warrant its rejection.

2. Ethnicity is an inherently problematic concept, as is that of culture, and we should be much more skeptical about them than intellectuals nowadays are. We may properly want to lend some clarity to Hispanic (and other forms of) ethnicity for ordinary and political purposes, but we should not expect it to admit of much specification. Perhaps we can say, roughly, that someone is (a) Hispanic when she is relevantly (especially ancestrally) connected to some member of the peoples who inhabited Spain or Portugal during the early Renaissance days of Iberian consolidation, American exploration, and African enslavement. Still, we should not expect to be able to determine with much precision just what the relevant connection is, nor just who are the people to whom a Hispanic must be so connected. That imprecision may not require a negative answer to the metaphysical question of whether there are or can be Hispanics or members of other ethnic groups. Nonetheless, it does warrant embracing a measure of skepticism about ethnic affiliation, and preferring a deflationary account of it. That suggests we do well to discard the concept of ethnic identity and to follow the lead taken by Naomi Zack and K. Anthony Appiah in racial matters, rejecting ethnicity's alleged moral import and

regarding it with skeptical detachment. Contrary to the view of some contemporary enthusiasts for ethnicity and race, I think we should consider these concepts so murky, indeterminate, and problematic that the prudent person ought to accord them only quite limited significance in her or his self-image, and in the way she or he thinks about others and relates to them. In contrast, I suggested earlier that near the end of his book Gracia comes close to exalting ethnicity, and without much effort to explain or defend that emphasis.

3. Gracia's Familial-Historical View of Hispanic ethnicity (being Hispanic) is deeply problematic in its central imagery of family and perhaps incoherent as an account of anything so grand as Hispanic identity. We can acknowledge the complex historical connections among the peoples of Iberia, the Americas (especially South and Central America and the southwestern regions of North America), and Africa to which Gracia repeatedly and insightfully draws our attention. However, we do well to rest content with this web of historical relations and to stop short of Gracia's (2000c) effort to squeeze from them a metaphysical tangle of "new realities," a single "community," a Hispanic "family," transcontinental "unity," and ethnic "identity" (88ff.).

NOTES

1. Gracia (2000c:chaps. 1, 3) notes that some do or might prefer such terms as 'Latina/o' or 'Latin American,' or 'Ibero-American' to pick out a larger or smaller subset of the ethnic group(s) he has in mind and, despite his book's title, carefully argues for the superiority of the term 'Hispanic.' I find his reasoning cogent and, for that reason, and for the sake of consistency and simplicity, hereafter I talk simply of "Hispanics" and of being "Hispanic."

2. One difference is that some people do talk of identity in these contexts (e.g., "identity politics"). However, some of us think they shouldn't, and one thing a philosopher should do here is to query this sort of naive practice and explore ways of justifying its presuppositions.

3. I am aware that Frege, Strawson, and Geach, among others, have denied that identity itself is a relation (Morris 1984:esp. chaps. 2, 5). I don't want to beg that question. My claim here is only that meaningful identity-talk must naturally lend itself to (or, minimally, must allow) formulation in two-term language. This is the test that, whatever the nature (if any) of identity itself, talk of identity across time and across possible worlds passes, and talk of ethnic identity fails.

4. "This [i.e., Gracia's] conception of who we are is open and pluralistic, allowing the coexistence of other, multiple, and variegated identities" (Gracia 2000c:69).

5. Philosophers have sometimes called this an individual essence or *haecceitas*. It is not obvious we should concede that these exist, since it is not clear what it is that they are supposed to explain, there being no alternative to X's being what it is (i.e., X), even if it could have been different from the (qualitative) way it is.

6. "We do not know what properties will be pertinent for Hispanic identity in the future. The set of properties which Hispanics share [and which makes them Hispanic] could change, and so could the proportion of qualities necessary for qualification. . . . Our identity is flexible and subject to evolution and transformation. . . . If tigers could be bred to lose their stripes, there is no reason Hispanics could not become quite different from what they are today or were in the past" (Gracia 2000c:60). I think the remark about tigers is not illustrative but irrelevant and misleading. Scientifically, being striped is not part of what makes an animal a tiger, even if having an inborn and genetic propensity for stripes were. In contrast, what Gracia is discussing for Hispanics is precisely our identity, which he understands as what it is that makes us Hispanic. At the American Philosophical Association Eastern Division session devoted to his book, when I pointed out difficulties in the notion of changing identities, Gracia said that he does not commit himself to the claim that ethnic identities themselves change. That may be true. Nevertheless, he does state, "Our identity is flexible and subject to evolution and transformation." This plainly commits him to the view that ethnic identities can change. Since that view still generates the problem that concerns me, I have here slightly reformulated my objection, now focusing on this weaker, modal claim.

7. Note that conceptions of ethnicity differ across cultures and also change over time within a culture.

8. "Group and ethnic identities are the result of both social construction and factors outside the power of societies" (Gracia 2000c:46).

9. Here and throughout, I treat Hispanic as an ethnicity. Since it embraces other ethnic classifications, it is sometimes considered a "pan-ethnic" (better, a transethnic) category (e.g., Gracia 2000c:198n.14). I ignore this complication.

10. I need not commit myself here on the question whether these deflationary accounts of truth succeed, a claim I think dubious. For an introduction to the topic, see Craig (1998:s.v. "truth").

11. He does meticulously argue, what some denied, that there are such things as both Hispanic and Latin American philosophy (Gracia 2000c:esp. chaps. 4, 6).

12. Sometimes Gracia (2000c) commits himself only to the weaker claim that we can discern no such quality: "Nor can my position be construed as implying that there are no common properties to Hispanics at all times and places. My point

is only that there are no properties that can be shown to be common to all Hispanics at all times and in all places" (56).

13. For X and Y to be numerically the same, if there is such a thing, must be understood as their sharing all qualities. Hence, Leibniz's principle of the Indiscernibility of Identicals.

14. Gracia may have gotten ahead of himself here in not qualifying this claim by restricting it, as he does elsewhere in this section, to discernible elements. A few pages later, as we have noted, he explicitly states that his view, as developed to that point in the text, does not entail that "there are no common properties to Hispanics at all times and places" (Gracia 2000c:56). This doesn't matter much, however, for Gracia soon repudiates these qualifications and issues a more sweeping declaration: "There cannot be a fixed list of properties in which [all] Hispanics [at all times] share. . . . Note that I began by allowing the possibility that in principle there could be such a list of properties even if we cannot identify it. Now, however, it should be clear that I am not willing to allow the possibility of such a list even in principle" (60).

15. I do not deny that the kind of similarity and dissimilarity found among, for example, the Acostas may be given a strict characterization, nor that it may exist in nonbiological groups. My point is only that, in such cases, we still need some other explanation of how the individual entities have come so to resemble and differ from one another.

16. Should we say, then, that culture determines not whether she is Hispanic but how Hispanic she is? That suggestion is initially appealing. However, I think closer, critical examination of Corlett's (1999) rigorous recent attempt to develop just such a position would reveal insurmountable shortcomings. See my criticism in García 2007:46–47.

17. The wording of Gracia's account is somewhat odd, but in calling Hispanics those who inhabited "what *were to become* the [Spanish and Portuguese] colonies" (emphasis added), he doesn't seem to mean only those who lived there prior to colonization, thereby excluding today's Latin Americans.

18. One matter that some will find offensive is Gracia's emphasis on the year 1492, notorious for the expulsion of the Jews from Spain and for Columbus's first journey to the Americas. He treats and defends the centrality of this (rough) date in the second section of chapter 4 of Gracia (2000c).

19. Gracia (2000c:33ff.) himself observes that identification (and reidentification) is (are) an epistemological matter, while identity itself is ontological.

7. THE BOUNDARIES OF
HISPANIC IDENTITY

RICHARD J. BERNSTEIN

In the concluding remarks of his splendid book, Jorge J. E. Gracia (2000c) tells us, "I feel as if the theses I have proposed raise more questions than they answer, but that is as it should be" (189). The aim of his book is to provoke fresh thinking about the issues he explores. It is in this spirit that I want to offer my criticism. Gracia's book is filled with insights, provocative claims, and valuable information. It is a courageous book, because Gracia takes on difficult and thorny issues—and he does this with verve and lucidity. I admire his ability to avoid clichés about the "politics of identity" and the "politics of difference" and to avoid the extremes of a misguided essentialism and a debilitating nominalism that dissolve questions about one's identity and solidarity with others. Furthermore, his pluralism and his sensitivity to the heterogeneity of Hispanic identity are laudable. He takes on the battery of arguments against the very idea of naming a group "Hispanics" or "Latinos/ as" and forcefully argues for the thesis that there is a Hispanic identity. His understanding of Hispanic identity is flexible, pluralistic, heterogeneous, and dynamic. Some of the most informative chapters deal with the beginnings of Hispanic philosophy and the character of Latin American philosophy.

Nevertheless, there are problems in his *positive* case for affirming Hispanic identity. Throughout the book, there is an unresolved tension between a more descriptive pole (where Gracia describes how Hispanic identity has been conceived) and a more prescriptive or normative pole (where he advocates how we *ought* to think about Hispanic identity). I want to focus on two clusters of issues: the positive case that Gracia makes for Hispanic identity, and his reflections on the possibility of a Hispanic-American philosophy. The subtitle of the book, *A Philosophical Perspective*, has a double meaning. Gracia, as a philosopher, not only uses the conceptual tools of philosophy to deal with the problem of Hispanic identity but also is explicitly concerned with developing the character of Hispanic, Latin American, and Hispanic-American philosophy.

After forcefully arguing "that there are no common properties to all those people whom we wish to call Hispanics," no common properties that Hispanics share at all times and all places, he emphatically declares,

> My thesis is that the concept of Hispanic should be understood historically, that is, as a concept that involves historical relations. Hispanics are the group of people comprised by the inhabitants of the countries of the Iberian peninsula after 1492 and what were to become the colonies of those countries after the encounter between Iberia and America took place, and by the descendants of these people who live in other countries (e.g., the United States) but preserve some link to those people. It excludes the population of other countries in the world and the inhabitants of Iberia and Latin America before 1492 because beginning in the year of the encounter, the Iberian countries and their colonies in America developed a web of historical connections which continues to this day and which separates these people from others. (Gracia 2000c:48–49)

Gracia continues by insisting that

> this group of people must be understood as forming a unity which goes beyond political, territorial, linguistic, cultural, racial, or genetic frontiers. It is not even necessary that the members of the group name themselves in any particular way or have a consciousness of their identity. . . . What ties them together, and separates them from others, is history and the particular events of that history rather than the consciousness of that history, a unique web of changing historical relations supplies their unity. (49)

I find it at once disturbing, and indeed a bit artificial, to assert categorically that the "origin" of Hispanic identity begins in 1492, a year so symbolically associated with the violence of the expulsion of the Jews from the Iberian Peninsula, and the beginning of the history of the brutal violence of what Gracia calls the "encounter" between Iberia and its colonies. Gracia's proposal departs from the ways in which many of those who think of themselves as Hispanics conceive of their identity. When the expression is used in the United States or even in Latin America, it is not commonly used to include ancestors or current residents living in the Iberian Peninsula. And I doubt that those residents of the Iberian Peninsula after 1492 (and their descendants) think of themselves as Hispanic—and certainly not as Latinos/Latinas.

By itself, this is not yet an objection to Gracia's thesis, because he knows that he is advocating a way of thinking about Hispanics that departs from common usage. He is making a normative recommendation, how Hispanics ought to think of their identity. According to Gracia, it is not even necessary that Hispanics have a consciousness of their identity. Nevertheless the disparity between Gracia's recommendation and actual usage focuses attention on what is so central for him—the importance of history and historical relations. I believe it is fair to say that one of Gracia's primary motivations for extending the domain of the name 'Hispanic' in this manner is because it helps to highlight the richness and diversity of Hispanic history and tradition. But I want to argue that Gracia overburdens the concepts of *history* and *family* in his positive characterization of Hispanic identity. I also think that when we analyze these concepts (as Gracia uses them), they fail to single out a distinctive Hispanic identity. Let me spell this out.

It is important to emphasize that 'history' does not name a "natural kind." We are always implicitly or explicitly appealing to some principle of *selection* in dealing with history. For example, I am a philosopher and also an American Jew born in New York (Brooklyn) whose ancestors came from Russia. What constitutes my history? Depending on what aspect of my history one *selects*, different histories will be relevant—the history of Jews, the history of Brooklyn and New York, the history of immigrants from Russia, the history of the philosophic traditions within which I work, and so forth. Identities are complex and shifting, and so are one's relevant histories. Gracia is certainly aware of the point that I am making. Indeed, he argues that for certain purposes the fact that one is Cuban or Cuban American may be more important than the fact that one is also Hispanic, but this is not an argument against speaking about Hispanic identity. I agree, but this is not my point. It is rather that the appeal to history or historical relations is not in itself *sufficient* to justify singling out the class of Hispanics. It is not history per se that justifies the "unity" of this group of people. Gracia is (at least, implicitly) appealing to some *other* characteristics that justify singling out this history as a distinctive history. But it is not clear what precisely these characteristics are. Indeed, I think Gracia is caught in something of a double bind. He denies that there is a set of characteristics or properties that all Hispanics share. Yet he seems to appeal to something like a "unity" in claiming that Hispanic history is a distinctive history. Gracia never really squarely confronts the issues of how we do and how we *ought* to carve up history—and why. Instead, he comes close to a type of essentialism that he so effectively criticizes. Consider some of his phrases. He speaks of "historical *unity* founded on relations" (Gracia 2000c:50), "a historical reality that *unites* us" (51), "*our* reality" (52), "a web of *concrete* historical relations" (52), and "*our* history" (65). But I fail to see either that Gracia focuses his attention on the words that I have italicized or that he indicates the rationale for the principle of *selection* that singles out the concrete, historical reality that distinguishes Hispanics from other groups. An appeal to a common history makes sense only if one gives some account of what makes this history "common." He wants to rule out political, territorial, linguistic, ethnic, racial, and genetic characteristics as being necessary for distinguishing Hispanics from other groups. And he thinks that appealing to history supplies the "unity" he is looking for. But it doesn't—unless we specify what makes a given history a unity.

There is another important distinction that Gracia tends to gloss over—a distinction that is all-important if one is to speak of Hispanic identity, or indeed any sort of ethnic or cultural identity. This is the distinction between a *third-person* view of history and a *first-person* (singular or plural) sense of one's history. Perhaps it is more accurate to say that Gracia is aware of this distinction but does not think it is important for the case he wants to make for Hispanic identity. In a passage that I quoted earlier, Gracia (2000c) says it is not necessary that a group should "have a consciousness of their identity as a group" (49). One can see why Gracia asserts this, but it has some awkward consequences. Gracia is certainly aware that many of those that he names as "Hispanic" do not think that their identity is bound up with their Iberian ancestors or with the current residents of Iberia. Yet according to his definition, these are all members of the group he identifies as Hispanic. So one's first-person consciousness cannot be a sufficient condition for singling out one's identity as Hispanic. But unless a people or a group has some sense or consciousness of its identity and of the significance of that identity for defining who its members are, it is difficult to discern what role the concept of identity is playing. After all, if we go back far enough, most human beings are historically related to one another (unless we are simply referring to their identity as human beings).

Earlier I spoke of a tension that pervades Gracia's book. And here it comes to the fore. Why is Gracia so concerned to make the positive case for Hispanic identity? Because naming oneself as Hispanic can be a source of empowerment, because when a people names itself (instead of having a name imposed upon it), the naming can be a source of pride and recognition. But "empowerment," "pride," or "recognition" simply do not make any sense unless one has some consciousness, some self-awareness of one's identity. In this respect, I think that Gracia (2000c) is just wrong when he asserts "knowledge does not determine being" (49)—at least in regard to a knowledge of one's own identity. The self-understanding and the self-knowledge of who one is, what one's allegiances and relevant history are, are *constitutive* of one's own being. This is a point that has been persuasively argued by Linda Alcoff, Hans-Georg Gadamer, Charles Taylor, Axel Honneth, and Nancy Fraser. It raises a much larger issue that Gracia neglects but which is essential in any discourse about a people's identity: the subtle interplay between history and cultural memory. History (especially third-person history) and cultural memory are not the same. But in the past few decades there has been an explosion of interest in the dynamics of cultural identity and memory—how cultural memory is formed, how it changes, and how it shapes one's outlook. Gracia's thesis about nurturing an encompassing Hispanic identity would be far more convincing if he had addressed the question of the formation of cultural identity and memory. Despite his excessive reliance on history and historical relations, I believe that what Gracia really wants to argue is something like the following: Hispanics *ought* to *expand* their self-understanding and self-knowledge of who they are in order to encompass the richness and diversity of their history—a history that spans the historical interactions between the Iberian Peninsula and those Hispanics living in Latin America or in other countries. It is this *enlarged mentality* that he thinks can *empower* the Hispanic community. But I have another reservation about Gracia's analysis. I find it a bit too theoretical and it doesn't deal with the hard realities of political power. He puts too much stress on self-naming as a source of empowerment. He tells us that "the point that needs to be emphasized is that to adopt a name and define one's identity is both a sign of power and an act of empowerment. It is a sign of power because those without power do not even have the prerogative of doing it. . . . To adopt a name and define one's identity is, moreover, an act of empowerment because it limits the power of others to name and identify us" (46).

One can certainly grant that a condition for empowerment is that people take some pride in identifying themselves as a group with a distinctive history and traditions. But as the history of many oppressed groups shows (including those who proudly call themselves Hispanics), the act of self-naming is hardly sufficient to empower a group in any meaningful sense. I want to make a stronger claim. An adequate examination of Hispanic identity demands a detailed analysis of political empowerment. But Gracia's remarks about power and empowerment barely scratch the surface. Gracia's inclusive understanding of the range of who is Hispanic actually weakens any collective sense of identity—at least an identity that can empower. But stretching one's identity to include all those who have been living in the Iberian Peninsula since 1492 and all those descendants living in other countries can weaken any strong sense of solidarity.

Sometimes Gracia shifts his emphasis to the concept of a family in order to make his case for Hispanic identity. He does not want to "reduce" Hispanic identity to a matter of racial or genetic identity. He goes to great lengths to defend the concept of *mestizaje* as a primary feature of Hispanics. He even criticizes Wittgenstein's famous distinction of "family resemblances" because "it appears to require a genetic connection which in fact is not required" (Gracia 2000c:50). "Indeed, the very foundation of a family, marriage, takes place between people who are added to a family through contract, not genesis. And in-laws become members of families indirectly, again not through genesis" (50). I can appreciate Gracia's spirit of openness in characterizing Hispanic identity, and his adamant rejection of any suggestion of racial and/or genetic purity. But the way in which Gracia uses the concept of a family is a bit too open and generous. If we flesh out the consequences of what Gracia affirms, it would mean that if a woman from Portugal marries a German businessman and goes to live with him in Frankfurt, then her husband is Hispanic! After all, he married into a Portuguese family. Sometimes relatives by marriage do take on some of the characteristics of the families into which they marry, but if this happens it is not because of the formal contract of marriage but rather because they adopt some of the cultural characteristics of their spouse's family. Gracia tells us that "Hispanics display the kind of *unity* characteristic of families rather than the unity characteristic of sets or classes based on shared properties" (54), but he does not tell us what kind of *unity* is characteristic of families. Despite Gracia's effort to show that his definition of Hispanic is not too thin, I am not persuaded that he has been successful. Consider, for example, the descendants of those Jewish Marranos who managed to survive in Iberia after 1492 but who subsequently moved to Amsterdam, Istanbul, or Tangier. According to Gracia's definition of Hispanic, they are Hispanic—even if they are presently Israeli citizens.

After all, they share a common history—even if they lack any consciousness of it.

In short, I do not think that Gracia has been successful in showing that the appeal to "historical relations," "historical events," and "historical reality" is sufficient for providing a robust sense of Hispanic identity. And I do not think that his use of the concept of a family helps to rectify this deficiency. These are "formal" objections. As a philosopher, Gracia is concerned that his formal definition of 'Hispanic' should stand up against objections. But I believe that the real problem lies deeper. Because Gracia seeks to expand the concept of Hispanic identity to include all those who are descendants of the encounter between Iberia and America after 1492, and because he wants to avoid any suggestion of racial purity, homogeneity, or shared common properties, he appeals to historical relations. But I also think that even Gracia realizes that "third-person" history is not adequate to make the case for a Hispanic identity that truly empowers. *There must also be a sense of one's identity and pride in being Hispanic.* In this sense Gracia's hope is that Hispanics will *appropriate* the richness and diversity of their history. It is the making of history into one's *own* history, absorbing it into the fabric of one's being, that is crucial for Gracia's normative claims.

Finally, I want to consider briefly some of Gracia's reflections about Hispanic American philosophy. I have already indicated that Gracia does an excellent job in showing the richness of the tradition of Hispanic philosophy. I also think that he illuminates the character of Latin American philosophy (with its conflicting culturalist, universalist, and critical strands). My queries concern his sketchy remarks about *Hispanic American* philosophy when he is referring to the philosophy of Hispanics living in the United States. Gracia notes that at present there are very few professional Hispanic American philosophers—especially when we consider the size of the Hispanic American population living there. Hispanic Americans still play only a marginal role in the philosophic community of the United States: "Hispanics, regardless of how we actually speak, look, or behave, are perceived as foreigners, belonging elsewhere, and as not being true Americans" (Gracia 2000c:182). But still, it isn't entirely clear what Gracia has in mind when he speaks of Hispanic American *philosophy*. I can well understand the desire to see that there are more Hispanic Americans who enter the philosophic profession, and that it is important that some philosophers (Hispanics and non-Hispanics) should be concerned with the issues that are central for the Hispanic American community. It would be desirable if the history of Hispanic and Latin

American philosophy were taught in our colleges and universities. Perhaps this is all that Gracia has in mind. But at times he seems to suggest something more—that Hispanic Americans ought to cultivate a philosophic orientation that is somehow distinctly Hispanic American. But if this is so, it is not clear what this concretely means. Perhaps all this will change in the future. With the anticipated growth of the Hispanic American population in the United States, the day may come when there are far more Hispanic American philosophers who focus on the problems of their community and their heritage. Although Gracia discusses the work of the few (unfortunately, too few) Hispanic American philosophers who have dealt with issues of their community, I do not think he has succeeded in making a case for a Hispanic American *philosophy* that is distinct. Let me be fully explicit. I am not questioning that there is Hispanic philosophy or Latin American philosophy, or even that some Hispanic Americans in the United States are concerned with their history and traditions. I am questioning whether there *now* exists something that we can identify as Hispanic American philosophy. But then again, perhaps my skepticism is not quite warranted. Gracia might serve as a model of a Hispanic American philosopher who honors the highest standards of philosophy and deals with problems of the Hispanic American community in a fresh, illuminating, and provocative manner. It certainly would be desirable if there were more Hispanic American philosophers who exemplified his virtues!

8. HISPANIC IDENTITY, ITS ORIGIN, AND HISPANIC PHILOSOPHERS

ROBERT GOODING-WILLIAMS

Jorge J. E. Gracia's *Hispanic/Latino Identity* (2000c) is a valuable contribution to contemporary philosophical discussions of racial and ethnic identities. In my commentary here, I will more or less ignore chapters 1 and 2 of Gracia's book, the first of which reviews in detail some arguments against using the expressions "Hispanics" and "Latinos/Latinas" "to name us," as Gracia puts it, and the second of which analyzes the relation of names to ethnicity and identity. Rather, I begin my remarks with a look at chapter 3, which is Gracia's positive account of Hispanic identity. I then proceed briefly to consider three other topics: Gracia's description of the origins of Hispanic identity; his discussion of political justifications for the use of a common name; and his treatment of the status of Hispanics in American philosophy. My aim in all of this is to probe Gracia's arguments, to raise some questions regarding his conclusions, and, most of all, to invite him to further clarify his views.

THE ARGUMENT FOR HISPANIC IDENTITY

Gracia (2000c:47–60) denies that there is an essence, a property, or a set of properties shared by all Hispanics at all times and in all places. Rather, he holds that Hispanics "constitute a family tied by changing historical relations which in turn generate particular properties which can be used to distinguish . . . [them] . . . from others in particular contexts" (xvii). Gracia's *familial-historical* conception of Hispanic identity stands at the heart of his book. In what follows, I argue that, strictly speaking, this concept does not pick out and distinguish from other groups the group of people Gracia wishes to pick out and identify as Hispanic. Put otherwise, the extension of the concept is broader than Gracia wishes it to be. As we shall see, Gracia also articulates a *geobiological* conception of Hispanic identity that, though he does not distinguish it from the familial-historical conception (in fact, he seems to believe that the two conceptions are identical), has a narrower extension than the familial-historical conception. It turns out, however, that the geobiological conception is too empty for Gracia's purposes, which is why it gives way, I think, to a *Hispanic-world* conception of Hispanic identity. In sum, Gracia develops three distinct notions of Hispanic identity, though he purports to develop just one.

Let me begin with Gracia's familial-historical conception of Hispanic identity. According to this conception, Hispanic identity is the identity of "a unique web of changing historical relations" (Gracia 2000c:49). To illustrate the sort of situation he has in mind, Gracia describes the case of four individuals, A, B, C, and D, where A is directly related to B, B to C, and C to D, though there are no direct relations between A and C, or between A and D, or between B and D. In Gracia's account, the relations that connect the members of the group ABCD are relations (1) that "tie each member of the group with at least one other member of the group" and (2) that "allow us to separate the group ABCD from other groups" (49).

How does Gracia conceptualize the relations he has in mind? He conceptualizes them, I believe, as historical events. He writes, for example, that "the history of Hispanics is a history of a group of people, a community united by *historical events*" (Gracia 2000c:50; emphasis added). More expansively, he asserts that the unity of Hispanics "is a historical unity founded on *relations*. King John II of Portugal has nothing in common with me, but both of us are tied *by a series of events that relate us* and separate us from Queen Elizabeth II and Martin Luther King" (50; emphasis added). In Gracia's view, then, to be Hispanic is to be a member of a community all of whose members are tied, or related, to at least one other member of the community by a historical event or a series of historical events.

Of course, Gracia wants the familial-historical conception of Hispanic identity to involve a bit more than this. To be Hispanic is to be a member of a *distinct and unique community* (again, what he calls "a unique web of changing historical relations") and not of just any community whose members are tied to one another by a series of historical events. Thus, Gracia wants also to identify a criterion for distinguishing the historical community of Hispanics from other historical communities. In other words, he wants to identify a criterion for distinguishing the historical events and multiple series of historical events that constitute the Hispanic community from the historical events and multiple series of historical events that constitute other historical communities. Gracia explains the criteria he identifies for this purpose by resorting to his conception of the Hispanic community as a sort of family.

"Now, families are formed by marriages," he writes. "So we are entitled to ask: Is there a point in history when our Hispanic family came to be? . . . We must find a point in history when we came together, and this, I propose, is the encounter of Iberia and America. It makes no sense to speak of Hispanics before 1492. Our family first came into being because of the *events* which the encounter unleashed" (Gracia 2000c:50–51; emphasis added).

It is obvious, I suppose, that being a historical event or a series of historical events that relates Hispanics cannot be Gracia's criterion for distinguishing Hispanic historical events and series of historical events from non-Hispanic historical events and series of historical events, for, in his account, being related by Hispanic historical events and series of historical events is precisely what makes someone Hispanic, or a member of the Hispanic community, in the first place. Thus, Gracia looks for a different criterion, which is *causal relatedness to a particular historical event.* That event, the encounter between Iberia and America, is what engendered the Hispanic community. For Gracia, it seems, the historical events and series of historical events that constitute the Hispanic community are exactly those events and series of events that were "unleashed" by Christopher Columbus's arrival in the Americas in 1492. As I interpret Gracia, then, he suggests that someone is Hispanic, or a member of the Hispanic community, if, and only if, she is related to at least one other individual through an event, or events, the character of which was causally conditioned by events stemming from—or, again, "unleashed" by—the encounter of 1492. For the sake of concision, I shall say that Gracia suggests that someone is Hispanic, or a member of the Hispanic community, if, and only if, she satisfies the familial-historical conception of Hispanic identity.

Now, the problem with this criterion, plainly, is that it is too broad. That is, it permits us to count as Hispanic indefinitely many more individuals than Gracia is willing to count as Hispanic. Consider, for example, the case of Dr. Martin Luther King Jr., whom Gracia does not count as Hispanic. It would be very difficult to show, I think, that his life, or that of any other African American, involved *no* events or series of events relating him to other people the character of which events or series of events was causally conditioned by events stemming from Columbus's arrival in America. Flip Wilson made the point better than I can in his 1967 televised comic monologue "Christopher Columbus":

> At thirty-five, he'd gotten out of grammar school. He arranged an audience with the queen, Queen Isabel. Isabel Johnson, that was the queen's name. She asked him about this American project. And Chris tells her, "If I don't discover America, there's not gonna be a Benjamin Franklin, or a Star-Spangled Banner, no land of the free, and home of the brave, and no Ray Charles." When the queen heard "no Ray Charles" she panicked. The queen said, "Ray Charles? You gonna find Ray Charles? He in America?" Chris said, "Damned right, that's where all the records come from." So the queen's running through the halls of the castle, "Chris gon' fine Ray Charles. He goin' to America on that boat. What you say." (quoted in Sollors and Dietrich 1994:6)

Martin Luther King Jr., Flip Wilson, Ray Charles, and, for that matter, millions of non-Hispanic and non–African American inhabitants of the United States satisfy Gracia's familial-historical conception of Hispanic identity, as I have construed it. Again, the familial-historical conception of Hispanic identity is too broad. That, I think, is why Gracia also sketches a geobiological conception of Hispanic identity. By doing so he suggests that satisfying the familial-historical conception is at best a necessary condition, but not a sufficient condition, for being a member of the Hispanic community that someone is Hispanic, or a member of the Hispanic community, *only if* (but not *if* and *only if*) she is related to at least one other individual through an event or events, the character of which was causally conditioned by events stemming from—or, again, "unleashed" by—the encounter of 1492. Thus, Gracia can justify the view that the Hispanic community includes neither King, nor Wilson, nor Charles.

Consider, then, Gracia's (2000c) geobiological conception of Hispanic identity, which tells us that "Hispanics are the group of people comprised by the inhabitants of the countries of the Iberian peninsula after 1492 and what were to become the colonies of those countries after the encounter between Iberia and America took place, and by descendants of these people who live in other countries (e.g., the United States) but preserve some link to those people" (48).

I refer to this conception as geobiological for it relies on geographical and biological criteria to limit the extension of the concept of Hispanic identity. The geographical criterion is being a post-1492 inhabitant of the region of Iberia or a post-1492 inhabitant of one of the regions of Latin America that was to become one of Spain's or Portugal's colonies. The biological criterion is being a descendant of people who live or have lived in one of these geographical regions and who preserve "some link" to the Iberian or Latin American Hispanics from whom they are descended. Through the reference to the year 1492, Gracia's geobiological conception of Hispanic identity alludes to the encounter between Iberia and America but does not entail that Hispanics be related to one another by events the character of which was causally conditioned by events "unleashed" by the encounter. Strictly speaking, then, the geobiological conception of Hispanic identity abstracts from historical events. In other words, it is logically possible, if not at all probable, that there exists someone, now or in the past, who satisfies the geobiological conception of Hispanic identity but not the familial-historical conception.

Gracia's geobiological conception of Hispanic identity is too empty. Although it mentions the year 1492, it makes no reference to the events of that year, or to any other historical events, and so fails to capture the historically formed, familial specificity of Hispanic life that Gracia wishes to capture. As we have seen, however, the familial-historical conception of Hispanic identity is also wanting. In my reading, Gracia's most persuasive attempt to do justice to the rich, historical distinctiveness of Hispanic life is in his discussion in chapter 5 of a *Hispanic world* characterized everywhere by *mestizaje* (roughly, "mixed-blood-ness"). Here he accords particular emphasis to the cultural mixture that animates the language, religion, art, architecture, music, and cuisine of the Hispanic world (Gracia 2000c:115ff.). Gracia's examples of cultural *mestizaje* suggest an approach to the question of Hispanic identity different from the ones he otherwise pursues. To be precise, they suggest that the contours of Hispanic identity will be most usefully limned not by philosophical attempts to say in a general and definitive way what membership in a transnational Hispanic community requires but by empirically dense and historically informed descriptions of Hispanic life that bring to light the specific, weblike, cultural connections that constitute the Hispanic world.

Let me now turn to the three topics that, in addition to the argument for Hispanic identity, I wish to discuss here.

THE ORIGINS OF HISPANIC IDENTITY

In connection to the question of origins, I have a small quibble. In particular, I want to question Gracia's emphasis, throughout his book, on the year 1492. By treating Columbus's appearance in the Americas as the event that spawns Hispanic identity, Gracia misleadingly separates the formation of Hispanic identity from the modern history of the Atlantic World that precedes Columbus's voyage. That history begins, arguably, in 1441, when Portuguese members of the Order of Christ (a military order first produced by the Crusades) landed on the West Coast of Africa. Indeed, some scholars have held that the Atlantic World was initially a world of the eastern Atlantic, an arena wherein Europeans and Africans forged a new social reality that was transported westward after Columbus's voyage, wreaking havoc on the world of the American Indians. By beginning his story in 1492 rather than 1441, and by permitting Africans to enter the picture only in 1518 (when the first license to bring slaves into the Americas was granted by Charles V), Gracia lets disappear from view the fact that many of the institutions and practices emerging in the New World after 1492—for example, black slavery and plantation agriculture—had their origins in the eastern Atlantic and in Portugal's encounters with Africa prior to 1492 (e.g., slave plantations in Madeira). Thus, he tends to obscure the roots of Hispanic identity in Europe's encounter with Africa and erroneously to accord Africans a secondary, belated role in a story line that highlights and gives primacy to Iberia's encounter with America.

COMMON NAMES/POLITICAL ARGUMENTS

I turn now to a second quibble. In his conclusion to chapter 3, Gracia (2000c) writes the following in response to the argument that Hispanic Americans need a common name to strengthen their political clout:

> This is, indeed, a strong argument. . . . The problem with it is that it does not properly take into account the diverse character and needs of the various groups which are covered by the name. Politically, the name does not produce the right results and may in fact be counterproductive. Puerto Ricans do not have the same needs as Chicanos, or Argentineans as Venezuelans, for example. Whether we speak of international or national politics, the use of one name need not be a good thing if the proper emphasis on the diversity of Hispanic groups is not maintained. The

justification of one name should not be based on politics, but on historical fact. (67)

My quibble here is with the notion of politics that animates Gracia's remarks. For example, I do not see a good reason for assuming that justification by appeal to political considerations and justification by appeal to considerations of historical fact are mutually exclusive. And I do not see that the particular political consideration in question—that Hispanics need a common name to strengthen their political clout—rules out taking into account the diverse character and needs of different Hispanic groups. To argue that, in some contexts, the use of a common name is politically needful is not necessarily to deny that there will be contexts in which pragmatic political considerations argue against the use of a common name. Finally, it seems to me that answers to questions like, Do Puerto Ricans have the same needs as Chicanos? will almost always be decided in the course of political arguments among Chicanos, among Puerto Ricans, and between Chicanos and Puerto Ricans regarding their respective needs/interpretations. Thus, I do not see a good reason to stipulate once and for all, as Gracia seems to do, that Puerto Ricans do not have the same needs as Chicanos, or Argentineans as Venezuelans, and so forth.

HISPANICS IN AMERICAN PHILOSOPHY

In summarizing his understanding of the status of Hispanics in American philosophy, Gracia (2000c) writes,

> The questions we want to answer have to do with the limited number of Hispanics in philosophy, the small number of established Hispanic philosophers, and the general indifference of non-Hispanic American philosophers and Hispanic-American philosophers to issues particularly related to Hispanics and Hispanic thought. My suggestion is that one reason behind all these facts is that Hispanics in general are perceived as foreigners; we are not thought to be Americans. (180)

Here Gracia argues that the perception of Hispanics as foreigners is an important factor in explaining the marginal status of Hispanics and Hispanic philosophical thought in the American philosophical community. And, to be sure, there is some truth in what he says. Still, my intuition is that

Gracia's argument needs some modification, precisely because, as he elsewhere acknowledges, the American philosophical community does not marginalize all other philosophers and traditions of philosophical thought that are perceived to be foreign (non-American), such as the English, French, and German traditions of philosophical thought. That being the case, one must be a bit skeptical of the claim that perceived foreignness per se explains the American philosophical community's marginalization of Hispanic philosophers and Hispanic philosophical thought.

An equally significant explanatory factor, I believe, is that Hispanic identity, as distinct, say, from English, French, and German national identities, is, in the United States, typically perceived as a nonwhite, nonblack, and non-Asian *racial identity*. This was evident, for example, when in the first sentence of a recent *New York Times* article it was reported that blacks and Hispanics are far more likely than whites to be stopped and searched by New York City police officers. And it was evident when, in the early days of the Ricky Martin craze, there was debate among my seventh-grade daughter and her friends as to whether Ricky Martin was "really" Hispanic, for his hair and fair complexion made him *look* white. So, again, Hispanic identity in the United States is, at least in part, a socially constructed racial identity. Thus, Hispanics, as distinct from English, French, and German "Euroforeigners," are perceived as racial others, and Hispanic philosophy, in contrast to the philosophy of English, French, and "Euroforeigners," is perceived as the philosophy of racial others. If American philosophy marginalizes Hispanics, it is in part, I suspect, because Hispanics, having been racialized as nonwhite, are subject to anti-Hispanic racism. Sometimes anti-Hispanic racism is explicit, but more often, in professional contexts like that of the American Philosophical Association, it takes the form of what Adrian Piper (1996) calls second-order discrimination. In this respect, the situation of Hispanics in American philosophy is not dissimilar to the situation of African Americans in American philosophy.

9. THE ROLE OF CULTURE IN

HISPANIC IDENTITY

GREGORY PAPPAS

In *Hispanic/Latino Identity*, Jorge J. E. Gracia (2000c) argues that "there is a way to understand the concept of Hispanic that allows us to speak meaningfully of, and refer effectively to, Hispanics, even when the people named by it do not share any property in common at all times and places" (48). The kind of unity behind the justified use of 'Hispanic' is historical and not one of commonality. Gracia explains that "King John II of Portugal has nothing in common with me, but both of us are tied by a series of events that relate us and separate us from Queen Elizabeth II and Martin Luther King. There is no need to find properties common to all Hispanics in order to classify them as Hispanics" (50). There is a historical reality that unites people of the Iberian nations, of the United States, and of Latin American countries after 1492.

Once one understands Gracia's starting point and aim and follows his careful reasoning throughout the book, it is hard not to come to agree with his conclusions. But this does not mean that he has worked out all the important details and that he is immune from criticism. My overall assessment is that, although Gracia (2000c:56) provides us with the right view about Hispanics, there are aspects of the experience of Hispanic identity that he unnecessarily downplays or underemphasizes because of the philosophical starting point, assumptions, and commitments that guided his inquiry. In particular, his opposition to essentialism may have led him to neglect the important function of cultural commonalities in the affirmation and creation of a Hispanic identity. As a result I am concerned that (as an unintended consequence) his theory may strike many as minimalist, thin, empty, and formal.

As indicated by the subtitle of the book, there is a particular "philosophical perspective" assumed in Gracia's treatment of Hispanic identity. I would like to make explicit some key assumptions of this perspective because I believe they affect the conclusions he reaches and inhibit him from reaching others.

To understand Gracia's view we must consider his starting point, concerns, and theoretical enemies. He shares with his enemies, the essentialists, the assumption that any good theory of Hispanic identity must be universal in the sense that it must account for all Hispanics across time and space and irrespective of context-relative criteria. He acknowledges that in a particular context Hispanic identity may be based on common properties, although they do not extend beyond that time and place. Therefore, common properties cannot be the basis of Hispanic identity: "Particular physical characteristics, cultural traits, language, and so on can serve to distinguish Hispanics in certain contexts, although they cannot function as criteria of distinction everywhere and at all times" (Gracia 2000c:56). The basis of Hispanic identity must be something universal and objective and not relative to context. Gracia thinks that beyond particular contexts and the experiences of individuals there is an undeniable and solid historical reality that justifies our name. Since so much of philosophy is done from this peculiar universal standpoint, it is fitting for him to call his view of Hispanic identity philosophical. Needless to say, there are plenty of contemporary philosophical views that would question his confidence in history (or his particular take on it) as the "reality" to anchor our identity. For Gracia there is a fact of the matter: the "historical reality" that ties us together whether we are aware of it or not and regardless of our present opinions of one another as a group. I am not going to question here his historical realism, but I do think it should be mentioned as a key assumption that guides his inquiry. He shares with essentialism the enthusiasm for a reality that is immune from relativistic and skeptical challenges.

If, as Gracia (2000c) admits, there is a criterion in context, that is, "at every time and in every period, some Hispanics have properties that tie them among themselves and distinguish them from other groups" (56), then is not this sufficient to account for Hispanic identity? What if one held the view, against Gracia and the essentialists, that there is no universal Hispanic identity but that relative to a particular time and place (context), there is a rough and general set of characteristics that are used to distinguish Hispanics from others? This would mean that there are as many correct theories of Hispanic identity as there are times, places, and reasons for coming up with a criterion.

This is, of course, problematic. It fails to account for the intuition (and fact) that different Hispanics at different times and places are related in some way and thereby merit the same name. This is the strength of Gracia's view. It accounts for this without falling into essentialism. But I question his resistance to integrating context-specific views about Hispanicity as an essential part of his overall theory. If a rough set of general characteristics is the actual basis on which particular people at different times base their contemporary sense of Hispanic identity, then should not they be presented as an integral part of any complete theory of Hispanic identity?

Gracia will answer that these characteristics are not necessary. Sure, they are not necessary in presenting a theory that is immune to counterexamples by other philosophers, but this does not mean that they may not be necessary for a theory that accounts for the Hispanic identity experienced by many Hispanics at different times and in different places. Most of the Hispanics whom I know care about their identity "right here, right now" and not about a universal identity that connects them to people in the previous centuries, like King John of Portugal. As a philosopher Gracia is careful not to make hypothetical and controversial generalizations about most Hispanics at any given time or in specific parts of the world; but this strikes me as having more content and relation to concrete experiences of identity than a theory that is based only upon abstract historical links from a universal standpoint. Perhaps he thinks that these vague and empirical issues are better left for sociology and anthropology. If so, he may be following the general tendency among philosophers to disregard what is most present, changing, contingent, particular, and empirical. To be sure, to base Hispanic identity on history instead of on a Hispanic essence, form, or soul is a move toward what is contingent and particular. But are not context-relative cultural similarities among Hispanics (however nonuniversal, changing, and hard to articulate into a theory) part of the "life and blood" of a lived Hispanic identity?

Gracia resists context-specific views about Hispanicity based upon commonalities because he is skeptical that such claims can even be made. He admits that "there is no reason why, in principle, all Hispanics could not have some properties in common which tie them together and distinguish them from others at some particular time," but then he says, "the reality appears different. For Hispanic ties, even at a particular time, tend to be familiar and historical rather than across the board" (Gracia 2000c:54). But even if no Hispanic group is tied to all other groups in the same strict way presupposed (in fact, even if each is unique), that does not mean that all Hispanic groups may not have something in common (i.e., similar) in comparison with some other groups. Gracia must be using 'common' in a different way. Indeed, and this is important, it must be so, because I fail to see how all attempts to base identity upon commonalities commit one to essentialism or to homogenizing what is heterogeneous.

Gracia's criticisms against seeking identity in commonalities are based on a particular "philosophical perspective" assumed when he uses the terms 'common' and 'identity.' In chapter 2 of *Hispanic/Latino Identity* he is very explicit about this. He claims that identity is not similarity. The former "precludes difference" and the latter "requires difference" (Gracia 2000c:42). Under these assumptions it is understandable why Gracia (or anyone) cannot find a common cultural identity among all Hispanics. Indeed, why stop there? There is no identity among even the most particular and similar of groups, for there are always differences that one can point to. Gracia would find this as disturbing as I do. In fact, he points out that among many Hispanics there has been a "general retreat from the more encompassing position of identity" (190). But he thinks this is a consequence of trying to find common properties on which to base identity. The search for an essence leads to separatism in light of the differences among even the most similar groups of Hispanics. He does not consider that perhaps the source of the problem may be the assumption that to share an identity is to deny differences. When one's standard of people's sharing things in "common" is unreasonably high, one can appreciate only differences.

In the metaphysics that I share with many classical American philosophers such as John Dewey, William James, and Charles Hartshorne, there is no absolute identity—that is, without differences. In my general view of things every thing is unique and not absolutely identical with anything else (heterogeneity is ontologically basic). However, there are also similarities and continuities as relations between things that allow me to make functional identity claims. Similarities and differences are everywhere, and it is our decision (or because of selectivity) to emphasize one or the other in different contexts and for different purposes. For example, I am Puerto Rican when I am distinguishing myself from other Hispanics or when I need to affirm what I share or a certain historical unity with "Nuyoricans" and Puerto Ricans from the island. But among Puerto Ricans I can make the case that I am actually Texa-Rican. And even among Texa-Ricans, if I still cared to emphasize differences, I would point out that I am different from the Texa-Ricans born and raised in Texas, and I could with that in mind give myself (ourselves) a name.

There are other contexts in which I am Hispanic. And as Gracia (2000c:189) says, it is founded on being part of a historical family, but it is also based (at the moment) on sharing some common (similar) things and to different degrees with most people who are part of that family.

Identity claims are based on relations, not just historical relations but actual sameness and actual differences and relative to the context in which the issue is raised. There are places and people in the world that I can identify with culturally but not historically, and there are other people to whom I have strong historical ties but with whom, for whatever reason, there is very little that we share culturally.

General ethnic names (e.g., 'Hispanic') are useful because they allowed me in particular contexts to emphasize relations. Sometimes such an ethnic name may be based upon a claim about a common culture. But the "same" culture does not imply homogeneity, which seems to be Gracia's overriding concern in avoiding identity claims based upon culture. For example, I am perfectly comfortable with claims about a common or identical Western culture. I am able to identify myself as a Westerner because there are some very general traits that we share in comparison with other world cultures. This does not compromise heterogeneity so long as we understand these claims as nothing more than generalizations or abstractions based upon similarities that we make for certain purposes. The same can be said about Hispanics. I can say that all Hispanic cultures, at some general level of comparison with other cultures in the world, have common elements, and I can do so without compromising our irreducible differences.

Furthermore, I believe that these vague commonalities serve an important role in creating a sense of identity and union, one that would be lacking if there were only the historical relations that Gracia emphasizes. Once again, and in fairness to him, at least in principle he does not deny this. But I think he does not stress enough their actual importance in making possible a unity that goes well beyond our historical ties. In a more flexible and context-relative understanding of "what is common" (not the one assumed by Gracia and essentialism), Hispanics can be said at different times and places to have shared a culture, one that is experienced as part of what we are at that time and place.

For Gracia, Hispanic identity is based either on historical relations or on relations of commonality. There are no common properties to all those people whom we wish to call Hispanics, and therefore he concludes that "our identity is not founded on common properties" (Gracia 2000c:189). But beyond the doubts that I have raised about what his criterion for "common" is, I am also wondering why those things that are "common" must be found in all members of the group. Must all members of a group have the same traits for those traits to be part of the identity of the group? What if the common traits that identify Hispanics are traits that belong to the group as a whole but that may not belong to all of its parts (i.e., only to most people)? What could be wrong with the view that I am Hispanic because I am related (historically) to a group of people most of whom speak a certain language or share a certain way of living in comparison with, for example, Anglo-Saxons? This would still be Gracia's view in the sense that it is the historical relations that determine the extension of the term 'Hispanic.' However, there is also an appeal to a common culture as a distinguishing aspect of identity without presupposing absolute sameness across the board. In fact, under this definition I may be Hispanic without having some of the common traits that define us as a group. My intention here is not to lay out or defend an alternative theory. I am merely suggesting that Gracia has set as his task to argue against an extreme view and in the process may have neglected more moderate and plausible views based upon sharing a culture while avoiding homogenization.

I am very sympathetic with Gracia's concern about the dangers of basing Hispanic identity solely on a quest for common traits. He considers homogeneity and essentialism as a dangerous "human invention" (Gracia 2000c:191). General names can be very unfair to the rich diversity and differences of the things designated. He is correct in arguing that this is especially true of Hispanics, and I hope his book may help to educate the world about this. But I think it is equally dangerous for people to overemphasize differences at the expense of denying commonalities and continuities. A balanced celebration of both differences and commonalities seems to me the ideal to be embraced. My hope is that the use of the general term 'Hispanic' may help to counteract the endemic tendency among Hispanics to affirm their differences only and at all costs. We have failed to affirm commonalities and continuities. Absolute heterogeneity as well as absolute homogeneity are dangerous fictions. For me the mistake is in the absolute character of the claims. The alternative to essentialism is not to drop all attempts to seek commonalities but to understand that "common" is never anything more than "similar," that is, that there are always differences.

Gracia and I may be concerned about different dangers, but we agree at some general level that the answer or the best thing we should all be doing is to "recognize our unity in difference." However, we disagree about the role of culture in such unity. For me there is more to our unity than our history.

For Gracia if we acknowledge our differences but also are proud of our historical relations, we have a good basis for a Hispanic identity. I agree that these two things are necessary but question whether they are sufficient to continue to affirm our identity. It seems to me that if we ignore commonalities (understood in a more flexible sense than Gracia allows), we are left with very little resource to unite and make connections. The things we share right now, and to different degrees (and not necessarily with all Hispanics for all times), and in comparison with other groups of people, are what make it worthwhile affirming our historical connections. I see no danger in emphasizing these generalities as long as we are aware that essentialism is false.

I may be related to other people in very solid and objective historical ways, but I see no point in affirming a group identity (or coming up with a name for us) because we do not share something worth building an identity about. Although I have not done my research, I am sure that there have to be in history groups of people for whom the only things that unite them are the historical ties. And that because of this no one has been interested in building or claiming a group identity and name. Certain people are Hispanic because they are linked historically, but why have we selected these historical links over others and called them Hispanic? Granted the fact that certain people are related historically is a good theoretical explanation about why they share certain things, but their sharing certain things may be prior and assumed by the explanation. I suspect that it is because most Hispanics have shared at different times and to different degrees (and relative to other groups) some common outlook or characteristics that their identity is important and that we are interested in their history. Why would anyone want to write a book about Hispanics if there is nothing special about them? It is because we share a unique culture of *mestizaje* that we stand out among other people in the world who are linked historically. It is because most Hispanics share some things or are similar in some respects (and to some degree) that the new sense of Hispanic identity created in the past ten years by Hispanics in the United States (e.g., by Univision) has been able to substantiate itself as not being a mere myth.

I agree with Gracia that we must fundamentally appreciate ourselves as part of a historical family, but I think we must also base our identity on affirming our contingent commonalities and continuities without thereby denying differences (or assuming homogeneity). Unless we have at least some vague sense of cultural unity, our historical identity, no matter how objective and precise, is something very formal and empty. It is something that may be used in counting who is or is not Hispanic in a census, but it is not a reason to affirm, to be proud of, and to celebrate identity. This is true even of families. Gracia is right in thinking that the values, traditions, and ways of being shared by a particular family are not the basis (necessary and sufficient conditions) to identify who is a member of that family. But who can deny the important role these things play in family identity? Without them the historical ties would disintegrate and be nothing more than trivia in history books.

I think Gracia's theory could accommodate all of my concerns had he said more about the function of culture in identity. He does claim that historical relations tend to generate shared cultural traits (at certain times and places). His theory "allows for common properties at certain times and places arising from particular historical relations" (Gracia 2000c:192). But is this all there is to culture? Is he suggesting that cultural commonalities are nothing more than accidental or merely external consequences of historical relations and not part of who we are (our identity)? Gracia holds that historical relations "generate particular properties which can serve to distinguish Hispanics/Latinos from others in particular contexts." Does he mean that commonalities are nothing more than contingent epistemic criteria or useful indicators but not part of who we are (ontologically) in specific times and places? How many of the "web of concrete historical relations that tie us together" are made out of these common properties so that without them we would not care about a Hispanic identity? Why cannot we accept the historical basis while also acknowledging an important function of culture in talking about Hispanics? In his efforts to emphasize history Gracia may have underestimated culture. He says that "the concept Hispanic should be understood as a historical concept" (53). Sure, but only historical?

Note that there are those who claim that Hispanics in Latin America hardly ever make any claim about a general Hispanic identity, but this is only because they live in a context where they have not been called to unify and to dwell on their similarities and continuities. In South America the Venezuelan is ready to distinguish herself from the Colombian and he to distinguish himself from her, but when they are living in the North American pluralistic context, they are more prone to notice their commonalities in comparison with others. The context in which identity claims are made creates a significant difference.

It is important, as Gracia insists, that we recognize that there is a history that unifies us, but is there only a history? It is my belief that the majority (not all) of Hispanics have such similar cultures in comparison with other groups of people that we can speak safely of sharing more than being part of a history of events. This is not to downplay differences. There is no under-lying cultural common denominator or substratum that we all have, but rather there is the sort of family resemblance or overlapping that Gracia approves of. What is shared (to whatever degree and however contingent to a time and a place) is important to Hispanic identity and unity as an experience, though it may be irrelevant to the extension of the term 'Hispanic.' The Hispanic that only shares a historical link with other Hispanics is a Hispanic, but her sense of identity and unity (of "belonging to") with other Hispanics is thin and weak in comparison with others who have adopted the ways of living (i.e., culture) of most Hispanics. Furthermore, culture is important to any His-panic identity worth affirming or preserving, and to have a strong cultural "glue" (beyond the historical one) is better than not to have it. Again, there is no reason why Gracia in principle cannot agree with all of this, but his fears about essentialism and homogenization may have prevented him from mak-ing this sort of affirmation. What is at issue in evaluating Hispanic/Latino identity is what counts as a good theory of Hispanic identity. Gracia's stan-dards in this matter are to some extent determined by his philosophical train-ing. He is satisfied with nothing less than the precise and well-argued set of necessary and sufficient conditions of Hispanicity. So many treatments of this topic are full of incoherence, vagaries, and unsubstantiated prose that it is about time a philosopher like Gracia stepped forward to clean and advance the quality of the discussion. Although *Hispanic/Latino Identity* is an im-portant book written for a larger audience, it has the intellectual rigor, con-ceptual analysis, and impeccable reasoning of professional philosophers. But that Gracia ends up with what may seem a minimalist account of Hispanic identity may also be the result of his philosophical expertise. In my opinion, this has been the fate of most treatments of many concrete-lived issues by philosophers. Too often our philosophical standards prevent us from allow-ing more content to our conclusions. A view of Hispanic identity must be something well argued and immune to objections but it must also address the identity experienced (lived and felt) by Hispanics in different contexts.

I must confess that I am very uncomfortable in even raising these minor criticisms of such an excellent book. *Hispanic/Latino Identity* is a book that I will continue to use in my Latin American philosophy classes, and I shall refer to it as the authority on the issue of Hispanic identity. Gracia has shown that ethnic identity is a legitimate and worthwhile subject matter of philo-sophical investigation.

10. THE LANGUAGE PRISM

ILAN STAVANS

This chapter is based on impromptu remarks I made while participating in a debate with K. Anthony Appiah and Jorge J. E. Gracia in September 2012 at the University of Buffalo on Gracia's own oeuvre.

I started by surveying my own career as a reader of his work, then pointing to specific texts by him I have found pleasing over time, among them his reflections on Jorge Luis Borges as a "visual" thinker as well as his discussions on ethics. I also talked of a collaboration he and I had just completed, a volume of conversations called *Thirteen Ways of Looking at Latino Art* (2014), in which together we selected a handful of pieces of Hispanic art, from a parodic triptych by the brothers Einar and Jamex de la Torre to a graffiti mural, from Andrés Serrano's controversial *Piss Christ* to a painting by José Bedia, and turned them into an occasion to reflect, uninhibitedly, on a broad range of topics, all rotating around the act of "seeing." As a result of that collaboration, I said, Gracia and I became friends. What I cherish most in that friendship is the capacity to think ideas through regardless of where they lead to and, equally important, the invitation to disagree without hurting the other's feelings. For the premise of humanist discussion is precisely the ability to differ cordially. That is what civility is about.

While I offered Gracia lavish appreciation, my remarks in Buffalo focused on a fundamental critique I have: his failure to look at language as a prism through which to analyze human experience. In order to allow the audience to understand this critique, I delved into one of Gracia's favorite themes: Hispanic identity. His reflections on the theme are contained in two books: *Hispanic/Latino Identity* (2000c) and *Latinos in America* (2008b). The scope of each of these books is different. The first addresses how Hispanics in general call themselves and the way the link between identity and ethnicity plays out in them. He then proceeds to examine the search for identity in Latin America from the colonial times to the present. The second book is an outgrowth of the first, although it isn't a sequel per se. In it he focuses exclusively on Latinos north of the border. Let me analyze each of these two books separately.

In the first, he starts with the assumption that it has been the philosophers who have delved into the question of identity: Do Latin Americans know who they are? If so, who are they? What distinguishes them from other people? Is there a unifying core that brings the identity of the twenty-two disparate countries in the region together? Should one use history as a homogenizer? Ethnicity? Culture? These questions foster another, crucial one: if it has been left to philosophers to ask these questions, one must assume there is such a thing as a Latin American philosophy. Gracia believes this is the case; I disagree—with a caveat. In my opinion, the Latin American philosophical tradition is a rather paltry one, not because it hasn't had first-rate thinkers but, instead, because the great thinkers of Latin America, at least those who have written on Hispanic identity, have never seen themselves as philosophers.

Instead, they have been essayists, anthropologists, political scientists, and thinkers in the model of Montaigne, whose job it was to think about culture and not, like Descartes, to think about thinking. I'm considering here a list that goes from José Enrique Rodó to José Carlos Mariátegui, from Ezequiel Martínez Estrada to Borges and Octavio Paz. Gracia traced the roots of Latin American philosophy by looking at those who have meditated on identity, starting with the pre-Columbian "creation story" in *Popol Vuh*, moving to the sonnets and plays by the seventeenth-century Mexican nun Sor Juana Inés de la Cruz, continuing to figures such as José Vasconcelos, whose *The Cosmic Race* ([1925] 1997) is a prophetic treatise on *mestizaje*, and moving onward to the present. Of all these thinkers, only Vasconcelos presented himself as a philosopher, although his half-baked erudition and convoluted arguments leave much to be desired. Other more conventional philosophers like Ramón Xirau have had only a limited impact.

In order to prove that the Latin American philosophical tradition does exist, Gracia proposes three approaches. Ironically, two of them affirm its existence while one of them, the crucial one, negates it. The first approach, known as Universalism, argues that philosophy, like mathematics, reaches conclusions that don't depend on special circumstances. Latin American philosophy is the philosophy done by Latin Americans, who produce the same type of philosophy others do as well. The second approach, Culturalism, argues that knowledge is always perspectival, meaning that Latin American philosophy is the philosophy that only Latin Americans will produce. The third approach, in Gracia's view, is shaped by concrete social conditions. This means, in his own words, that "Latin America doesn't have the social conditions necessary to the development of an autochthonous philosophy." That is, Latin Americans could engage in Universalism and Culturalism but they can't because the conditions to achieve an autochthonous philosophy are unavailable. Still, Gracia offers a chronological study of how identity has been shaped by the region's thinkers across time.

The second book by Gracia deals with Latinos in the United States and considers two concepts: minority and ethnos. An immigrant himself who came to America from Cuba to enroll in undergraduate school, he perceives himself to be a member of this minority. In fact, his dual position as an insider and an outsider here enables him to take a privileged position: that of observer. In this case, he talks about identity in an immigrant society and uses the marketplace, affirmative action, and linguistic rights to develop a view of how Latino identity is formed.

Needless to say, this theme has also been the subject of heated discussions. I have contributed to the discussions in several places, including, most recently, the volume *What Is la hispanidad?* (2011), coauthored with Chilean historian Iván Jaksić, who is one of Gracia's distinguished graduate students and the editor of this volume. Until the 1980s, there were a number of national groups with ancestry in the Hispanic world: Mexicans, Dominicans, Cubans, Puerto Ricans, Colombians, and so forth. These groups did not yet coalesce into a single unit, an *unum*; instead, they were understood as a *pluribus*. Collecting them in one rubric caused all sorts of complications. Eventually, to the rubric of nationality one needed to add ethnicity. Could one really talk of a Latino identity, one shared by every member of this disparate group? It was difficult since not only aren't Latinos unified in national terms but also racially they are a many-sided bunch, whose members are white, black, Asian, and all colors in between.

For that reason, the concept of minority, even if imperfect, became less ethereal, more tangible. I don't believe a one-fits-all identity is possible when addressing Latin America. Nor do I think one can apply such a view to Latinos in the United States. Is there a European identity? Yes, but it is loosely formed from an addition of Italian, German, French, Portuguese, Spanish, Greek, and so on—so loosely, in fact, as to evaporate into thin air. I have the same opinion of a Latin American identity. *X-ray of the Pampa* (Martínez Estrada [1933] 1971) and *The Labyrinth of Solitude* (Paz 1950) are probing meditations in the tradition of Latin American identity. But they address different topics and reach different audiences.

In any event, the historical roots of the Latino identity in the United States date back to before the arrival of the *Mayflower* in Plymouth, Massachusetts. The Spanish soldiers, missionaries, and explorers of the sixteenth century spread themselves from Florida, Texas, and New Mexico to California and Oregon. Their interaction with the aboriginal population, which leads to what we have come to understand as Hispanic American civilization, precedes the formation of the nation.

As is usual in Gracia's work, he offers a patient, detailed analysis of ethnos and minority in regard to Latinos in the United States. To it he brings the viewpoints of journalists, sociologists, anthropologists, literary critics, historians, and political scientists. That he approaches it as a philosopher brings a breath of fresh air. His examination succeeds not because he is a philosopher but because he is a humanist: he understands the problem of identity not from one viewpoint but from several. He does it in large strokes, introducing elements such as physical traits, ancestry, belonging to a group—say a family, a community, or a congregation, a country—and, crucially, it allows him to consider individual self-identification, which, in a democratic, pluralistic society, is a key factor. Ironically, what he doesn't do is embark on the same quest he accomplished in the first book; that is, he resists looking chronologically at the history of how the identity of Latinos has been conceptualized by the ethnicity of the minority itself as well as by extraminority viewpoints.

This is a pity, because that history is a mirror in which the minority sees itself reflected. My suspicion is that Gracia isn't fond of history as a discipline; I say this because in the articulation of his arguments, historical facts are seldom presented. Within the United States, the words 'Latino' and 'Hispanic' have a contested legacy. Those preferring 'Hispanic' believe it links the minority to its Iberian past (Spain, during the Roman period, was originally called Hispania), whereas those opting for 'Latino' see it as a bridge to Latin America, even though what makes Latin America "Latin" are its Roman roots. Prior to these words, there were others: 'Latin (as opposed to Latino) people,' 'Spanish-speaking,' and 'Spanish' are only three.

All these rubrics fall under what could be called general typology, an attempt to look at the minority as a whole. There is also a "particular typology," which is frequently invoked by those implying that Latinos are not a minority after all but a sum of parts. Rather than stressing the qualities bringing everyone in the minority together, they emphasize national backgrounds: I'm Cuban American, rather than Latino American, or Mexican American, Dominican American, Colombian American, and so on. In any case, Gracia meditates on Latino identity in the present, failing to offer the proper historical context.

I now finally come—somewhat morosely—to my main critique of his work: the absence of what to me is one of the most significant elements shaping the identity of Latinos in the United States, as well as the theme that forms my own way of looking at life: language. Among other places, I have written about this in my memoir *On Borrowed Words: A Memoir of Language* (2001), as well as in my lexicon *Spanglish: The Making of a New American Language* (2003), and in the essays included in *Dictionary Days* (2005). Other than Latinos, no minority in the country has held to its immigrant tongue with equal commitment. None has delayed its integration to the mainstream for such a lengthy amount of time.

Spanish is the link to the past but also the ticket to a bicultural identity. Some members of that minority are monolingual (Spanish, English, Spanglish), some are bilingual (Spanish-English, Spanish-Spanglish, English-Spanglish), and, of course, some are trilingual. Another set of divisions across linguistic lines might be implemented: people who speak Spanish but don't write it, and so on. The level of fluency determines the identification they might feel toward the minority. There are also varieties of Spanish: Puerto Rican in the mainland, Argentinean Spanish, and so forth. Of course, one should push this dimension even further: people who speak the type of Spanish used in Sonora, Mexico, vis-à-vis Chiapas, Mexico. Geography therefore is a link to linguistic belonging. By ignoring language as a factor determining identity, Gracia bypasses a crucial manifestation of culture, one dangerous to ignore.

In my remarks, I talked of Spanglish as an element in the linguistic triumvirate of the Latino minority. Spanglish isn't a standard language. Instead, it is a jazzy, spontaneous way of engaging that comes about with explicit strategies: code switching, meaning the back-and-forth between two standard forms of communication; simultaneous translation, whereby the speaker uses one language to express thoughts formulated in another; and the abundant

formation of neologisms, false cognates, and barbarisms that belong neither to one language nor to the other. In truth, Gracia ignores language
tangentially. *Latinos in America* includes a section in which he discusses
bilingual education, not from the perspective of identity but from the viewpoint of language rights. Should the government of the United States fund
programs geared toward the acquisition, endurance, and profitability of an
immigrant language that competes with English in various areas, from home
to school, from politics to business? Does the learning of that language fall
under First Amendment rights?

Gracia does consider the best way to educate children in general and
immigrant children concretely. As I mentioned, he talks about immigrants'
linguistic rights. His own view is that the English Only and English First
movements function under worrisome premises. He ponders those premises
but never fully acknowledges language to be a lens through which Latinos
perceive themselves and, consequently, a useful tool through which to understand the shaping of their identity.

This limitation not only pertains to Gracia's *Latinos in America*; it is also
patent in *Hispanic/Latino Identity*. In fact, it is present throughout his entire
work. In Buffalo, I encouraged him to take this issue into consideration, invoking Ludwig Wittgenstein's memorable *Philosophical Investigations* (1953),
most suitably those dedicated to language. If, as Wittgenstein states, the limit
of one's language is the limit of one's world, and vice versa, the structure, the
fluidity, the transformation of that language, as it is used in history, reflect
the changes of the world. From the Second Punic War, in 210 B.C.E., to its
polyphonic, multifaceted dimensions today, when it is used by approximately
450 million people in Latin America, as well as by another 40 million on the
Iberian Peninsula, by some 60 million who employ it as a second language,
and, crucially for the debate in Buffalo, by a large portion of Latinos in the
United States, the development of the Spanish language is also the development of Hispanic identity, a way to access the ways this civilization has perceived itself over time.

Who are the purveyors of language? The people themselves: all of us. To
appreciate how Latin America has changed from the viewpoint of identity,
one might look to Sor Juana, Rodó, Mariátegui, Vasconcelos, Borges, Paz, and
Mario Vargas Llosa for inspiration; and, if and when one agrees to bring in
Spain, at Jorge Manrique, Lope de Vega, Miguel de Cervantes, and Miguel de
Unamuno. (I've always wondered why Iberian thinkers rarely make it to the
canon of Hispanic identity, when that canon, even while looking at only its

Latin American side, springs from the colonial outpost of the Roman Empire known as Hispania.) Similarly, to understand change one might look at the parlance of the classroom, the supermarket, the music hall, and the TV show, from Buenos Aires to Ciudad Juárez, from Havana to Madrid.

In sum, language isn't only how we conceive of the universe. Language is the universe itself. As Ralph Waldo Emerson put it, "You can never say anything but what you are."

11. THE SECOND *RECONQUISTA*

EDUARDO MENDIETA

I would like to begin by paraphrasing and summarizing a review that I wrote of Jorge J. E. Gracia's *Hispanic/Latino Identity* (2000c). Gracia is without question one of the best-known Hispanic/Latino philosophers in the United States and abroad. He was a founding member of the American Philosophical Association committee on Hispanics, and its first chair. This book of his is not only unique but also peculiar, for the kind of philosopher Gracia is and has made his reputation as. He was trained as a medievalist and has written extensively on metaphysics and the philosophy of history. His areas of expertise are late-medieval philosophy, the problem of individuation, a central topic within ontology, or more broadly defined metaphysics. Why this book may be considered peculiar is because scholars trained in such fields tend not to be concerned with contemporary matters, social reality, and the vagaries of identity politics. Yet Gracia has taken on a topic that prima facie could be construed as being inimical to and even unworthy of his own philosophical orientation and his philosophical attention. As he declares in the preface he writes not as a leader, or prophet, or even ideologue of a movement. Instead, he avows that he writes as both a Hispanic and an American who is concerned with the fate of the nation and its people, who just happens to be a philosopher. And this is what makes this book peculiarly refreshing and insightful. Gracia is not in the business of peddling or catering to intellectual fashions or the latest philosophical fad. Nor is he compromising his intellectual orientation in order to make it fit some political agenda. Gracia demystifies a lot of sacred cows and is able to question many presuppositions taken for granted in identity movements and philosophy. There is a lot of honesty and clarity in this book (Mendieta 1999b:41).

I begin with this paragraph because I want to underscore two essential characteristics of this book: its oddity and its lucidity. Both, of course, were a great source of philosophical pleasure to me. Here is a philosopher who by training would seem to be inured to philosophical fashions taking up one of the most fashionable topics today in the United States: the politics of identity. On the other hand, for people who have read Gracia before, who have studied his clear, precisely written essays and books, it is a delight having him use his argumentative skills to clear much confusion when it comes to the question of ethnic identity. Respect and appreciation, however, do not hinder criticism. Criticism, in turn, does not extinguish knowledge. Notwithstanding the criticisms one may raise, one is sure to have walked away from this book much more knowledgeable.

For those who have not read the book, I will give a very summary description of the contents, then I will proceed to my criticisms and concerns.

I

The book is made up of seven chapters. Four of them deal with the question of Hispanic. These four chapters deal individually with four questions:

1. What should we call ourselves: Latinos, Hispanics, Iberoamericans, or individual national names, like Colombians?
2. The relationship between naming and cultural and ethnic identity: here Gracia's discussion deals more broadly with the power of cultural labeling and the need that social groups have to affirm their own labels.
3. What could or should be the foundation for a cultural identity, or the name of a sociocultural group, when race, language, religion are not all present in all its members as necessary conditions for their being identified as belonging to that group?
4. Finally, Gracia turns to the history of the emergence of the Hispanic people out of intercontinental encounters, mythical inventions, and *mestizaje*.

The second half of the book contains three chapters. These turn to relating Hispanic to philosophy. Chapter 5, for instance, deals with the issue of whether there is something called Hispanic philosophy, and why it has been exiled from the canon of Western philosophy. Chapter 6 deals with the question of whether there is a Latin American philosophy. And the last chapter turns to the status of Hispanics/Latinos within the discipline in the United States. This is a very rich book: filled with excellent arguments, clear and pedagogically useful typologies, forgotten but indispensable history, and even proposals for research agendas and curricular recommendations.

II

Now let me turn to my criticisms and concerns. I will raise four main criticisms. One has to do with the issue of naming ourselves Hispanic; the other three deal with philosophical issues.

The first concern that Gracia's book raised for me was whether in fact he was globalizing the concept of Hispanic. I discern an unintentional, although equally suspect, thrust to project a name, or what some call pejoratively a sensus rubric, upon unsuspecting and uninvolved peoples. One of the central arguments of the book is that we should call ourselves Hispanic. This is Gracia's answer to the question: What should we call ourselves? But for whom is Gracia asking the question? Gracia is clearly answering a question that Hispanics/Latinos in the United States are asking. It is they who are trying to forge an identity vis-à-vis other ethnically diverse groups who are making similar identity claims for very specific sociopolitical and economic reasons. The question to which Gracia is offering an answer is not a question that most Latin Americans ask with the same urgency that we ask it in the United States. Does a Colombian, a Peruvian, a Guatemalan, a Mexican ask the question, What should we call ourselves? From day to day, they are Colombian, Mexican, and so forth; sometimes they make a claim to a Latin American identity, and then, occasionally, to a Spanish identity. For the most part, Hispanic is a strange moniker.

The matter of who is asking the question and for what reasons do not become explicit themes of the book, notwithstanding the chapter dedicated to the issue of the power of naming oneself (chapter 2, which otherwise is highly insightful and informative). I think that inattention to these two questions leads Gracia to neglect the very specific U.S. context of the question of ethnic identity, but also, in turn, to inadvertently press upon Latin Americans an identity that they might not be so eager to embrace. In both cases, the consequences are disastrous. I take the question of Hispanic/Latino identity to be of great importance in the United States. Hispanics presently (i.e., as of 2010) constitute about 17 percent of the U.S. population. We are the largest minority and the fastest growing. It is projected by the Census Bureau that Hispanics will become almost 25 percent of the population in the United States by the middle of the first century of the second millennium. These are impressive numbers, but more impressive are the negative numbers that this demographic explosion entails. Hispanics will be the youngest, the most undereducated, the ones with least social capital, and so on. What I see is the profiling of a new underclass, a new social malady.

For reasons specific to the United States, one of the ways in which social inequality has been dealt with, at least since the New Deal and the Good Society, is through identity discourses. The welfare state was originally designed to alleviate the hardships of the working class. During the 1950s and 1960s, the liberal discourse of the welfare state was captured by the civil rights movement. Now, the state itself was to alleviate ethnic and racial inequity by distributing social resources claimed on the basis of ethnic and racial identity. In other words, insofar as the welfare state was supposed to remedy the unfair inequities suffered by groups on the basis of the ascribed identities, it was on the basis of these very same identities that these groups could make claims for social resources: if you wanted access to political and economic power, then you made identity pronouncements that purportedly entitled you to such benefits.

In the United States, in short, distribution of social wealth is directly linked to recognition. This is why we have such a belligerent and entrenched culture of the politics of identity in the United States. And this is why we Hispanics/Latinos are having the kind of debates Gracia is intervening in.

The problem, however, is that the welfare state is under attack. Its ability to alleviate social inequality is distrusted. The rich have revolted. In turn, identity politics has become suspect. Society in general has become cynical and skeptical of identity-claims, especially when they are supposed to entitle the claimant to some sort of social benefit.

On the other hand, we have the Latin American reality on one side and the Spanish reality on the other. I think that Spanish problems are of a very different sort from Latin American problems. Spain was a world power for at least two centuries and then became a second-class nation, politically backward, culturally confused. Latin America is accosted and weighed down by an interminable list of problems: political immaturity occasioned by the atrophy of its civil society brought about by perennial external interventions;

cultural schizophrenia; and a maniacal need to create identity by mixing. I cannot possibly in the space here give a list of the problems that confront both cultures. But let me just point in the following direction. Let me summarize what I take to be the central differences between these three different groups: Hispanics/Latinos face problems as a minority in a context in which identity discourses are obsolete, or are on the way to becoming obsolete. Latin Americans face questions of nation-state building, economic development, and outdated forms of nationalism that were the only way in which Latin Americans could live out their citizenship. Spain, on the other hand, while enjoying a fairly stable sense of nation-statehood, is presently forging a new political identity: beyond totalitarianism, toward a new form of constitutional republicanism. Such different struggles and contexts cannot be dealt with fairly and without gross generalizations by one same name. At the very least, projecting 'Hispanic' upon all those people that because of historical reasons share certain family resemblances can lead to eviscerating the very specific political and strategic content that the term may have for a very specific group of people: peoples of Latin American descent in the United States who share a unique history of racial, ethnic, and class oppression that has rendered them second-class citizens. At the very worst, such a gesture can turn into a *reconquista* launched upon Latin America, and the Iberian Peninsula, from the United States by exiles, *despatriados*, and *desterrados*. Of course, philosophically and even historically, there is a profound irony and lesson in such a gesture. Existentially, politically, and culturally, it is highly questionable.

Second, my next concern has to do with Gracia's idea of philosophy. One of the chapters of *Hispanic/Latino Identity* deals with the case of Hispanic philosophy. I found this chapter confusing and to be working at odds with the goals of the book. On the one hand, Gracia defends the importance of Spanish philosophy in the sixteenth and seventeenth centuries. He defends its importance by arguing that this philosophy laid down the foundations of most modern political philosophy, the theory of the rights of nations, and the transformation of natural law into the rights of cultures. I agree with Gracia that the philosophy produced under the colonial period is of paramount importance for understanding contemporary Europe, and what we take to be modernity. On the other hand, Gracia thinks that most of the philosophy was epigonic and servile. Most of the philosophy produced in both Spain and the colonies during the sixteenth century, in Gracia's opinion, was *philosophia ancilla theologiae*, and to this extent Gracia agrees with the kinds of positions that would like to see Spain and Latin America as never having undergone

either a Renaissance or an Enlightenment. And here is where I would disagree. Gracia seems to operate with a very strict, academic, discrete understanding of philosophy as an academically autonomous discipline. I think
that on this point Gracia has anachronistically projected backward a very
modern notion of philosophy into a past when we did not yet have the separation between universities and churches, the emergence of a public sphere
of critical discourses, or, furthermore, a division between state, Church, and
a third sector, what Hegel called civil society, that could allow philosophy to
acquire enough autonomy to act as a critical tool of self-reflection of society.
Notwithstanding this lack of differentiation between these different aspects
of society, criticisms were pronounced and they were powerful. I am referring to the work of Bartolomé de Las Casas, which Gracia does not discuss
because of its explicit theological character. Curiously, he does discuss Francisco de Vitoria and Francisco Suárez, who were nevertheless also working
out of a medieval context. In any event, historically Las Casas had a profound
impact in the way the Spanish Crown dealt with Amerindians, more so than
Juan Ginés de Sepúlveda, whose treatise on the justification of waging war
against the Amerindians was not published until the twentieth century.

It is my contention that Gracia's restricted understanding of philosophy
leads him to be unreceptive to those elements in sixteenth and seventeenth
century Spanish philosophy that could be claimed as sources of inspiration
for contemporary Latin America. Gracia's lack of receptivity on this front also
prevents him from furthering his own argument of the family resemblance
that exists between Spaniards and Latin Americans. I think, for instance, that
the work done by Enrique Dussel, Germán Arciniegas, Silvio Zavala, and
Leopoldo Zea in rescuing and taking up the philosophical challenges of the
encounters between Amerindians and Spaniards is directly linked to that
work produced during the sixteenth century. Further, for many of these
thinkers, such projects of reconstruction and retrieval were directly linked
to the project of forging a viable, liberatory, and critical Latin American identity. For some of these thinkers such an identity had to negotiate the Scylla
of Europe's imputation that Spain had betrayed the Enlightenment and the
political revolutions of the eighteenth century, and the Charybdis of the cri-
ollo rejection and extermination of the Amerindian. This hazardous trek
was partly negotiated through the rescue of figures like Las Casas and Vitoria, who had spoken up and militantly organized in the defense of the
Amerindians but also projected an alternative route to and through European modernity, which was then just about to be born. Recognition of this

would have allowed Gracia to make a stronger case for the kind of bridge building he is advocating between European Hispanics and Latin American/North American Hispanics. Furthermore, to discuss the sixteenth and seventeenth centuries in their own terms, that is, without the blinkers provided by the twentieth-century academization of philosophy, would have allowed Gracia to argue in stronger ways for a greater recognition of Spanish, or Iberian, philosophy within the canon of Western philosophy. It would have allowed him, and many like me, to argue for a more expansive understanding of the different false starts, the never taken, missed opportunities, of a modernity that remains a normative ideal, in the sense meant by Jürgen Habermas and Enrique Dussel, that although opposed act as complementary and mutual correctives.

Third, one of the most interesting chapters in Gracia's wonderful book is the one dealing with Latin American philosophy. I liked it because of the extremely useful way in which Gracia offered a typology of the different attitudes toward the question, Is there a Latin American philosophy? Gracia distinguishes three positions, although he seems to end up talking about a fourth. The three positions that he distinctly marks out he calls the universalist, the historicist, and the critical. The universalist position holds that all philosophy is always the quest after eternal truth, *perennis philosophia*, and as such it is untouched by its context. For universalists, therefore, it is not that there is no Latin American philosophy, it is that there is no German or Greek or Spanish philosophy *überhaupt*. Philosophy is always philosophy, *sin más*. The historicist position argues the opposite, namely, that philosophy is always its time comprehended in thought, as Hegel put it. The argument is that Latin American philosophy is Latin American ipso facto, by the very fact that it is thought by Latin Americans. The critical position divides into two. The first stance argues that hitherto no Latin American philosophy has been produced because Latin Americans have lived under conditions of inauthenticity and therefore their philosophy is not a real reflection of their existential situation. The argument is that all philosophy thus far has been at the service of the colonizers and imperialists.

This first stance distinguishes itself from a second and different critical stance: here the argument is that this philosophy has not been produced because philosophy in Latin America has yet to assume itself as both subject and object from the standpoint of liberation. One may argue that these two critical stances are really one position at different times. There is also a fourth position, which Gracia discusses briefly and with a dismissive tone but which

I think is of paramount importance, especially today. This is the position to which Gracia refers with the pejoratively taken adjective 'postmodern.' I think this is a recent, insightful, and extremely viable position, best represented by the work of someone like Santiago Castro-Gómez, who in *Crítica de la razón lationamericana* (1996) develops an archaeology of discourses about "Latin America." I think, however, that Gracia does not see that Castro-Gómez's position is one that is shared by a whole host of philosophers and intellectuals working on the borders of philosophy, social theory, literary criticism, post-colonial, and cultural studies. Under this rubric of the 'postmodern' we would have to include the works of Nelly Richards, Walter Mignolo, Mabel Morana, Ileana Rodríguez, and Román de la Campa, but also the now classic Roberto Fernández Retamar (Beverly, Oviedo, and Aronna 1995; Lange-Churión and Mendieta 2001; Mendieta 2006).

Now, being familiar with two of Gracia's most recent works that address directly these questions, namely of the nature of philosophy, I am already aware of the lack of sympathy he has for deconstructive, poststructuralist, postmodern, postcolonial perspectives (Gracia 1999c:95–110, 2000d:193–211). In fact, it is not just an emotive attitude. Gracia has developed in the aforementioned articles excellent arguments against such positions. For the moment, however, let me conclude with my comments referring to this third concern that I have with Gracia's book. I think that there is a fourth position that has developed concerning "a Latin American philosophy." This fourth position has attempted to understand both the institutional and the ideological power such a question has deployed not just in Latin America but also in the United States and Europe. I think, furthermore, that this new position allows for a more dialectical mediation between Europe, the United States, and Latin America. When we ask to what extent we have made "others" of ourselves for the sake of a colonial gaze, we are also asking to what extent the colonial subject has constituted itself as a gazer of another who presents herself as other, that is, as native, autochthonous, virginal, and thus to be violated, or as a someone who has been violated already by the encounter.[1]

Fourth, my last concern, which is linked to my prior concern, pertains to the issue of Gracia's indictment of the philosophical establishment in the United States. Had I read Gracia's book before making my decision for philosophy as a Ph.D., I would have thought about it long and might have been negatively persuaded. The book yells: Do not become a philosopher, especially if you are Hispanic. It declares: The discipline in the United States has no respect for your culture, your history, your language, and if you make it out as a Ph.D. in philosophy, it is likely to segregate you in nonphilosophy departments. I think that Gracia is right in his tone. Most of the people who will read his book are colleagues in the discipline who will be so shamed that they will want to carry out some of the changes Gracia suggests. Notwithstanding this important shaming goal, I think that we also need another kind of discourse, and that is a discourse that tells the young that they should become philosophers, and it should give them good reasons for becoming so. Why should a poor Latino kid want to become a philosopher? I do not think it is because of the pay, prestige, or cornucopia of opportunities. There is something extremely idealistic, romantic, and selfless about wanting to become a philosopher, especially in a U.S. culture that is so materialistic, hedonistic, and ostentatious.

I think that this is where Gracia failed to tie the knot. On the one hand, we have the question of identity. On the other, we have the question of the nature of a discipline, philosophy. I think they are related. By becoming a philosopher one can contribute to the forging of a new cultural identity: as much of the United States as of one's people. Philosophy is a tool for self-understanding but also a hermeneutical quest for cultural self-reflexivity. We cannot allow others to tell us who we are. We must be able to claim our identities, and, in this struggle, philosophical clarity, depth, precision, of the sort that Gracia exhibits, are of great importance.

In the end, I wished Gracia had ended on a more positive note: become a philosopher, despite and against all the odds, because it is a stand as well as a gift, a stand against social anonymity and the offering of a gift of cultural affirmation to a "new people" that is becoming.

NOTE

1. I develop at greater length some of these arguments with Gracia in a paper presented at the 1999 meeting of the Society for Phenomenology and Existential Philosophy (Mendieta 1999a). The paper was presented to a panel, to which Gracia (1999a) and Mignolo (1999) also presented papers.

12. HISPANIC/LATINO IDENTITY

a response

JORGE J. E. GRACIA

Under the rubric "Hispanic/Latino identity" are included several topics. The roots of their discussion go back deeply into the history of Latin American thought but have recently become controversial among philosophers in the United States. Other disciplines also have addressed these topics, as one would have expected, particularly disciplines such as sociology, anthropology, literature, and art, but in increasing numbers philosophers have added their voices to these exchanges.

Hispanic/Latino Identity was the first systematic philosophical attempt at coming up with a theory that is not descriptive of the views of Latin Americans on these topics, and for this reason has functioned as a catalyst for their philosophical discussion, eliciting a considerable number of criticisms and comments, including those presented here. The criticisms fall roughly into several main categories, only to some of which I am able to respond for reasons of parsimony. The most important concern the view of Hispanic/Latino identity I have proposed. Almost every critic whose commentary is included in part II of this book, as well as Lawrence Blum (I:4), has echoed one or more objections to it. A different kind of objection, voiced by J. L. E. García, questions the very legitimacy of the notion of ethnic identity and its application to Hispanics. A third comprises objections by García, Richard J. Bernstein, and Robert Gooding-Williams against my historiographical claim concerning the importance of 1492 for Hispanic identity. Another series of objections addresses what my critics consider my neglect of certain factors that they deem essential to ethnicity, such as race (e.g., Gooding-Williams, who echoes a point made by Linda M. Alcoff [I:2]), history (e.g., Bernstein and Ilan

Stavans), language (e.g., Stavans), and culture (e.g., Gregory Pappas). Gooding-Williams also questions my thesis that the perception of being foreign explains to a great extent the marginalization of Hispanics in American philosophy today. And Bernstein also asks me to explain how I see the role of Hispanics in American philosophy, and their contribution to it, and, second, a point echoed by Eduardo Mendieta, to issue a more edificatory call to young Hispanic intellectuals in the United States to join the ranks of philosophers. From all this it should be clear that my critics have covered the most important, and frequently debated, questions one may raise concerning Hispanic/Latino identity and its impact in the United States.

In order to present a clear and coherent response for the sake of readers, I shall gather the objections that appear to be similar, or closely related, under eleven questions.

1. Should we talk about ethnic identity?
2. Do we need an account of Hispanic identity?
3. Is my account of Hispanic identity adequate?
4. What role does history play in an account of Hispanic identity?
5. Does my view account for Hispanic/Latino identity over time?
6. Does my view do justice to the social and political conditions of Hispanics/Latinos?
7. At what point in history does it make sense to begin speaking of Hispanics?
8. What is the role of culture and language in ethnicity in general and in Hispanic/Latino identity in particular?
9. What should the role of Hispanic/Latino philosophy be in American philosophy?
10. Is my conception of Hispanic and Latin American philosophy adequate?
11. What are the consequences of the perception of Hispanics/Latinos as foreigners?

SHOULD WE TALK ABOUT ETHNIC IDENTITY?

Let me begin with the most fundamental or, if you will, the most general objection. This, as formulated by García, is that the very notion of ethnic identity is so "problematic" and "dubious . . . as to warrant its rejection." If García is right, the enterprise of developing a theory of Hispanic/Latino identity is misguided and I should do well in abandoning it. Indeed, a more radical, and less generous, critic than García might argue that we need not bother with anything else I have said concerning Hispanics/Latinos, insofar as everything that is said about ethnic identity or the identity of this ethnic group is necessarily muddled because it depends on the very notion of ethnic identity, which is itself muddled.

García gives three main reasons that specifically support his rejection of this notion. After careful examination, however, they do not appear to me to be sound. Indeed, these reasons either beg the question or depend on rather controversial philosophical assumptions. All three repeat a basic point under slightly different modalities: in order to make sense, identity-talk must be relational, requiring two-term expressions, such as A and B, in which the identity of one with the other is considered through qualitative changes, across time, in different possible situations, and so forth. This disqualifies, or puts into question, issues that have to do with what it is to be a sovereign, a citizen, a Muslim, a dishwasher, or for that matter Hispanic; that is, with essences. García supports his point with a quotation from Adam Kuper (1999), in which the latter says that "the concept of identity is an oxymoron [when] used in relation to an individual, because an individual cannot correspond to himself or herself. . . . The notion of identity is connected rather to the idea that the self has certain essential properties and some contingent ones" (234).

First, let me note that García explicitly formulates his objection in terms of language. We need two linguistic terms in order to make identity-talk meaningful. But, actually, all identity-talk, regardless of what it refers to—and this includes Hispanics/Latinos—can be rendered this way. This applies even to essences; that is, what it is to be a sovereign, a citizen, a Muslim, and so on. To talk about the conditions that have to be satisfied by things that are chairs is precisely to talk about this and that thing both being chairs, and this thing being a chair as opposed to some other thing that is not a chair. Yet I certainly can talk about one person, regardless of time, in terms of identity, a case García would have to regard as illegitimate. Indeed, the case of ordinary language is overwhelming. Don't we talk about someone's ID, or proof of ID, someone's identity, or proof of identity? Or of a person's mistaken identity? Or about someone's false identity? All these expressions appear to depend on a use of 'identity' that does not involve the use of two terms. And if we turn away from ordinary language and to philosophy, the case is very clear. Or have we forgotten the famous example of 'Cicero is Tully'? (Cicero and Tully are two names for the famous Roman orator.) Of course, some philosophers have doubted that to say that Cicero is Tully is informative or even meaningful, but in order to support their doubts about what appears on most counts to be a perfectly meaningful and ordinary statement, they have had to devise extraordinarily complicated theories. Moreover, the issue has yet to be settled. So, it just won't do for García simply to say that the talk of identity requires two linguistic terms and this disqualifies group or ethnic identity from the category of meaningful talk.

Second, if García's quarrel is not really with language, in spite of the way he puts his objection, but with things, something similar applies. Assume that what García means is not that sentences that include the term 'identity' require two other linguistic terms but rather that identity is a relation between two things and, therefore, it cannot apply to one thing alone, unless that thing is considered at two different times or at two different points in a process. This is clearly not an uncontroversial claim. Indeed, it has been under dispute on and off since as far back as the Middle Ages. So, again, it cannot be used, without support, to dismiss other views of identity, including mine.

Third, as for Kuper's quote, I am not sure Kuper quite understands what an oxymoron is, but let's leave this aside. More important for us is that Kuper appears to support the very notion of identity García opposes. Indeed, Kuper (1999) says that "the notion of identity is connected rather to the idea that the self has certain essential properties and some contingent ones" (234). From this I gather he believes that the notion of identity has to do with the essence of the self, that is, certain conditions that make the self what it is. And such conditions are precisely what I am talking about when I talk about achronic ethnic identity, and what García tells me makes no sense.

Now, in the final version of García's commentary, prepared after I had responded to his earlier criticisms, he adds that Kuper's last remark opens the door for me to construe identity as personal essence. And he notes that this is contrary to both my antiessentialist approach and my claim that persons can have multiple identities. What García ignores is that I do not take Kuper's bait insofar as I do not construe all identity as personal. Clearly, García does not understand all identity as personal identity (more on this later), without offering any reasons for it, but in my view identity is a broader notion than personal identity. Otherwise why do we need the qualifier 'personal' to refer to it? Indeed, we talk about identity—for example, the Principle of Identity—even in logic. Furthermore, my theory is not about personal identity at all, but about ethnic (Hispanic/Latino in particular) identity. That persons may share in multiple ethne does not entail that they have more than one personal identity or one essence (if instead of 'identity' we wish to use the term 'essence'). Just as the fact that I am a citizen of Cuba and Canada does not conflict with the fact that I am also an American citizen, or the fact that I am the brother of Mercedes does not conflict with the fact that I am the brother of the late Ignacio. In short, García's rejoinder does not help his case but rather further confirms the sources of his misunderstanding. (For more on this, see Gracia 2008b:chap. 1.)

DO WE NEED AN ACCOUNT OF HISPANIC IDENTITY?

Considering that García rejects the notion of social or group identity, it should not be surprising that he also rejects the need to account for Hispanic identity. Indeed, he argues that the concept of what it is to be Hispanic is not needed for affirmative action and other political/legal/social policies. Of course, this does not mean that he thinks we do not need to identify Hispanics for affirmative action. He grants that we do, but in order to identify them we do not need, in his judgment, to deploy the notion of Hispanic identity.

Frankly, I do not understand how García can claim this. If we do not have a concept of Hispanic, and, let me add, presumably a good one, how can we identify Hispanics? To be able to talk about conditions of identification seems to require that we also talk about what Hispanics are, what it is to be Hispanic, and what Hispanics have in common, if anything. That García does not like the term 'identity' to refer to this, for reasons we saw earlier, does not change this fact.

IS MY ACCOUNT OF HISPANIC IDENTITY ADEQUATE?

Under this heading I include several objections, some of which are based on confusions between four different questions, for which I cannot blame my critics in particular since they are widespread in contemporary philosophy. These confusions lead some of my critics to say that I have more than one theory, my theories are mutually inconsistent, or my theory does not do what it is intended to do when in fact they refer to one part of my theory and a task that, in my view, is supposed to be done by another part. Let me proceed, then, by clarifying the three questions that are the source of confusion and by making explicit the parts of my theory that answer these questions. I label these questions *metaphysical, historical,* and *epistemological,* respectively.

The *metaphysical question* can be formulated in this way: What is the metaphysical nature of ethnicity in general, and of Hispanic/Latino ethnicity in particular? By this question, I intend to ask for a categorial characterization of ethnicity. Let me give an example of what I have in mind. If I ask for the categorial characterization of "human being" within, say, an Aristotelian metaphysics, the answer is "substance." This means that, within an Aristotelian categorial scheme, human beings are considered substances. If I ask the same question of "white," the answer is "quality." And if I ask the same question of "three feet long," the answer is "quantity," and so on. If, instead of an Aristotelian categorial scheme, I use a Humean one, I end up by saying that a human being is a bundle of perceptions perhaps, and that white is an idea, because those are the most general metaphysical categories that Hume uses to classify these things. Now, I may ask the same question of other things. In fact, I can ask it about anything, and this is what metaphysicians regularly do. They try to categorize colors, minds, tables, and events according to categorial schemes they have previously postulated or developed (Gracia 1999b, 2014).

In my theory, I use this procedure to deal with ethnicity in general and Hispanic/Latino ethnicity in particular. The question is: Within which general category does ethnicity fall? Is ethnicity a quality similar to white? Is it a relation, like motherhood? And so on. In answering the question, I put considerable emphasis on the denial of views that consider ethnicity either a property or a set of properties that accompany every member of an ethnic group. Ethnicity cannot be explained in terms of a set of necessary and sufficient conditions that apply to members of an ethnic group, because the properties that accompany the members of the group change with time and place. On the positive side, I argue that ethnicity is best understood as a family resemblance that, unlike Wittgenstein's theory, is conceived in historical and relational terms.

Consider the Gracia family—we could consider any family and any family name, including matrilineal families and family names. This is a group of people we know by the last name 'Gracia.' What is it that makes the individual persons members of this group? It is a set of historical relations, the members of which are contingent and do not necessarily apply to all members. My grandmother Gracia became a Gracia through marriage to my grandfather Gracia. My father Gracia became a Gracia because he was the issue of my grandmother and grandfather Gracia. My wife is a Gracia because she married me. My cousin Estevan is a Gracia because he was adopted by my uncle Gracia. And so on. In many ways one could say, with the disciples of Wittgenstein, that the only thing that all Gracias have in common is that they are called Gracia (Bambrough 1960–1961). But this is really not sufficiently informative, because we call ourselves, and are called by others, "Gracia" because of particular properties that turn out not to be the same for all of us, even if they are the same for more than one of us. These properties are founded on relations that are historical and contingent but that nonetheless tie together the members of the family. Similarly, the reason why I am in a certain context considered Hispanic might be that I speak Spanish and was born in Cuba. The reason Ignazio is taken as Hispanic is that he speaks Spanish and lived for a long time in Argentina; the reason for Joan Miró is that he was born in Catalonia and spoke Catalan. The reason my daughters are Hispanic is that they have Hispanic parents, one Argentinean and one Cuban. All these reasons point to historical and contingent properties that have nothing to do with the metaphysical categorization of Hispanic, except insofar as they confirm that categorization as familial, relational, and historical.

This metaphysical issue should not be confused, in turn, with the *historical question*. When we are talking about metaphysics, we are speaking of categorial characterizations of the most general sort and, if you wish, *sub specie aeternitatis*. The historical question is a different one for several reasons. For one, it does not concern the general category we are dealing with, or, to put it differently, the class; rather, it concerns individuals. The metaphysical question in the case of ethnicity and Hispanics is about the general category, or categories, within which ethnicity and Hispanicity fit. And the answer is that they fit within the category of a familial-historical group, rather than within the category of a property-sharing group. The historical question, on the other hand, concerns the temporal, contingent situation of particular ethnic groups, and in our case Hispanics.

Also, in the case of the metaphysical question we are concerned with necessary conditions of the most general sort that apply across time and place. In the case of the historical question we are concerned with contingent conditions that apply to individuals and are contextual and historical. The sorts of questions involved in the latter, then, have to do with historical location. In the case of historical entities, like ethnic groups, these questions involve factors that lead to the formation of the groups, the moment or moments of group origin, and the relative unity and diversity of the groups throughout history. To answer that the Gracia family began in the twelfth century in a little town of Aragon, when the name 'Gracia' was given for the first time to some long-forgotten male ancestor of mine, is not to contradict that to be a Gracia does not entail a property common to all those people who are called Gracia and belong to the Gracia family. It is merely to confirm the fact that, metaphysically, the Gracia family is a historical entity unified by a set of contingent relations throughout history. Likewise, to say that the use of the term 'Hispanic' for an ethnic group begins to make sense only after 1492 is to confirm that Hispanics are an ethnic group, that they do not necessarily share properties that are common to all of them, and that they are tied together by a series of relations that are historically contingent. So, yes, all Hispanics are tied in some way to 1492, but this tie is historical and contingent and serves its purpose only contextually, which is one of the requirements established by the first part of my theory. So, contrary to Gooding-Williams's contention, this does not constitute a second theory of identity and it does not contradict the purported first theory. It is merely a part of my overall theory.

Still, there is another source of confusion, which concerns a third issue, the *epistemic question* of how one can tell whether someone is a member of an ethnic group or not, or, more pointedly, whether someone is Hispanic or not. How do we know that Martin Luther King Jr. does not count as Hispanic but Gracia does? And how can I tell whether a Sephardic Jew who lives in Morocco is or is not Hispanic? The issue here concerns necessary and sufficient conditions also, but the conditions in question are conditions not of being but of knowing. Because of this, and because knowing involves knowers and the means of knowing, and the horizon of knowing is always contextual and limited, the conditions involved do not need to coincide with the metaphysical or historical conditions of which I spoke before. There may be metaphysical conditions of identity that are beyond the powers and means of knowing of particular knowers. And there may be criteria of identification that are effective within a context and not outside that context.

Let me illustrate. Consider an isolated part of this world in which only human beings know how to swim, and in which, for this reason, there are no animals of any other kind that know how to swim. In this part of the world one could use knowledge of how to swim as a criterion of humanity. If someone knows how to swim, he or she is human. And yet, this is a contingent fact, and certainly contextual. Visitors from some other place would find this criterion insufficient because in their part of the world other beings besides humans swim. The point, then, is that members of ethnic groups are identified in context, and the same applies to Hispanics. We can be identified here, or there, for reasons that cannot effectively function outside these particular contexts as necessary and sufficient conditions of identity or identification. Again, then, the existence of contextual necessary and sufficient conditions that function epistemically does not contradict my view but actually supports it. Nor does acknowledgment of this constitute a third theory of identity, as Gooding-Williams suggests, and least of all one that contradicts my Familial-Historical View.

Of course, some of my critics will not be satisfied with this answer. They will argue that I have not provided enough guidance to determine whether X belongs or not to group G. In the case of Hispanics, whether Jorge Gracia or Martin Luther King Jr. belong to the group of Hispanics. Indeed, although most of those who argue in this way explicitly reject essentialism, they in fact assume it in their arguments: they want necessary and sufficient conditions for every case and outside a context, and when these are not forthcoming, they argue that no distinction is possible. In other words, they borrow from essentialists the criteria of effective class participation and when it is clear that such criteria cannot be found, they deny that distinctions are possible and make distinction an arbitrary matter that depends on individual whims.

The root of the problem is a misunderstanding common to both essentialists and nonessentialists concerning the very nature of ethnic groups. Ethnic groups are neither like a triangle nor like the foods I choose to eat. The first is fixed by conditions that apply universally and noncontextually; the second is a matter of what I like. The identity of ethnic groups is based on changing factors, and the boundaries of the groups are not strict. The identity changes because historical events often alter the conditions of membership, but this does not entail that the conditions are arbitrary, or have to do with personal preferences, as happens with the foods I like. The boundaries of ethnic groups are not strict because membership in such groups depends on the number and closeness of the ties of each individual with other individuals, and these vary in a group. Some people are more closely tied to others, some less. In an ethnic group, we have a spectrum, with a thick core and an ever thinning periphery. It would be nice for conceptual reasons, perhaps, to have neat and clear boundaries. But this is not the way ethnic groups are, and therefore to expect them to be this way is futile. Moreover, it is counterproductive to expect that theories about the nature of these groups should make them what they are not. My theory correctly reflects an important fact: the membership of some members of an ethnic group is unquestionable, whereas the membership of others is questionable and, therefore, open to legitimate disagreement. Indeed, I have argued elsewhere that most of our commonly used concepts, such as "most of X," as used in "most members of this class," function in a similar way, so there is nothing unusual for ethnic group concepts such as "Hispanic" or "Latino" to do so (Gracia 2005b:59–60).

Now consider the case of Sephardic Jews raised by Bernstein as a counterexample to my view. In this case, there are relations that tie this group to the group of Hispanics—some Sephardic Jews still speak Spanish, for example, and maintain relations with core members of the Hispanic group—whereas in others these relations are missing—some Sephardic Jews do not speak Spanish and have severed their historical ties to other Hispanics. How do we classify Sephardic Jews, then? Surely this appears to be a matter of argument and degree. Perhaps all Sephardic Jews should be excluded from the category of Hispanic, perhaps the first group should be included and the other excluded, or perhaps both groups should be included. The issue is not one that can be easily determined. And certainly, as I have argued, the context needs to be taken into account. For example, if we put a group of Mexicans and Sephardic Jews from Morocco in a room together with a group of Andalucian Spaniards, Chinese peasants, and some Englishmen, how do you think the group would break up?

WHAT ROLE DOES HISTORY PLAY IN AN ACCOUNT OF HISPANIC IDENTITY?

A tenet of my view is that history plays an important role in ethnic identity in general and Hispanic/Latino identity in particular. However, Bernstein finds difficulty with the issue of demarcation, of determining who qualifies as Hispanic. My theory, he believes, does not provide sufficient guidance in this respect. Echoing an argument voiced by K. Anthony Appiah (2000) against W. E. B. Du Bois, he frames his objection in terms of the use of history I make.[1] History, he objects, is not specific or particular enough to be able to demarcate Hispanics from other groups. History is general; it can be your history or mine, this history or that. So my emphasis on historical relations as what unifies Hispanics fails. Bernstein is aware that I speak not of history in general but of "our history," that is, the history of Hispanics, but he argues that I need to point out something that turns "history" into "our history" and that I do not effectively do this because I deny that there are common properties to the group of Hispanics throughout history and because the notion of family that I use to further clarify the issue is ineffective without such properties.

At this point he adds the suggestion that is behind many of the difficulties that he and some others find with my view. He writes that it is the sense or consciousness of history as "ours" that is missing from my theory and could be used to supply the missing element. By consciously appropriating history, by identifying ourselves with certain events, we effectively particularize history and become a group. This amounts to a view in which self-identification is either a necessary or a sufficient condition of ethnic identity. I do not know whether Bernstein would go so far as to claim that it is a sufficient condition, although he does make clear it is necessary ("there must also be a sense of one's identity and pride in being Hispanic").

I find both claims unacceptable. The first is unacceptable because ethnic groups function as groups even when they lack a sense of themselves. Self-identification is a long and protracted process that often depends on conditions external to an ethnic group and takes a long time to emerge. There is plenty of empirical evidence in the work of anthropologists to suggest this to be the case. The second claim is unacceptable because people can be taught to think of themselves in many ways that are contrary to facts; they can be indoctrinated, and facts can be covered up or misrepresented. A child may grow up thinking she is a natural offspring of her parents when in fact she is adopted. Consider the pathetic case of the Nazis and all the self-delusions in which they engaged!

Like Bernstein, Stavans is concerned with history, but his concerns are somewhat different. He argues that my characterization of Hispanic/Latino identity "resists looking chronologically at the history of how the identity of Latinos has been conceptualized by the ethnicity or the minority itself [in the United States] as well as by extraminority viewpoints." Indeed, he concludes by observing, "My suspicion is that Gracia isn't fond of history as a discipline" because in the articulation of my arguments "historical facts are seldom presented." Note that Stavans's argument is not only different from Bernstein's but also weaker insofar as it is not just self-reflection and self-identification but knowledge of the history of self-reflection and self-identification that seems to be presented as necessary for a social identity such as Hispanic/Latino identity.

First a comment about Stavans's voiced suspicion that I am not fond of history because I do not use historical facts in my arguments in support of my position concerning Hispanic/Latino identity. Contrary to what he believes, this suspicion cannot have a solid foundation insofar as I was originally trained as a historian and a very considerable amount of my work is painstakingly historical, in reference to both medieval philosophy and Spanish/Hispanic/Latin American/Latino philosophy and thought. It is not the case that I am not fond of history. Indeed, I am particularly fond of it. Nor is it accurate to say that I do not make reference to history or historical facts in my discussion of Hispanic/Latino identity. A good part of the two books to which Stavans refers (Gracia 2000c, 2008b), in addition to many articles in journals I have published over the years, contain considerable historical analysis and argumentation, particularly the first book. Moreover, I have also published substantial discussions of the views of Latin Americans about Hispanic/Latino identity. One is an anthology of the most pertinent texts on this topic written in Latin America, coedited with Iván Jaksić: *Filosofía e identidad cultural en América Latina* (completed in 1983 but published in 1988). Another is a recent book I edited, *Forging People: Race, Ethnicity, and Nationality in Hispanic American and Latino/a Thought* (2011), that discusses Latin American ideas that have particular bearing on the question of Hispanic/Latino identity. Nonetheless, Stavans is right to say that I do not, in the books he mentions, dwell to any great extent on the history of Hispanic/Latino ideas about Hispanic/Latino identity. So, why don't I do it, and is this something essential to a proper view of Hispanic/Latino identity?

It seems obvious that the history of self-reflection and self-identification by Hispanics/Latinos, and by others on Hispanic/Latino identity, is a relevant subject of discussion when one considers Hispanic/Latino identity. Indeed, as I just noted, some of those who have engaged this issue have gone so far as to argue that self-identification is a necessary and/or sufficient condition of Hispanic/Latino identity: to be Hispanic/Latino requires to self-identify as such, and such self-identification may suffice for it. Others have argued that knowledge of the history of self-reflection is essential for Hispanic/Latino identity: I cannot be Hispanic/Latino if I do not know about the history of self-reflection by Hispanics/Latinos.

I believe, however, that these views make a serious mistake in the case of Hispanic/Latino identity, although they might not do so in the case of some other ethnic identities. Let me identify some reasons.

First, they fall into the kind of confusion between the epistemic and the metaphysical to which I called attention earlier in this chapter. To put it in more ordinary language, it confuses what we think about ourselves with what we are. I can be something that I do not think I am, and I may not be what I think I am. One can think of oneself as charming and in fact be the contrary, and vice versa. The history of what Hispanics/Latinos think we are, qua Hispanics/Latinos, may be accurate or not, depending on many factors. Second, knowledge of our history is surely not a requirement of Hispanic/Latino identity. Most Hispanics/Latinos, except for academics and the like, know very little of our history, except for the immediate facts that concern our families, and least of all of what those who have theorized about Hispanic/Latino identity have said about it. Third, it is difficult to find cases in which Hispanic/Latino identity requires this kind of knowledge of those who have that identity.

My general view about ethnic identity, and this applies to Hispanics/Latinos (as I argue in Gracia 2000c, 2005b, 2008b), is that it does not require a set of properties common to all members of the group. And one of the properties that may not be common is that the members of the group be self-reflective, and least of all be aware of the history of self-reflection in the group, about our identity. Ethnicity is too contingent on circumstances to require it. True, some ethnic groups require such awareness and self-identification. And in such cases those who give an account of the ethnic groups must make a place for them in their account. But Hispanic/Latino identity is not like that, and so it is immaterial to bring such reflection and its history into play. This is one reason why I did not feel compelled to include it in the presentation of my view; it is not necessary to account for Hispanic/Latino identity.

Let me cite the example of a well-known Mexican philosopher, Samuel Ramos (1962), who thought hard and wrote much about Mexican identity. Did he try to find a set of properties that characterize Mexicans? Yes, although I do not find his list convincing. But did he provide a history of views about Mexican identity to preface his own view or buttress it? No. Why? Because he did not think it necessary. He was talking about what Mexicans are, not about what Mexicans think they are.

I may be wrong about ethnic identity in general or Hispanic/Latino identity in particular, but regardless of that, it is important to maintain a distinction between what one is and what one thinks one is. Surely, I do not want to think I am Napoléon when I am not. And, although in some cases what one thinks one is becomes relevant for what one is, at other times it is not. I saw my task in *Hispanic/Latino Identity* as providing a theoretical account of Hispanic/Latino identity, not of what Hispanics/Latinos, or for that matter what non-Hispanics/Latinos, have thought and written about our identity.

But there is still one other consideration that I think might be useful to bring up. This is that the discussion of Hispanic/Latino identity that Bernstein and Stavans find wanting is fundamentally philosophical, not historical.

Historical accounts consist in narratives that present and interpret historical facts and use historical arguments, whereas philosophical accounts
involve conceptual analyses that do not necessarily require reference to
historical facts or historical arguments, although they may use them. The
former is the job of the historian, which, as I mentioned, I have also done
but do not do to a great extent in the context of my philosophical analysis of
Hispanic/Latino identity. Consider, for example, a metaphysical analysis
of a human being. This would end up with a conclusion such as that a human
being is a substance that thinks (Descartes), or a composite of form and
matter (Aquinas), and so on. And none of this requires a history of the views
about human beings.

I bring this matter up not so much because I am trying to defend my
position. Rather, I want to make clear some of the basic requirements of developing an acceptable discussion of Hispanic/Latino identity, which in my
view include that we keep clear the distinction between a philosophical analysis and a historical one, as well as between what Latinos/Hispanics are and
what we, or others, think we are, that is, between fact and opinion.

Naturally, at this point one might ask: But doesn't this separation of the
philosophical from the historical entail that you have abandoned the interdisciplinary approach you claim essential for a full understanding of race,
ethnicity, and Hispanic/Latino identity in *Surviving Race*?

The answer is that "interdisciplinarity" does not entail "confusion." One
thing is to claim that different disciplines need one another, and another to
distinguish them or the ways they proceed. Surely physics needs mathematics, but this does not entail that one is the other or that mathematics is empirical and physics is not. That I keep philosophical and historical claims
separate does not mean that I have abandoned the claim that philosophy
needs history and history needs philosophy. Nor does the claim I made earlier in this book—that philosophy does not have a specialized method—mean
that we cannot do philosophy without using a historical method. It all depends on the part of philosophy in question. Consider, for example, logic and
the philosophy of history. Logic requires no historical analyses, whereas the
philosophy of history does. My analysis of ethnic identity in general is
fundamentally metaphysical and therefore can dispense with the history of
ethnic facts without betraying the belief that philosophy profits from the
results achieved by other disciplines.

This does not mean that self-identification and group identification cannot be part of the conditions that play a role in ethnic identity, or that the

appropriation of history by a group does not play a role in that group's self-identification. It certainly can and often does. When I say that "knowledge does not determine being," a claim Bernstein questions, I do not mean that knowledge does not affect being. What I mean is that the knowledge of a fact does not alter that fact, even if knowledge of the fact (1) may produce other facts that otherwise would not have been produced or (2) may modify certain facts that otherwise would not have been modified. My knowledge of who hit me over the head may alter my future conduct, but that knowledge cannot alter the bump I have on my head or the identity of the person who caused it. This is a distinction that, surprisingly, is often missing in discussions of these issues.

Here is also the answer to another criticism made by García, who takes a strong position against the notion of socially constructed identities. He argues that I flirt with the idea that ethnicity and ethnic identity are socially constructed, by which I think he means that in my view they are completely or exclusively social constructions. Clearly, from what I have just said, this criticism is unfounded. A sense of identity often plays a significant role in the development of identity, but it is neither a necessary nor a sufficient condition of it. The issue is more complicated than Bernstein, Stavans, and García seem to believe.

My view in this matter is that a sense of identity and the appropriation of history are certainly part of history, but they are not necessarily or exclusively what make history ours, or yours for that matter. So what does? An effective answer to this question needs to consider four factors. The first is that certain historical events affect certain people directly. Clearly, the initial encounter in 1492 between the persons aboard the Castilian ships and the natives of San Salvador affected these people directly in rather obvious ways. The second is that some events affect only some people directly and not others. The initial encounter did not directly affect Russian peasants or Chinese bureaucrats living in Russia and China at the time. The third is the number of events that take place. A few isolated events cannot compare with chains or clusters of many events. Consider the difference between the Vikings' landing in Newfoundland and the landing of the Castilian ships in San Salvador. The fourth is the significance of the events. It is one thing to give a few colored beads to natives; it is another to change their way of life and impose a foreign model of government over them. It is one thing to settle in a place but keep separate from the native population, as the English tended to do in North America, and it is another to mix freely with the population, as Iberians did.

If we take all four factors together, I think it becomes clear that certain historical events effectively tie some peoples together while at the same time separating them from others, whereas others do not. Indeed, this is very much what happens with a family: a marriage unites the persons in question and separates them from others, and it does so in a different way from trading. History becomes ours precisely because of the particular history it is. It creates us as groups by uniting us and by generating relations and properties that, in context, serve also to separate and distinguish us from others.

My position, then, allows for the discussion of historical conditions and properties for Hispanics. There is no reason why, for example, we cannot speak of certain features of Hispanic philosophy or thought in the nineteenth century. It also allows for the discussion of criteria of identity within a historical context. But all this has to be understood within the relational and nonessentialistic metaphysical framework I have provided. This is why I can, without contradiction, discuss such features of Hispanics as *mestizaje*. On the one hand, to make this, or any other feature associated with *some* Hispanics, part and parcel of the nature of *all* Hispanics is to fall back into the kind of essentialism that distorts the nature of ethnicity and is responsible for much oppression and discrimination in human history. On the other hand, to reject the metaphysical framework is to give up on understanding what ethne are and how they work. It condemns us to a kind of superficial, and culturally biased, description of ethnic phenomena without a foundational understanding of them, or to the kind of description that is more properly undertaken in such fields as sociology and cultural anthropology. So I must reject Gooding-Williams's suggestion in this direction. I must also reject the views of those who see coloniality, domination, exploitation, and the like as idiosyncratic characteristics of Hispanics, Latinos, Latin Americans, or other ethnic groups (for suggestions of this sort, see Mignolo 1999:36–41).

DOES MY VIEW ACCOUNT FOR HISPANIC/LATINO IDENTITY OVER TIME?

Apart from objections concerning the number, consistency, and adequacy of my theory, García questions both the notion of an identity that changes over time and my claim that Hispanics have no shared properties. He puts the first criticism thus: "If what it is to be (a) Hispanic is different at Time One from what it is at Time Two, then there really is no such a thing as being (a) Hispanic, no such quality or essence—let alone identity." His point is that I cannot consistently hold that there is a Hispanic identity when such an identity changes over time.

But here again we see a begging of the question. According to García, to say that an identity changes over time is in a sense like saying that there is an identity and there is not an identity—a clear contradiction. But this is not what I say. I hold that Hispanics have an identity over time, but not that the identity itself changes. What changes is something else. The source of the trouble for García is that he assumes that for Juan to have a Hispanic identity at time$_1$ is for him to have a certain characteristic that if Pedro does not have at all, or Juan does not have at time$_2$, makes both Pedro and Juan at time$_2$ not Hispanic, or not Hispanic in the same sense as Juan is at time$_1$. But this is not my position. I speak, rather, of a group (or a set or a class, if you will) and what makes something belong in it. My point is that human beings belong to ethnic groups because they are related in certain ways, but not necessarily in the same ways, even when they do not share the same properties. What makes Juan and Pedro, and Juan at time$_1$ and Juan at time$_2$, Hispanic is that they are related to other members of the group of Hispanics, not that each of them has a property that the others do not have. To reject my view by saying that, if there is no property in common there cannot be a group, is simply to beg the question. It is to reject my conclusion, not to give an argument that undermines it. And to say that different members of a group belong to it because they have different properties, rather than the same properties, is not anything I have claimed.

García also puts forth a group of three arguments, all aimed at disputing my claim that Hispanics do not share properties (García prefers to call them "qualities," but I will retain my terminology since nothing hangs on this and it may prevent confusion). All three arguments have a similar target: García aims to show that, contrary to my claim, my theory implies shared properties among Hispanics. According to the first argument, it is because the very notion of Hispanic identity is a property Hispanics share; according to the second, because each Hispanic is such because of some property, so that all Hispanics must share at least the disjunctive property composed of the properties each Hispanic has; and according to the third, because the very intelligibility of identity requires a shared property.

I have said enough about the third reason before and, therefore, do not need to address it again: it is merely an assumption García makes and one that has been disputed by many philosophers, so to accept it as an argument without any substantiation other than mentioning it is ineffective. About the first two reasons, I need not say much either except that, when I speak of properties, I am speaking of something more than identity or disjunctive properties. If identity is a property at all, it is a property quite different from other properties and certainly different from the kinds of properties used to identify ethnic groups, such as language, food, and customs. Moreover, identity is what needs to be explained, not what can be assumed. Disjunctive properties have peculiar problems that I shall put aside for the moment, but I should at least add that what I said about identity also applies here. Indeed, I have no objection if García insists on calling them properties (or "qualities" in his own terminology) and includes them among the properties ethnic groups have. My quarrel is not with their name or with these kinds of rather empty properties but with more substantial ones. So I do not find that these objections pose a serious difficulty for my theory.

García also questions my Familial-Historical View of Hispanic identity by arguing that, by refusing to follow Wittgenstein in accepting a genetic link in families, which is then used to explain resemblance, I make "the analogy [with a family] impossible to follow and apply." Against this I respond that the rejection of a necessary genetic link is precisely what makes the analogy work. Consider that games—an example of family resemblance Wittgenstein used—are not genetically linked. Different kinds of games form a family even though they have no genetic link, so their resemblance is not explained through genetic links, as García purports. The point, which Wittgenstein may have missed, is precisely that even in families genetic links do not tie all members—think of adopted children and husbands and wives—if his view accords with García's interpretation of it.

The objections to my theory that I have thus far discussed have been metaphysical, historical, or epistemic, corresponding to three of the four kinds of questions I distinguished earlier. Now I turn to some *sociopolitical* objections.

DOES MY VIEW DO JUSTICE TO THE SOCIAL AND POLITICAL CONDITIONS OF HISPANICS/LATINOS?

Considering the climate of opinion today, it would have been strange not to have had someone raise an objection based on sociopolitical considerations. And, indeed, several of my critics do, particularly Alcoff (I:2), and Gooding-

Williams and Mendieta here. Alcoff argues that I neglect to pay attention to the close connection between fact and value, assuming the possibility of a valueless objectivity that is not possible. The close connection between fact and value is a reason why, for Alcoff, facts are not very far from politics, a point that we have debated and on which we have disagreed in print (Alcoff 2005b, 2005c; Gracia 2008b:chap. 3). Gooding-Williams also raises this point, but it is Mendieta who dwells more extensively on it, making it perhaps the core of his criticism.

Mendieta objects to what he calls my globalization of the concept of Hispanic based on its political and social consequences. Apart from the question of whether Latin Americans might be willing to embrace such a global concept, he claims that adopting it would be "disastrous." The reason is that the political and social challenges that Hispanics face in the United States, Latin Americans face in Latin America, and Spaniards face in Spain are quite different. My proposal, according to him, does not do justice to the particularity of these "struggles" and in fact "can lead to eviscerating the very specific political and strategic content that the term ['Hispanic'] may have" for particular groups.

Let me make clear that I am very sympathetic to the view that the particular should not be swallowed up by, or reduced to, the universal. After all, one of the first books I ever wrote was about individuality, not universality, and I have always emphasized the importance and reality of the particular (Gracia 1988). Also I am sympathetic to the notion that Latin Americans, Iberians, and Hispanics residing in the United States face different social and political challenges and that it is important to take the particularity of them into account. (For this, see also what María Cristina González and Nora Stigol [III:15] have to say, and my response [III:17].) But I do not see how this undermines the validity or usefulness of my theory. Indeed, it seems actually to support it insofar as broader categories are necessary to understand the relations between narrower ones. The history, identity, and culture of Iberians, Latin Americans, and Hispanics in the United States are inextricably tied together and they cannot be fully understood independently of one another. Failing to understand how they are related causes serious misunderstandings of those histories, identities, and cultures, and of the relations between these peoples and other peoples, such as Anglo-Americans, the French, and the English.

Consider for a moment someone like José Vasconcelos. What is he? Mexican by nationality; mestizo by race; and a mixture of Spanish, Amerindian, and African in terms of culture, where the Spanish element is rather predominant (there is also a veneer of Anglo-American culture resulting from a period of residence in the United States). Does it make sense for him to say that he is Mexican and not Latin American? That he is Latin American and not Spanish? That he is African and not Amerindian? That he is white or not white? Of course, Vasconcelos can think (or could have thought, since he is dead) whatever he wants. But the place of his birth is not negotiable and is part of his identity; his DNA is not negotiable and is also part of his identity; and the sources of his culture are not negotiable and again are part of his identity. So, does it really make sense for Vasconcelos, and this goes for Mendieta also, to forget, for reasons of a political and social agenda, the facts that make him up?

This brings me to three objections I have against the underlying assumptions behind Mendieta's criticism of my view.

1. It is shortsighted. By focusing on particular social agendas, it misses the big picture. But by missing the big picture, it actually misses the smaller ones as well. Mendieta wants an identity that forgets history and its results, and this is a serious mistake. A fictional history is dangerous because it is always invented by the stronger. The only defense the weak can muster against the myths of the powerful is the power of facts, not the myths of the weak.

2. It is misguided. To try to have politics and social agendas dictate metaphysics, or, to put it differently, to have ideology and values dictate facts leads to mistakes. Of course, it may be that Mendieta does not believe there are any facts. If this is so, then there is no point in engaging in any discussion, for then the only way to settle disagreements is through force. But I do think he believes there are facts, just that the facts he believes there are, are not the facts others believe in. Indeed, would he not consider that Spanish is his native tongue a fact, and an unquestionable one?

3. And it is inconsistent. For Mendieta to argue against the global understanding of 'Hispanic' and in favor of narrower labels such as 'Latin American' and 'Mexican' lead to incoherence. If we are to be consistent and use only labels that reflect "particular struggles," then we surely have to abandon all totalizing—to use a fashionable adjective—labels, including 'Latin American' and 'Mexican.' Indeed, in many ways the sociopolitical issues that face such countries as Argentina—which has never really considered itself Latin American—and Chile are very different from those that face such countries as Mexico and Ecuador. The differences may in fact be greater than the ones

in the issues faced by Argentina and Spain. Likewise, it is quite clear that national labels like 'Mexican' need to be rejected as well, for there are many groups of people in Mexico (let's not forget Chiapas) who see themselves as having political and social agendas that are quite different from the ones the mestizos from the big cities have identified for the country.

In short, the objections that Mendieta uses to reject my theory can be used to reject his. Should we reject the use of global, regional, and national labels then? Of course not. As I have said, we need all these for an adequate understanding of social realities. The problem is that Mendieta does not understand the need for, and place of, more general labels. Once this is understood, then we can keep and use these labels along with less-general ones. The root of this misunderstanding is a false dilemma between general and particular identities, and between eliminativism and essentialism, which are themselves rooted in essentialistic assumptions, as I explain in *Latinos in America* (2008b:chap. 1). But when are we justified in using these labels, and particularly the 'Hispanic' label? This leads me to the next topic.

AT WHAT POINT IN HISTORY DOES IT MAKE SENSE TO BEGIN SPEAKING OF HISPANICS?

My view is that it makes sense after 1492, but Gooding-Williams, Bernstein, and García question the importance I attach to this year. Bernstein's reason is that it is "disturbing, and indeed a bit artificial" because of its association with the violence of the expulsion of the Jews from the Iberian Peninsula and the violence initiated by "the 'encounter' between Iberia and its colonies," and García echoes this sentiment. Gooding-Williams claims that 1492 effectively leaves Africans out, insofar as they enter the picture only in 1518, and therefore obscures the importance of the Portuguese encounter with Africans and the many institutions that arose therein and were transferred in time to America. His suggestion instead is that the significant year should be 1441, when the Portuguese first encountered Africans.

With respect to Gooding-Williams's point, I do not wish to dispute the important role of Africans in the formation of Hispanic identity. Moreover, there is evidence that the influence of Africans in America started much earlier than 1518, an official date; this evidence indicates the presence of Africans in the Caribbean at least ten years earlier. Consider, for example, that there are earlier artifacts, of Caribbean origin, in which African influence is quite evident. And there is evidence of the presence of Africans in the Iberian Peninsula—and I am not speaking of North Africans—much earlier still. Slavery was common in Europe throughout the Middle Ages, and African slavery was known in the Iberian Peninsula long before slavery became widespread in America. The issue, then, is not about the significance of the African presence in America. It is rather about whether we should push the date for the beginnings of a Hispanic identity back to 1441 in order to do justice to the African presence.

Even though I sympathize with Gooding-Williams's concerns, I would rather retain 1492 for various reasons. First, 1441 would not do insofar as African slavery was known before then in Europe and many of the trappings of slavery were well in place before 1441. Second, the impact of Portuguese explorations, although important, never reached the level of impact of the first Spanish encounters with America. This can be seen in the historical record insofar as the legal and ethical issues that surfaced as a result of 1492 had not arisen before. There is also a question of numbers. It was only in the early sixteenth century that Africans were brought to America in sufficiently large numbers to have a major impact on the formation of the Hispanic ethnos, even if some of the encounters with them by Portugal in prior years contributed to the establishment of some cultural patterns and institutions that would become part of the cultural framework of America. Third, there is an issue of regional impact. The impact of Africans on this cauldron was initially regional, and it continued to be so for quite a while. In large measure it was confined to the coastal boundaries of the Caribbean and the coast of what is today Brazil. This means that it does not make much sense to overemphasize the early overall significance of the presence of Africans, even if with time their impact acquired enormous proportions. Finally, it must be kept in mind that I do not claim that Hispanic identity is fully constituted starting in 1492. To do this would certainly be absurd, and obviously so. My claim is that 1492 is a year in which several events set in motion the process of development of a Hispanic identity. Indeed, I explicitly prefer to talk about "encounters" rather than "an encounter" as significant for the formation of a Hispanic/Latino identity. The significance of 1492 therefore should not be misunderstood.

With the call by Bernstein and García for attention both to the expulsion of the Jews and to the brutality of the Iberian conquest of America, I agree fully. Indeed, I note both in the book. The violence involved in them is undeniable, and it is difficult to find harsh enough terms to condemn them. Still, this violence is irrelevant to the importance of the year for the beginning of the constitution of Hispanic ethnicity. Indeed, most ethne begin with violence and only those who wish to glorify particular ethne should be disturbed by this fact. My analysis was concerned only with formation, not judgment, and both the expulsion of the Jews and the first encounter are significant for the formation of Hispanic ethnicity. I say quite a bit in *Hispanic/Latino Identity* about this, so I need not belabor the point here. But perhaps I should mention that the expulsion of the Jews is a sign of a growing sense of themselves, among Iberians, as separate from what they considered to be other peoples. This sense was partly based on religious grounds, as indicated by the way they referred to Castilian, the language they identified with themselves, as "Christian" (*cristiano*). The expulsion of the Jews, together with the defeat of the Moors, who were driven out of Granada shortly before, are two additional steps in the direction of an increasing separation of Iberians from the world that did not include America and to a closer association with America.

This analysis points to the importance of history in an account of Hispanic/Latino identity. But what kind of history is involved and to what extent is it required? These are the questions that I brought up and explored earlier in the context of the criticisms by Bernstein and Stavans. Next I turn to a different question, having to do with the role of culture and language in ethnicity and Hispanic/Latino identity.

WHAT IS THE ROLE OF CULTURE AND LANGUAGE IN ETHNICITY IN GENERAL AND IN HISPANIC/LATINO IDENTITY IN PARTICULAR?

Pappas criticizes my view because, in his judgment, it does not give culture the place it deserves. So, is he right? I'm afraid he is not.

First of all, I should make clear that I have never said that culture plays no role in ethnicity, or that the role it plays in Hispanic/Latino identity is insignificant. My point rather is that culture is (1) a living, evolving phenomenon that is not homogeneous and uniform throughout time and history and (2) the result of historical relations. Culture results from the reaction of humans to their environment and to one another. It depends, therefore, on at least two factors: human needs and human responses; and it develops in the context of historical events. Human needs and responses are always contextual, although often guided by more basic needs and responses. We need to eat and we have to move from place to place. But the food we eat and how we move depend on what we have available at a particular moment in our history and the historical context in which we find ourselves. So, yes, Hispanics/Latinos are culturally different here and there from non-Hispanics/Latinos, and many of us may share certain cultural characteristics here or there. But all these cultural traits are historically related and dependent on historical relations. In short, I do not neglect culture, rather I place culture where it belongs.

More specifically, Pappas's objection is based on two distinctions: one between "culture" and "history" and the other between "common" and "similar." He argues, first, that I emphasize history to the detriment of culture and, second, that I conceive the term 'common' in too narrow a way, thus precluding the notion of a common culture. According to Pappas, this leads me to argue against the view that ethnicity involves common properties, whereas in fact ethnicity is based on such properties. Instead of this narrow conception of commonality, Pappas offers one in which commonality is understood more like similarity, thus allowing for differences and permitting some members of a group, who are said to share something in common, not to share the property or properties in question.

Let me first answer the second point, about my presumed narrow conception of 'common.' This seems to be a mere verbal issue. Pappas calls "common" what I call "similar," so that when he speaks of members of an ethnic group as sharing something in common what he says can be translated into my terminology by saying that members of the group share something similar. Now, I have made clear that I am perfectly willing to accept, and that my theory allows, similarity among the members of a group. So I am not sure Pappas has succeeded in sufficiently distinguishing the substance of his view from mine in order to be able to criticize mine. Indeed, he readily grants the point I make, that to talk about ethnic identity is to talk about members of a group not all of whom share the same properties. What he does not seem to like is that, instead of using the term 'common,' I use 'similar.' But because I mean by 'similar' what he means by 'common,' there is no quarrel I can discern.

With respect to the criticism that I emphasize history too much to the detriment of culture, thus rendering my view formal and empty—terms also used by Gooding-Williams and García in their criticisms—I have this to say: Pappas himself grants repeatedly that my theory in principle allows for cultural properties to be shared *in context* by members of ethnic groups. So his objection, although phrased in this way in several places, must involve something more than this in order to be distinguished from my view. I surmise the difference is that I give priority to historical relations over cultural properties, whereas cultural properties, in Pappas's view, are fundamentally important insofar as they are the bases of the consciousness of the identity of an ethnic group.

Here I detect a confusion between two sets of concepts. The first is between cause and effect; or, put in another way, between the position of the cart and the horse. It seems to me rather obvious that two or more persons have cultural properties in common—say, that they speak the same language—because history brought them together, or brought some of their ancestors together, and not vice versa. And this is so for a reason I have earlier noted, namely, that culture is a result of attempts by humans to cope with their circumstances; culture results from human action, which in turn is prompted by circumstances. So, if by 'history' (and I have in mind human history rather than natural history or any such thing) we mean past human actions, then those actions are prior in principle to culture. Of course, this does not mean that cultural factors may not prompt actions and therefore cause history. They do. But this is not the point, is it?

The second confusion I detect in Pappas's discussion is between the consciousness of similarities that we use to construct concepts of ethnic identities and the historical facts that tie members of ethnic groups together. In reflection, we begin in consciousness, with what appears to be common. Only after we consider these commonalities, finding that they are inadequate to account for ethnic unity, do we come to the underlying historical framework. So, yes, epistemically cultural traits come first, but that is only because of the epistemic immediacy of culture. Let me repeat a point I made earlier: we must be very careful not to confuse "ethnic identity" with "consciousness of ethnic identity," or, as it is sometimes put, "identity" with "a sense of identity," for this confusion is the source of much oppression and segregation. Finally, let me make clear that this distinction does not imply that cultural facts play only epistemic roles. Indeed, the reverse is the case: they play epistemic roles because they are facts. I can be effectively known as a speaker of Spanish because I speak Spanish. If I did not speak Spanish, it would be a mistake to think of me as a speaker of Spanish. In short, cultural facts occupy an important place in my theory, but they are important contextually and contingently. Speaking Spanish is neither a necessary nor a sufficient condition of being Hispanic/Latino; it may be so only here and now, or then and there.

The example I just presented leads me to the second criticism of my view that Stavans voices:

> My main critique of his work [is] the absence of what to me is one of the most significant elements shaping the identity of Latinos in the United States. . . . Spanish is the link to the past but also the ticket to a bicultural identity. . . . The level of fluency [in Spanish] determines the identification they [i.e., Latinos] might feel toward the [Latino] minority. . . . By ignoring language as a factor determining identity, Gracia bypasses a crucial manifestation of culture, one dangerous to ignore.

There is no question that Stavans brings up an important factor in Hispanic/Latino identity, namely Spanish. Language is an extremely important part of culture insofar as it is through language that we not only express ourselves but also think. Moreover, it is true that I do not emphasize language as much as Stavans would like me to do. But, again, there are reasons why I do not.

Let me first point out that the main language that Hispanics/Latinos use is not, as Stavans assumes, Spanish. A good portion of us in the United States and Latin America do not speak Spanish at all. Some of us speak Portuguese, and others speak Amerindian languages and speak Spanish only as a second language, and often not at all. Stavans confuses Hispanics/Latinos with recent immigrants, as he and I are, to the United States, and with those of us who are Spanish speaking. Indeed, the diversity of languages we speak is one of the reasons why I explicitly reject our identification with being Spanish speaking and why I de-emphasize Spanish in my discussion of our identity. Spanish is neither a necessary nor a sufficient condition of Hispanic/Latino identity, and it is a serious mistake to believe that it is since the facts are clearly against it. This does not mean, however, that for those of us who speak Spanish, this language is not important, although even in this case perhaps not as important as Stavans believes.

Now, in none of my writings on Hispanic/Latino identity have I addressed the issue of what the properties are that make us be so. The reason is that, as I have noted before, there is a long history of those who have tried to compile such a list and have failed. They have failed precisely because such a list does not exist except in the minds of those who wish it existed. Hispanics/Latinos are not held together through a set of properties that are common to all of us throughout our history. We are more like a family in which some of us share properties with some others, but no property is common to all the members of the group. No empirical evidence exists that anything to the contrary is true.

However, Stavans does not agree with this position and in fact believes in cultural essences not just for Hispanics/Latinos but for various different cultures and ethne (Stavans and Gracia 2014). And he is not alone. This is a popular position, strongly favored for purposes of nation building in Latin America (and in the United States), although close scrutiny shows that it is unwarranted. It is at most an unsubstantiated hypothesis and possibly a myth that many hold and believe but that so far has remained speculative.

Stavans concludes that "ignoring language as a factor determining identity . . . [is] dangerous to ignore." Actually I think the reverse is true. The idea that ethnic groups have properties that define them, including languages, tends to fuel the kind of nationalistic and ethnic feelings and policies that have caused much harm and pain to humans. Not having an essence, not having to speak Spanish and still be Hispanic/Latino, is reassuring, and I think a preventive to all kinds of possible curtailments to individual freedoms and rights. Think of the movement to make English the official language of the United States or Spanish the official language of Mexico. Doesn't this oppress those Americans and Mexicans whose native tongues are not English or Spanish? If English were the official language of the United States, I would not feel quite American, and the fact that Spanish is the official language of Mexico may be one of the reasons the Maya do not feel a national kinship with Spanish-speaking Mexicans. (More on the issue of linguistic rights in my response in III:17.)

WHAT SHOULD THE ROLE OF HISPANIC/LATINO PHILOSOPHY BE IN AMERICAN PHILOSOPHY?

In the closing chapter of *Hispanic/Latino Identity* I raise the question concerning the role of Hispanics/Latinos in American philosophy. This leads Bernstein to ask about the role and contribution of Hispanic philosophy to American philosophy, what Hispanic philosophy in particular would be like, and how it would be related to American philosophy. These questions are important for my theory, for I have claimed that there is nothing peculiar and idiosyncratic that is characteristic of Hispanics or our philosophy. How can I argue, then, that we should be taken into account and that we have something to contribute to American philosophy?

First, let me make clear that I have not argued that Hispanics/Latinos as a group, or Hispanic/Latino philosophy, just as Hispanic/Latino individuals themselves, do not have *any* properties or that they do not have *distinguishing* properties. To have said this would have undermined much for which I argue. My point is that there are no common properties that run throughout our history. The properties of Hispanics/Latinos and Hispanic/Latino philosophy are the result of familial-historical relations and therefore are contextual, contingent, and restricted to particular periods and historical locations. Yes, during the early part of the colonial period much of, and I want to emphasize *much of* because there are always many exceptions to any rule one cares to formulate concerning historical matters, Hispanic philosophy, whether in the Iberian Peninsula or in Latin America, had many characteristics that separated it from Anglo-American philosophy (one, of course, being that there was no Anglo-American philosophy to speak of at the time). The themes, the issues that it addressed, the language in which it was written, and so on were part of these properties. But these properties were not universal in the Hispanic/Latino philosophy of the period, even if they were very widespread, and most of them did not survive subsequent history.

The same can be said about Hispanic or Latin American philosophy in the twentieth century or during the nineteenth century, or about the philosophy in the Río de la Plata in the eighteenth century, and so on. A historian will find groups of texts that, because of particular historical circumstances, may be characterized in certain ways that will more or less easily distinguish them from texts that come from other periods or texts that come from other places. For example, much has been written in Latin American philosophy about the problem of whether there is or can be a Latin American philosophy or a Latin American identity during the first three-quarters of the twentieth century. Hence, one would be tempted to characterize Latin American philosophy as having this particular property in contrast with the Anglo-American or French philosophy of the period. Yet to do this would be to distort the record in important ways, because it would give the impression that all Latin American philosophy produced during this period had this property. And this is not true. Much Latin American philosophy at the time is not distinguishable from Anglo-American or French philosophy in this respect.

Second, there is a long history of philosophical speculation in Latin American societies that in time produced Hispanic/Latino philosophy. Even if one does not count pre-encounter philosophical thought in Latin America or the Iberian Peninsula, philosophy has had an important presence that continues to this day in Latin America. So, although there is no philosophical body of work that is homogeneous, there is a body of work that addresses a large variety of themes and topics for a period of five hundred years, and it does so from perspectives that, although not uniform, are generally different, in context, from those adopted by Anglo-American philosophers.

Third, because Hispanic/Latino philosophy has generally been marginalized within the European and Anglo-American context, it constitutes an excellent subject matter for those who wish to see how philosophy develops in the periphery, at the margins of the hegemonic ideological currents that dominate the world. Hispanic/Latino philosophy is an excellent case study where one can observe the role power plays in philosophy. I have not yet seen this point made in the literature. Yet it is important, for this is an area where clearly Hispanic/Latino philosophy can contribute to American philosophy. This point leads me to advocate for the study of Latin American philosophy in the United States, *malgré* García's argument to the contrary.

In short, then, without claiming a homogeneous nature, a spirit or *Geist*, for Hispanic/Latino philosophy—which is humbug in my view, and dangerous to boot—I see that the study of Hispanic/Latino philosophy can add something valuable to American philosophy. It can give American philosophy a point of contrast from which to examine itself and philosophy in general; and it can provide a balancing point to what is often too one-sided and hegemonic. Finally, we must keep demographics in mind. With the number of Hispanics/Latinos growing at a fast rate in the United States, it is vital that the country provide a cultural space for them. In a democratic society, it is essential that all groups be encouraged to participate in the cultural life of the nation (Gracia 2000a, 2008b:chap. 5). So it is necessary for the well-being of American society that Hispanics/Latinos, with the issues that they bring with them, be encouraged to participate in this life. And philosophy, as the self-conscious reflection it is, has a particularly important role to play in this process. (More on this in my response [III:17] to Howard McGary [III:16].)

So much, then, for what Hispanic/Latino philosophy can contribute. Now, for the other question: What would Hispanic/Latino philosophy look like? I am not sure I can consistently answer this question, for according to my theory, a philosophy takes on a particular look depending on the circumstances, and I do not know all the circumstances that will affect the introduction and study of Hispanic/Latino philosophy in the United States. The best I can do is to say that, if the unity of Hispanic/Latino philosophy, as the unity of Hispanics/Latinos in general, is based on a historical set of familial relations, Hispanic/Latino philosophy in the United States will have relations with the rest of the philosophy produced in the Hispanic/Latino world, unlike American philosophy today. This means that Hispanic/Latino philosophy in the United States will take into account developments in philosophy in the Hispanic/Latino world and keep in touch with them. These texts, whether from the past or the present, will play a role in shaping Hispanic/Latino philosophy in this country and not just in the philosophy that Hispanics/Latinos practice and produce. It will do so because it will be tied in some significant ways to Hispanic/Latino philosophy elsewhere. But again, this does not mean that this philosophy necessarily has, or will have, the same enduring properties, for whatever properties it has had, has, or will have, are the contingent result of its history.

IS MY CONCEPTION OF HISPANIC AND LATIN AMERICAN PHILOSOPHY ADEQUATE?

Here I would like to focus on two sides of this question, although elsewhere in this volume (III:17) I expand on my view. One has to do with my overall claim about the identity of Hispanic philosophy; the other with my classification of the discussion of identity in Latin American philosophy. Mendieta finds both inadequate because, in his view, they neglect philosophers and philosophical currents that should have been included. The root of these exclusions, according to him, is that I have too "narrow" and "academic" a conception of philosophy that makes me unsympathetic to entire currents of philosophical development, such as postmodernism.

Mendieta's characterization of my view is inaccurate. Since he refers to some of my other works that are not particularly concerned with Hispanic/Latino issues, I believe I am entitled to use those very works to set the record straight. Indeed, in many places, including *Philosophy and Its History* (1992) and *Metaphysics and Its Task* (1999b), I have explicitly adopted a very broad conception of philosophy, which certainly includes the very authors Mendieta claims I exclude (Gracia 1992:55–60, 1999b:9–17). According to that conception, philosophy is a view about the world or any of its parts that seeks to be accurate, consistent, comprehensive, and supported by sound evidence. This view is so broad that the difficulties with it are more with exclusion than inclusion. So whatever view Mendieta says I hold, he did not find it in my works.

Furthermore, if the view Mendieta attributes to me is not mine, then it cannot be this view that makes me exclude the figures and currents I exclude. Indeed, Mendieta claims that I exclude "the work of Las Casas . . . because of its explicit theological character." First of all, no one will be able to find any statement of mine to this effect, or one from which this view could be inferred. The reason is that I do consider the work of Las Casas philosophical. It is true I do not mention him in the chapter of *Hispanic/Latino Identity* that deals with Hispanic philosophy and that I do mention Francisco de Vitoria (1483–1546) and Francisco Suárez (1548–1617), along with Alfonso Briceño (1587–1668), Antonio Rubio (1548–1615), and some others, but I do mention him in an earlier, longer version of this chapter, published as an article in the *Review of Metaphysics* (with which Mendieta is acquainted) (Gracia 1993). Indeed, contrary to Mendieta's suggestion, it would be very hard for me to argue, under any circumstances, that the work of Las Casas is theological (for my view of theology, see Gracia 2001a). The reason I do not refer to Las Casas in the mentioned chapter is that the philosophers to whom I refer are used as mere examples and that, in the overall picture of philosophical originality and acumen, although not in terms of social and political relevance, authors like Suárez and Rubio are much more important. Las Casas was a great popularizer, but many of his ideas were borrowed from already existing works by other thinkers. Moreover, his philosophical perceptivity must be questioned insofar as he did not see the inconsistency in his position with respect to Amerindians and blacks.

A similar answer can be given to Mendieta's objection that I do not pay due attention to postmodernists in the discussion of identity in Latin American philosophy. The reason again is not that I think these authors are not philosophers. The reason is that I think their views can be accommodated within the third category of approaches I claim are used to characterize Latin American philosophy: the critical approach. Their views are not sufficiently different from those of Augusto Salazar Bondy (1925–1974), Juan Rivano (b. 1926), Leopoldo Zea (1912–2004), and others to merit a separate category. Mendieta's enthusiasm for their work, of course, leads him to put them in a category of their own, but I am not convinced this is warranted. While I am willing to consider reasons why this should be so, so far none that is compelling has been offered.

At this point perhaps I should say something about Mendieta's last objection: that my portrait of Hispanic philosophy in the United States, although accurate, is discouraging and should be tempered with a call to Hispanics to join the ranks of philosophy. I certainly did not mean to sound discouraging, although the current situation *is* in fact discouraging. Now, I think that Mendieta's objection goes back to a deeper disagreement, based on our respective conceptions of philosophy. He appears to share with a long line of philosophers the view that philosophy should prompt action (Karl Marx) or be edificatory (Richard Rorty). Naturally, if this is so, or if one of the ends of philosophy is to be so, then the discourse of philosophy should be more like a sermon or a political speech. My own view of philosophy is different. I see the owl of Minerva flying at night. So my job is not to sermonize or harangue. I leave that for preachers and politicians. I see my task primarily as one of understanding, even though understanding may, and often should, lead to action.

WHAT ARE THE CONSEQUENCES OF THE PERCEPTION OF HISPANICS/LATINOS AS FOREIGNERS?

One of my theses in *Hispanic/Latino Identity* is that the perception of Hispanics/Latinos and Hispanic/Latino philosophy as foreign contributes to the marginal place we occupy in the American philosophical establishment. But Gooding-Williams questions my answer insofar as English, French, and German philosophy are also foreign to Americans and yet they are not marginal in American philosophy. Indeed, he suggests that racialization is the real culprit, and he draws an analogy with the situation of African Americans in American philosophy.

My response to this is, first, that I have not claimed that the perception of foreignness is the only factor involved in the marginalization of Hispanics/Latinos in American philosophy, so that in fact my view does not rule out racialization as a factor. In fact, I believe that racial prejudice has much to do with the discrimination that some Hispanics/Latinos experience, particularly those who look darker or have phenotypical features common among Native Americans. However, I also claim that the perception among Anglo-Americans that Hispanic/Latino cultural roots and intellectual heritage are different from their own causes many of the prejudices they have against Hispanic/Latino philosophy. In this, I should refer to the example Renzo Llorente (III:13) provides.

Second, English, French, and German philosophy are not considered foreign at all in the United States. Indeed, this is precisely one of the points I made in *Hispanic/Latino Identity*: American philosophers by and large consider themselves part of the non-Iberian, European philosophical heritage, and particularly the English, French, and German branches of it. It is philosophers who fall outside these lines of philosophical development, or outside American lines of philosophical development, that are considered "foreign." So the counterexamples cited by Gooding-Williams actually confirm my thesis rather than undermine it. Contrary to what he claims, the issue here seems to be culture and ethnicity rather than race, even though race may be a contributing factor.

Third, the situation of African American philosophy is certainly bad in the United States, but it really cannot be compared with that of Hispanic/Latino philosophy to this extent: African American philosophy is regularly taught in colleges throughout the United States (according to the American Philosophical Association survey that I mentioned in *Hispanic/Latino Identity*, at least 27 percent of colleges offer a course in African American philosophy every two years), whereas this is not the case with Hispanic/Latino philosophy. Besides, African American issues are regularly taught in other courses that have to do with racism and minority rights—in courses on ethics and political theory, for example—and again this is not the case with Hispanic/Latino issues. Finally, one need not look very far to see the many books and articles published in philosophy journals about African philosophy or African American issues. Indeed, there are whole series of books on these topics. But about Hispanic/Latino philosophy or Hispanic/Latino issues there is practically nothing. I cite some of these examples in the book, but many more have come to my attention since then (Mendieta 1999a:50–51).

The situation of African Americans in American philosophy, then, is quite different from that of Hispanics/Latinos, and although their situation is very bad indeed, it is not nearly as bad as that of Hispanics/Latinos. This leads to the question of rights, particularly linguistic rights and affirmative action, for Hispanics/Latinos, which I take up in my responses (III:17) to Llorente and McGary.

NOTE

1. Bernstein's objection should not be confused with Appiah's (2000) charge of circularity against Du Bois, which can also be used against my position. I have answered the charge of circularity in Gracia (2007a, 2008b:chap. 2).

PART III

HISPANICS/LATINOS

AND PHILOSOPHY

13. HISPANICS/LATINOS, LABELS, AND LATINO PHILOSOPHY

RENZO LLORENTE

Jorge J. E. Gracia's *Latinos in America* (2008b) is a spirited, informative, immensely enjoyable work, and a remarkably successful combination of applied philosophy, metaphysics, and metaphilosophy, to name just a few of the many fields covered in Gracia's exploration of Latino identity. The overall thematic cohesion that Gracia achieves in treating a formidable range of topics—for example, the nature of identity, the meaning of ethnic labels, the sociology of American philosophy, individuation, and linguistic rights—is likewise remarkably successful, as is his attempt to treat these and other topics in a way that will engage and satisfy professional philosophers without rendering his text inaccessible to nonspecialists.

For all its virtues, however, *Latinos in America* is not without its ambiguities, and some of the positions that the book defends appear rather questionable, as does the way in which it addresses certain problems.

In my brief remarks, I would like to focus on four aspects of the book that strike me as problematic in one way or another:

- Gracia's treatment of the relationship between Latino and Hispanic
- His defense of 'Latino,' as opposed to 'Hispanic,' as a group label
- His conception of Latino philosophy
- His treatment of the debate over language rights

As *Latinos in America* invites comparison with one of Gracia's previous books, *Hispanic/Latino Identity* (2000c), I will be making occasional references to the earlier text in the course of my discussion.

THE RELATION BETWEEN 'LATINO' AND 'HISPANIC'

Let me begin with the first problem that I mentioned, namely the relationship between 'Latino' and 'Hispanic.' Simply stated, the question is the following: What exactly is the relation between the two groups named by these terms? If we consult Gracia's account in *Hispanic/Latino Identity* (2000c), his earlier book, the answer to this question would seem to be relatively straightforward, for in that work Latinos are said to constitute a subset of Hispanics, the latter being defined as "the group of people comprised by the inhabitants of the countries of the Iberian peninsula after 1492 and what were to become the colonies of those countries after the encounter between Iberia and America took place, and by descendants of these people who live in other countries (e.g., the United States) but preserve some link to those people" (48; cf. 52). According to this earlier account, the class of Latinos excludes Iberians (Spaniards and the Portuguese) but includes their children born in Latin America and may or may not include the children of Iberians who emigrated directly to the United States (Gracia 2000c:5; cf. 2008b:38). (This kind of indeterminacy does not pose a problem for Gracia's [2008b] theses, for he stresses that "identities need to be conceived as flexible, contextual, historical, and relational" [16].)

Does Gracia assume the same view of the relation between Latinos and Hispanics in *Latinos in America* (2008b), a book whose arguments are based on the proposition that Latinos constitute a distinctive ethnos (i.e., ethnic group)? It is hard to say. To be sure, there are certainly good reasons to assume that Gracia conceives of Hispanics also as a distinct ethnos, in keeping with the thesis of his earlier book. For one thing, it is clear that Gracia (still) regards 'Hispanic' as an ethnic name, and the function of ethnic names is to refer to ethne (58). For another, Gracia's conception of the Latino ethnos— based on what he calls the Familial-Historical View of Latino identities—rests on the same kind of explanation as Gracia had proposed for making sense of Hispanic identity in his earlier book. (For a discussion of the Familial-Historical View, see Gracia 2000c:chap. 3; for a brief discussion of this concept, see Gracia 2008b:17.) Moreover, in *Latinos in America*, Gracia characterizes ethnicity as follows: "Ethnicity has to do with historical relations of various sorts that contingently tie people" (23). If this is the case, then it would seem to follow, especially if we bear in mind the other considerations that I have mentioned, that Latinos make up a subethnos within the broader Hispanic ethnos (to use the terminology that Gracia now favors). What we have, in other words, is one ethnic group nested within another, larger group. Latino would be to Hispanic as, say, Guaraní is to Latino, or Ashkenazi is to Jew (regarding intraethnic conflicts, see Gracia 2000c:128).

The problem is that in *Latinos in America* Gracia never actually acknowledges that Hispanics also make up an ethnos. Instead, Gracia (2008b) says, in referring readers back to *Hispanic/Latino Identity*, that "the term ['Hispanic'] should be used to refer to a cultural complex which incorporates both Latin American and Iberian elements" (56). This claim proves quite surprising given that the earlier book includes explicit references to "Hispanic/Latino ethnicity" (Gracia 2000c:43; cf. 42) and because an ethnicity is, we may assume, something rather different from a mere "cultural complex." Has Gracia therefore changed his mind not only with regard to the advisability of using 'Latino' instead of 'Hispanic' (which I shall come to in a moment) but also regarding the nature of the broader family to which Latinos belong? Does he now hold that Latinos constitute an ethnos within a larger family, Hispanics, which is itself not an ethnos?

THE PREFERENCE FOR 'LATINO' OVER 'HISPANIC'

The relation of Latinos to Hispanics is, then, unclear in the pages of *Latinos in America*, yet, as it turns out, a good deal hinges on the relation between these two groups. If we embrace the framework for classifying the identity of Latinos and Hispanics proposed in *Hispanic/Latino Identity*, Gracia's earlier book, it makes little sense to ask the question posed in *Latinos in America* (2008b), "Which of these two names ['Latinos' or 'Hispanics'] is more appropriate for the ethnic group in question" (49)? Asking which of these terms is more appropriate is akin to asking whether we should use the term 'New Yorkers' or 'Americans' for people who were born and reared in New York State. As in the case of (native) New Yorkers and Americans, the relation of Latinos to Hispanics is one of subset to set: all Latinos are Hispanics, but not all Hispanics are Latinos. And just as we may sometimes wish to foreground a person's status as a New Yorker rather than an American—or, to use a properly ethnic example, as a 'Guaraní' rather than a 'Latin American'—we may sometimes wish to stress a person's status as a Latino rather than as a Hispanic. Conversely, it may sometimes be desirable or necessary to use the more inclusive term in order to emphasize a person's membership in a larger ethnic group.

To be sure, Gracia (2008b) seems to concede this point, noting that "both 'Latino' and 'Hispanic' are helpful when thinking about various dimensions of the Latino experience, because each brings out something the other misses and therefore helps to increase our understanding" (73; cf. 58). The trouble is that this acknowledgment is somewhat at odds with Gracia's aim of settling on, or at the very least privileging, *one* name for referring to Latinos, or at any rate of establishing one name as the preferred name. The question, again, is not, Which name, 'Latino' or 'Hispanic' is more appropriate? but, rather, Which aspect, which group membership, do we wish to highlight in the case at hand?

If, on the other hand, Gracia does not regard the class of "Hispanics" as constituting an ethnos but, rather, simply a "cultural complex" (whatever that may entail), then the only suitable *ethnic* name for Latinos is indeed *Latinos*. 'Hispanic' may be useful for referring to Latinos in order to highlight a cultural dimension of Latino experience, but it should not be used as an ethnic label.

In any case, let us suppose, for argument's sake, that it is advisable to endorse only one of these two labels ('Latino' or 'Hispanic'), at least within the context of American culture, which is for the most part the context for Gracia's discussion. Should we, as Gracia contends, embrace the label 'Latino'?

In his earlier book, *Hispanic/Latino Identity* (2000c), Gracia claims that 'Hispanic' is the only term "which appears even remotely justifiable" (191). To be sure, this earlier work sought a framework that would gather both Latinos and Iberians in one group, but it is also true that in *Hispanic/Latino Identity* Gracia was likewise concerned above all with the Hispanic/Latino community in the United States (see, e.g., xii). In *Latinos in America*, his new work, Gracia does something of an about-face, for he now maintains that 'Latinos' is, generally speaking, with some caveats that I shall mention later, the more suitable term. Gracia's change of mind appears to have been motivated almost exclusively by arguments advanced by Linda M. Alcoff in an article that appeared after the publication of *Hispanic/Latino Identity*. While critical of Alcoff's arguments, Gracia (2008b) endorses her conclusion to the effect that 'Latino' is preferable to 'Hispanic' from a political perspective, since the term 'Latino' has a distinctive and appropriate regional connotation (Latin America) and, on the other hand, connotes or suggests something "backwater, marginal, unimportant, and poor" (57). At one point Gracia defends 'Latino' also because it connotes the "colonial situation of Latinos" (73), a rather surprising claim considering that Gracia argues at some length (56–58) that it is a mistake to employ the concept of colonialism, as Alcoff does, in analyzing the contemporary oppression of Latinos. At any rate, these connotations lend 'Latino' an advantage, Gracia contends, to the extent that this label "brings to the fore the disadvantaged condition of a certain group of people and helps in the development of an effective political strategy to address their grievances" (58). In short, 'Latino' is more valuable for political purposes (73), and these purposes are presumably—Gracia himself does not state this explicitly—of paramount importance.

There are a number of problems with this argument. First of all, Gracia does not tell us why the "regional" connotation of 'Latino' is politically significant, useful, or valuable. What exactly are the grounds for holding that geographical associations per se are politically important? A regional connotation in itself hardly carries the same evaluative-rhetorical force in political discussion as, say, the term 'oppressed,' or even 'colonial' (the latter term being, as we have seen, one that Gracia usually rejects). In short, unless we automatically conflate the Latino label's nonevaluative regional connotation with the evaluative connotations of "backwater, marginal, unimportant, and poor," Gracia's claim that the regional connotation is in itself politically significant seems highly questionable.

What about this latter claim—Gracia's second justification for preferring the label 'Latino'—that 'Latino' connotes something "backwater, marginal, unimportant, and poor"? Even if we grant that this is the case in the United States, it is implausible, I believe, to say that 'Latino' bears these same connotations in Latin America (as Gracia's argument assumes—'Latino' is intended to apply to Latin Americans, too—and as he himself insists [see, e.g., 2008b:58]). Consider the claim that 'Latino' connotes "marginal" in Latin America, too: Can it really be the case that Latinos are regarded as marginal, qua Latinos, in countries in which they make up virtually the entire population? Is it not more reasonable to suppose that to the extent that a Latino resident in a Latin American country is identified with that which is marginal, it is rather because, for example, she also belongs to another, minority ethnic group, or is poor, or belongs to some otherwise oppressed social sector? Likewise, it would seem implausible to claim that 'Latino' connotes "backwater, unimportant, and poor" in, say, Nicaragua, Colombia, Peru, Uruguay, or the Dominican Republic. Significantly, some of the examples that Gracia offers to illustrate the currency of the adjective '*latino*' in Latin American countries seem to actually contradict his contention that '*latino*' connotes "backwater, unimportant, and poor." He notes, for example, that "one finds *tiendas latinas* [Latino shops], *restaurantes latinos* [Latino restaurants], *comida latina* [Latino food], and so on, throughout Latin America" (Gracia

2008b:56n.17). It would certainly seem unwise of shop owners and restaura-
teurs to include the word '*latino*' in the names of their establishments if this
word is associated with the "backwater, unimportant, and poor."

To be sure, at one point Gracia (2008b) seems to qualify or restrict his thesis somewhat, suggesting that in Latin America (unlike the United States) it
is particularly in connection with "cultural endeavors" that the use of '*latino*'
is "deprecatory" (57). Of course, this already constitutes a significant qualification, whose implications I shall discuss in a moment. Before doing so,
however, I would like to register my own doubts regarding this even more
limited contention. Gracia's statement involves an empirical claim, of course,
and the claim may be true; but we certainly need evidence, which Gracia does
not provide. In any case, the one example that Gracia does provide hardly
shows that the use of '*latino*' is "deprecatory" in Latin America when used in
connection with "cultural endeavors." Gracia writes, "This [deprecatory use]
is quite clear in the case of philosophy. Latin American philosophy (*filosofía
latinoamericana*) in Latin America is taken to be inferior, weak, and derivative, in comparison with European or American philosophy" (57).

Notice, first of all, that the example refers to a usage of 'Latin American'—
'*latinoamericana*'—and not '*latino*.' Second, while it is no doubt correct to
say that Latin American philosophy is regarded by many Latin Americans
themselves as weak and derivative, and that this fact may cause, or at least
reinforce, the negative associations of '*latino*,' it is plainly not *because* (some)
Latin American philosophy is weak and derivative that it is called *latinoamericana*. (It is called Latin American/Latino because it is produced by, or addresses issues of concern to, Latin Americans, or because it originates in Latin
America.) In other words, the name for this enterprise is not due to a deprecatory usage of '*latino*' or '*latinoamericano*,' even if the disappointing quality
of much Latin American philosophy may contribute to the currency of such
a deprecatory usage. It is one thing for a word to be used in a deprecatory
fashion and quite another for an activity or practice to reinforce the deprecatory force of a word.

The upshot of these considerations is that 'Latino' as used in Latin America
seems to lack some of the connotations that it has in the United States and
perhaps elsewhere outside Latin America. Yet the connotations in question
are the very connotations that are supposed to account for the political value
of the 'Latino' label, and this in turn implies that the political value of
'Latino'—and hence the main reason, according to Gracia, for preferring this
label to 'Hispanic'—may be limited to the United States, or at best countries

outside Latin America. If the "regional" connotations of 'Latino' are indisputable but of little political significance, the deprecatory connotations (and "marginal" in particular), while politically significant, would appear to be associated with the term mainly outside Latin America. Perhaps, then, there are good reasons for preferring another term to designate Latinos living in Latin American countries themselves.

Before moving on to discuss Gracia's conception of "Latino philosophy," I should mention that these considerations seem to point to what is, to my mind, a more accurate conception of Latino identity. Gracia is undoubtedly right to insist on the property of "marginality" in connection with the Latino label: marginality, if not exactly constitutive of the notion of "Latino," is certainly one of its main connotations; but the marginality in question is, I submit, that which typically attends geographical displacement, dislocation, and uprootedness. In other words, the marginality originates with *immigration to non–Latin American countries.* For this reason, I would argue that it makes the most sense to use 'Latino' for Latin Americans who have emigrated to a non–Latin American country, along with the descendants of these emigrants who are born and/or brought up in these non–Latin American countries of destination. Indeed, I believe that contemporary usage tends to reflect a conception of "Latino" along these lines: Peruvians in Colombia may view themselves as Peruvians or Latin Americans, or perhaps even some hybrid of Peruvian and Colombian, but I doubt that they tend to think of themselves as "Latinos." Yet these very same Peruvians might be apt to see themselves primarily as "Latino" were they to emigrate to the United States or some other non–Latin American country. Accordingly, even if Gracia (2008b:xiii) is right in assuming that Latinos in the United States and (what he calls) Latinos in Latin America are ethnically the same, it may be unwise to use the label 'Latino' for both groups given that it has certain primary connotations that apply to one group but not to the other.

LATINO PHILOSOPHY

Let me now turn to Gracia's discussion of what he terms Latino philosophy. It is well to begin by noting that Gracia (2008b:chaps. 7, 8) performs a valuable service in highlighting and explaining the prejudice against Latino philosophy and Hispanic—or, if one prefers, Latin American and Spanish—philosophy. Here is an example from my own experience teaching Latin American philosophy (which Gracia would also call Latino philosophy). In the fall 2007 semester, I taught a course called Latin American Philosophy, and one of the men in the class was a visiting student from a university that is generally regarded as having one of the very best philosophy departments in the United States. At the beginning of the semester, I had a lengthy conversation with this student in my office. In the course of this conversation the student mentioned that he had told one of his previous professors, a well-known philosopher, that he would be taking a course on Latin American philosophy while studying abroad in Madrid. According to the student, the philosopher replied, "Well, that's not really philosophy." Now, I suspect that the philosopher who made this remark does not know the first thing about Latin American philosophy and has probably never in his life opened a book written by a Latin American philosopher. But the point is that the attitude he expressed is indeed pervasive—and pernicious: at the end of the semester the student seemed to be of the opinion that Latin American philosophy is not *really* philosophy, even though he had written his term paper on Alejandro Deústua's concept of aesthetic value, a perfectly orthodox philosophical topic.

Returning to Gracia's discussion of Latino philosophy, we should first note that the phrase 'Latino philosophy' is not nearly as current or well established as Gracia (2008b:137) would have us believe; that is to say, this name for a particular category or field of philosophy has not, to my knowledge, been widely used up to now. Gracia's reluctance to acknowledge his terminological revisionism produces some rather perplexing passages. For example, how are we to assess his claim, in explaining the neglect of Latino philosophy in the United States, that "Latino philosophy is not perceived as exotic enough" (168), when the category of "Latino philosophy" is itself so novel and unfamiliar? One might be inclined to think that Gracia is in effect simply proposing a different term for what has heretofore been called Latin American philosophy, and that his claim at bottom is no different from the claim that Latin American philosophy has been neglected in the United States because it is "not perceived as exotic enough" (which claim is both original and plausible). But the problem is not merely that Gracia employs a new term and category but that he also proposes a new conception of "Latino philosophy," which should be understood, he argues, as "ethnic philosophy," the philosophy of an ethnos (139–47).

I will not examine this conception at length here but will merely indicate one set of concerns. Gracia (2008b) maintains that "in ethnic philosophy what is important is the identity of an ethnos and what is considered philosophy for that ethnos" (147). Indeed, "criteria of inclusion in Latino philosophy" depends on "what counts as philosophy for the ethnos" (144, 142). These claims prompt a couple of questions. Is it really the case that, as far as other ethnic philosophies are concerned, the ethnos determines what counts as philosophy? (Is this true, for example, of Hispanic philosophy, of which Latino philosophy forms a part [173]? Or is Hispanic philosophy not an "ethnic philosophy"?) If this is indeed the case, should we endorse this conception of ethnic philosophy, or propose a different one? By "philosophy" Gracia understands "a view of the world or any of its parts that seeks to be accurate, consistent, comprehensive, and supported by sound evidence" (152; cf. 188). If we accept this conception of philosophy, it seems to me that we should either reject Gracia's view that the ethnos enjoys a privileged position in determining what artifacts count as ethnic philosophy or else opt for a word other than 'philosophy' to designate the corpus of works that are judged by the ethnos as forming a part of its "philosophy."

Quite apart from these considerations, or rather even if we accept both the name 'Latino philosophy' and the notion of philosophy that Gracia associates with it, we ought to ask ourselves whether it is advisable in practical terms—that is, for the purposes of promoting philosophy produced by, or bearing on problems of special interest to, Latin Americans and Latinos—to use this name. Recall that, according to Gracia, one of the principal advantages of using 'Latino' vis-à-vis 'Hispanic' has to do with the fact that the former connotes something "backwater, marginal, unimportant, and poor." If one of our aims is precisely to combat the marginality and neglect of Latin American (and Hispanic) philosophy within the milieu of Anglo-American philosophers, is it really desirable to adopt a name that conjures up something marginal, backwater, and unimportant? Might it not be the case, in short, that the very considerations that justify and recommend the adoption of 'Latino' in other contexts militate against the use of 'Latino' as an area label in philosophy? It is already difficult enough to gain acceptance for Latin American philosophy, even when it is not presented as a form of "ethnic philosophy"; promoting it as the latter in a profession whose members by and large bear a strong bias toward a form of philosophical practice that Gracia calls "universalist" will make acceptance still more difficult. Would it not therefore be preferable to eschew a name that will only add unfavorable sociocultural connotations to a tradition, or conception (depending on one's perspective), of philosophy toward which many Anglo-American philosophers already tend to display a dismissive attitude?

These problems suggest, it seems to me, that we would probably do well to maintain the more customary categories of "Latin American" and "Hispanic" philosophy (of which Latino philosophy is one component [Gracia 2008b:173]), for all their inadequacies. As Gracia himself observes, "In philosophy, perhaps more than anything else, the notion of a Hispanic, rather than just a Latino, community makes much sense" (177), for in this context "the use of the term 'Hispanic' . . . allows us to see historical connections that otherwise we would miss" (58). At the very least, we shall prevent additional confusion and avoid having to defend three unfamiliar categories of philosophy, when establishing the legitimacy of two of the categories is already work enough.

LANGUAGE RIGHTS

The last aspect of *Latinos in America* that I want to comment on concerns Gracia's discussion of "linguistic rights." The focus of Gracia's (2008b:chap. 6) discussion of linguistic rights is Thomas Pogge's argument for "English-first." Gracia does an excellent job of both analyzing Pogge's argument and revealing its fatal flaws; given the superficial plausibility of Pogge's argument, this analysis proves especially valuable. After disposing of the argument, Gracia ends his chapter on linguistic rights with a short section titled "A Worrisome Suspicion," in which he writes, "I suspect that behind its [the English First principle] use there is a commitment to English-only supported by a misguided sense of American nationality in which the United States is identified necessarily as an English-speaking country and those who are not proficient in English are not quite, or truly, considered American citizens" (124).

I believe that Gracia's suspicion is warranted, and it is for this very reason that his treatment of linguistic rights is, it seems to me, somewhat misconceived. For if this is the *real*, underlying reason for much, if not most, of the support for the English First principle (or the establishment of English as an official language) and opposition to bilingual education, would it not be more worthwhile to devote most of one's efforts to exposing and challenging the nativist assumptions and essentialist nationalism informing the debates over linguistic rights? Gracia's decision not to pursue this theme appears particularly surprising considering that *Latinos in America* opens with a quotation that expresses this very nativist/essentialist nationalist sentiment, suggesting that Gracia is well aware of its significance and pervasiveness. The words cited in Gracia's (2008b) preface come from an essay by Samuel Huntington (2004:30), who complains that "Hispanic immigrants . . . have not assimilated into mainstream US culture" and warns that these immigrants may end up "divid[ing] the United States into two peoples, two cultures, and two languages" (Gracia 2008b:vii). Let us ignore, for now, the obvious questions prompted by this passage: What's so great about "mainstream US culture"? What's wrong with two languages? Has there ever really been only one culture in the United States? Does Huntington deplore the Pilgrims' failure to assimilate into mainstream Native American culture? The point to underscore for our present purposes is that such remarks highlight the importance of challenging and discrediting nativist or nationalist assumptions—which are at bottom profoundly undemocratic—in developing the case for certain linguistic rights.

This source of resistance to linguistic rights suggests, I believe, that Gracia may understate the challenges that the legitimation and assertion of Latino identity pose to other ethnic and social groups. On the last page of *Latinos in America* (2008b) Gracia tells us that "there is no real threat with which we need to be concerned" (210). But if the increased respectability of Latino identity may entail that previously dominant groups lose some of their social power, does this increased respectability not represent a threat to these groups? Consider, again, the issue of language. There are lots of people in the United States who at one and the same time advocate English First and reject bilingual education at the primary school level while supporting the expansion and improvement of "non-English-language" education at the secondary and postsecondary levels. Is there not something of an inconsistency here? And if there is, might it not have to do with the respective beneficiaries of non-English-language education at the primary level and at the secondary (or postsecondary) level? Is it not true that second-language education at these different levels empowers different groups? Or consider political advertisements that appear in Spanish: Why do politicians who appear completely unsympathetic to bilingual education and the linguistic rights of Latinos nonetheless commission and run election advertisements in Spanish? In reflecting on examples such as this one, or on the inconsistencies in attitudes toward foreign-language education, one is inclined to agree with a point stressed by Argentinean psychologist and philosopher Aníbal Ponce (1974:58) some eighty years ago: in the United States, Spanish is studied for the purpose of furthering domination. When the study, or use, of Spanish does not serve this purpose, it is not encouraged.

The more general point, at any rate, is that the legitimation of Latino identity, whether or not it entails a greater acceptance of Spanish as a working language within the United States, may serve to empower some presently oppressed or disadvantaged groups, and this empowerment may work to the detriment of other groups (as may also be the case with affirmative action for Latinos, which Gracia advocates). Gracia (2008b) notes that his own, distinctive identities "function as sources of action" for him (26). Assuming that identities function as sources of action for others as well, the positive development of Latino identity may produce changes in American society that pose a threat of one sort or another to other social groups. As a nation, we should probably welcome these changes, but it would be a mistake to assume that no one will feel threatened by them.

14. ETHNIC PHILOSOPHY AND

LATIN AMERICAN PHILOSOPHY

SUSANA NUCCETELLI

Jorge J. E. Gracia's *Latinos in America* (2008b) offers insightful discussions of philosophical issues involving the rich experiences of Latin Americans and their descendants abroad. Of special interest to readers will be the book's novel proposal for categorizing Latin American philosophy, according to which it should be classified as a form of "ethnic philosophy" (140ff.). This way of understanding Latin American philosophy might resolve a number of questions concerning the discipline's name and boundaries that have been at the center of current discussions. But how does the proposal square with the *scope* of Latin American philosophy: that is, with the question of which works are to count as belonging to the discipline? Whose works should we include?

Clearly, the correct answer should be conservative enough to count as Latin American philosophy the work of current mainstream professional philosophers such as Gracia himself and Guillermo Hurtado, both of whom have devoted a significant part of their work to examining Latin American philosophy. But it should also have something to say about the work of many "borderline" thinkers about whom questions are sometimes raised regarding their inclusion in the discipline. These include works that, though not strictly philosophical in the technical sense, do plainly have philosophical import—for example, the work of pre-Columbian thinkers, some literary figures such as Sor Juana Inés de la Cruz and José Martí, and certain nineteenth-century leaders of the independence and national reorganization that followed, such as Simón Bolívar and Juan Bautista Alberdi—all of whom show originality and wisdom in their treatment of philosophical ideas and arguments arising in a Latin American context.

By Gracia's own lights, one advantage of construing Latin American philosophy as a type of ethnic philosophy (hereafter, "ethnic Latin American philosophy") is that this conception allows the inclusion of many valuable intellectual works by Latinos that would not be counted as philosophical if assessed by the standards prevalent in either the philosophies of other ethnic groups or the core areas of philosophy traditionally construed. If ethnic Latin American philosophy could accommodate certain nonstandard works—say, those of Bartolomé de Las Casas and Sor Juana—together with the mainstream analytic products of Héctor-Neri Castañeda and Ernesto Sosa, that would count very much in its favor. But here I shall argue that Gracia's conception falls short of delivering this result, since in the end it's unclear *which* works are to be included or excluded by it, and how we are to decide this in any case.

One problematic (and therefore interesting) case is that of the Maya folk cosmology narrated in the sacred book *Popol Vuh*. Gracia rightly lists this work among the disputed cases. Even so, *Popol Vuh* can be read as providing evidence of cognitive diversity of a sort relevant to philosophy in a number of ways (see, e.g., Nuccetelli 2002), so it could be treated as a test case for Gracia's view. It is, I think, an objection to that view that it leaves undecided this crucial case. (Although I suspect that it leaves undecided other borderline cases as well, I shall not attempt to show that here.)

|

Assessing Gracia's ethnic Latin American philosophy requires some comparative overview of major, rival views on an unresolved question: What, if anything, *is* Latin American philosophy? This question, however, is ambiguous, as can be seen by considering the parallel cases of, Is there French philosophy? or Is there a Latin American Thomism? for which answers may vary according to what is meant by 'French philosophy' and 'Latin American Thomism.' (For a discussion of ambiguity, see Nuccetelli 2003, 2010b.) Answers to the question about Latin American philosophy constitute a wide spectrum, with strong universalism (SU) and strong distinctivism (SD) at its opposite extremes, the central theses of which may be outlined as follows:

SU All of philosophy's theories, methods, and topics are strictly universal.

SD None of philosophy's theories, methods, and topics is strictly universal.

Since SU and SD are contraries, they are therefore incompatible (although they could not both be true at once, they could of course both be false). As it happens, sympathy for one or the other of these extreme views is not at all uncommon in contemporary Latin American philosophy. For a recent defense of a thesis that comes close to SU, we need look no further than Greg Gilson's (2006) interview of Mario Bunge in the *APA Newsletter on Hispanic/ Latino Issues in Philosophy*. Pressed on whether there is a distinctive Latin American philosophy, Bunge denies it on what appear to be strong universalist grounds. In his own words, "I don't think that Latin America constitutes a distinct area of philosophy. Latin America is philosophically just as pluralistic as North America, Western Europe, India, or Japan" (10). At the other extreme, a paradigm representative of a doctrine along the lines of SD can be found in the work of Leopoldo Zea (e.g., 1948, 1989). Statements such as the following generalize to all philosophical theories:

> The abstract issues [of philosophy] will have to be seen from the Latin American man's own circumstance. Each man will see in such issues what is closest to his own circumstance. He will look at these issues from the standpoint of his own interests, and those interests will be determined by his way of life, his abilities and inabilities, in a word, by his own circumstance. In the case of Latin America, his contribution to the philosophy of such issues will be permeated by the Latin American circumstance. Hence, when we [Latin Americans] address abstract issues, we shall formulate them as issues of our own. Even though being, God, etc., are issues appropriate for every man, the solution to them will be given from a Latin American standpoint. (Zea 1948:226)

Gracia, in proposing the category of ethnic philosophy without explicitly holding that all philosophy is ethnic, appears to reject equally *both* SU and SD. His views clearly represent a more moderate "middle way" somewhere between those extremes. Two possible candidates for such a view are weak universalism (WU) and weak distinctivism (WD):

WU Some theories, methods, and topics in philosophy are universal.
WD Some theories, methods, and topics in philosophy are not universal.

Unlike SU and SD, these have a chance of both being true at once. Clearly, these middle way theses are incompatible with either SU or SD. WD would be upheld by anyone who thinks that some philosophical theories, methods, and topics are characteristic products of certain ethnic or cultural groups. It is in fact compatible with other theories, methods, and topics being universal— that is, it is compatible with WU. Thus, the middle-way position allows us to say that there is a distinctively Latin American philosophy while insisting that other philosophical disciplines may be universal.

If I understand the view offered by Gracia in *Latinos in America*, it exemplifies one such middle-way combination of WU and WD: that is, it allows for both a characteristically Latin American philosophy, which he conceives as a type of ethnic philosophy, and universal disciplines such as ethics, metaphysics, and so forth. If this is right, then Gracia is committed equally to disagreeing with the extreme views of Bunge and Zea on the question at hand and to holding instead that Latin American philosophy is an instance of a category of distinctive ethnic philosophy. In fact, it would be odd (and probably self-defeating) for Gracia to endorse either strong universalism or strong distinctivism, since he would thereby be undermining the legitimacy of his own work, which is anchored in both the universal problems of philosophy (such as those of metaphysics) and the characteristic problems of Latin American philosophy (such as the controversy over *whether there is* such a philosophy at all). But since any middle-way position postulating the existence of a distinctive type of philosophy must produce a plausible account of the scope of that discipline, we need to look closely at what Gracia has to say about that.

II

Gracia's ethnic Latin American philosophy, then, is a middle-way position that has the advantage of committing to neither denying the existence of a distinctive Latin American philosophy nor taking it to consist merely of philosophy *in* Latin America. Furthermore, in contrast to both strong universalists and strong distinctivists, Gracia might be able to accommodate the celebrated works of many Latin American nonphilosophers who have produced philosophically interesting doctrines. (I count, e.g., Risieri Frondizi and Carlos Pereda among paradigm SU theorists who reject such works, and Leopoldo Zea and Augusto Salazar Bondy among paradigm SD theorists who do the same.) But, as noted, he'd need to provide a plausible account of who is to be included and why. This would require an individuation criterion that would explain what makes a theory, method, or topic part of ethnic Latin

American philosophy. Let's consider, then, the case of Maya folk cosmology to show that Gracia owes us such a criterion. This narrative, which purports to describe the origins of both the universe and the Maya-Quiché people, unfolds in ways that seem utterly alien to what we now take a philosophical theory to be. It is, however, analogous in important respects to the folk cosmologies of nearly all pre-Socratic Greek philosophers, who are standardly credited with raising the very questions that triggered the development of Western philosophy. Thus, the Maya folk cosmology seems to qualify as Latin American *proto*philosophy—a claim that can be held consistently *with* the view that more contemporary philosophical and scientific methods are needed *now* to discuss properly the philosophical issues raised by *Popol Vuh*.

In *Latinos in America* (2008b), Gracia considers the question of whether that work is eligible for inclusion in Latin American philosophy but demurs: "Is the *Popol Vuh* to be included in Latino philosophy? The issue now shifts to whether pre-Columbians can be considered part of the Latino ethnos and why. . . . Still, you probably want me to tell you what I think about the *Popol Vuh*: Does it belong or not to Latino philosophy? I do not want to answer the question, because I do not find it philosophically interesting" (142).[1]

The passage does provide a criterion (albeit a sketchy and conditional one) for inclusion of *Popol Vuh* in Latin American philosophy: it should be included if and only if the Maya are part of the Latino ethnos (here, "ethnic group"). But this cuts both ways. If it turns out that there are good reasons for counting the Maya as part of the Latino ethnos, then it would follow apodictically that *Popol Vuh* should be taken as belonging to Latin American philosophy. Now I would say that there are clearly good reasons for so counting them, so it's puzzling why Gracia withholds judgment on the issue. The argument is clear:

1. Given Gracia's individuation criterion, *Popol Vuh* is Latin American philosophy if and only if the Maya are part of the Latino ethnos.
2. The Maya are part of the Latino ethnos.
3. Therefore, *Popol Vuh* is Latin American philosophy.

Assuming that *Popol Vuh* has philosophical import, then, given Gracia's criterion, there is no reason to remain agnostic about the subject.

As usual, however, it may be that the devil is in the details. What, exactly, is meant by 'being part of a people'? The expression cannot refer to a relationship that is strictly actual, since that would lead to the implausible claim that, for example, ancient Greek philosophy doesn't belong to current Greek or European philosophy. *Today*, after all, the ancient Greeks (since none of them are still living) are not literally *part of* the current Greek/European people. But we don't, for all that, want to say that Plato's *Republic* is not to be included in Greek/European philosophy! So the denoted relationship must allow for historical chains: the products of the ancient Greeks are in this sense *part of* Greek and European people's culture today, and their philosophical works therefore eligible for inclusion in Greek/European philosophy.

Now according to the evidence of the social sciences, it is beyond dispute that perhaps more than any other pre-Columbian narrative, *Popol Vuh* is part of the culture of the present-day Maya people, who have received it mostly through an oral tradition. So, by Gracia's condition, we would not hesitate to include *Popol Vuh* in Latin American philosophy—unless of course we were persuaded that the Maya people do not qualify as Latin Americans. But plainly they do, as can be seen from the popularity of some contemporary Maya among Latin Americans. Rigoberta Menchú, a Maya-Quiché Guatemalan Nobel laureate, is widely revered as an advocate of human rights for the indigenous peoples of the Americas. Surely, in light of the historical, geographical, and cultural facts—that, for example, Menchú is an honored citizen in Latin America—it would make no sense to exclude her from the broader Latino ethnos—nor would it, mutatis mutandis, to exclude other indigenous leaders, such as the Aymara Evo Morales and the Zapotec Benito Juárez. Since Menchú in some ways represents the Maya people, it would likewise make no sense to exclude *these people* from the Latino ethnos, any more than it would to exclude the Aymara or the Zapotecs.

It follows that, if we reason by Gracia's criterion in the quoted passage, *Popol Vuh* comes out as included in Latin American philosophy. So it seems that one could remain agnostic on the subject only at the price of being stuck with a dilemma that has no obvious solution. On the one hand, one could argue that *Popol Vuh* cannot be read as a philosophical or protophilosophical text at all (i.e., one could simply *deny* my claim). But to support this would require setting up sound standards for what is to count as philosophy—an unpromising assignment. Or, on the other, one might try to argue that the Maya are *not* part of the Latin American people. But, for the reasons just provided, supporting this horn of the dilemma would be an equally difficult task.

III

Perhaps Gracia's agnosticism is rooted in his views on Latin American philosophy as ethnic philosophy and the identity of Latinos as an ethnic group. About the former, he tells us very little: only that it is the philosophy of an ethnos. About the latter, a topic not without controversy, he has a well-developed theory according to which there is no single property that Latinos all have in common. Rather, they share a net of family-resemblance relations that link the great number of subgroups referred to as "Latinos." Since they *have no single, common feature at all* but do bear to one another those relationships, they constitute an ethnic group. Now Gracia seems to link these two accounts: (1) Latin American philosophy as ethnic philosophy and (2) Latino identity as a net of family-resemblance relations with no single property in common. For he holds that the philosophical works belonging to Latin American philosophy need have no single, identifying feature at all. Moreover, they need share no feature at all with the philosophy of any other ethnic group. Furthermore, those works cannot be taken to capture a property shared by all Latinos (throughout their history), for there is no such property.[2]

But what is it that makes works as dissimilar as Jorge Luis Borges's short stories, pre-Columbian folk cosmologies, and analytic theories by figures such as Héctor-Neri Castañeda and Ernesto Sosa qualify as Latin American philosophy? Perhaps the individuation criterion in the previous passage about *Popol Vuh* could be generalized to state that any work would qualify as Latin American philosophy if and only if it could be considered part of the Latino ethnos. But this is too liberal, since then any work whatsoever that can be considered part of the Latino ethnos would qualify: Borges's short stories, Sosa's analytic epistemology, and even philosophical works in the style of European philosophy that have contributed nothing characteristically Latin American. To me, it is ironic to grant that status to, for example, the writings of Antonio Rubio (Mexican, 1548–1615), whose compendium of Aristotelian logic, the textbook *Logica mexicana*, was popular in Spain as well as in Latin America during the colonial era. Unlike *Popol Vuh*, Rubio's work passes muster with strong universalists and strong distinctivists alike—but not with anyone who regards as truly Latin American only works that broach subjects or methods that are originally or characteristically Latin American. I submit that more should be done by Gracia to sharpen an individuation criterion that, following the middle way between extremes, will capture what is distinctive about Latin American philosophy.

That said, I should add that I believe Gracia's book is an important addition to the Latin American philosophical canon, the sort of work from which anyone interested in the subject can learn a great deal. Gracia has for many years been one of the field's leading scholars, and it is always a signal event when one of his books appears. Latin American philosophers may disagree about many things, but not about Gracia's well-deserved scholarly reputation.

NOTES

1. In previous work, Gracia has seemed to deny that pre-Columbian thought could count as part of Latin American philosophy. For example, in a topical entry in a current dictionary of philosophy, Gracia and Elizabeth Millán (1995) write, "Latin American philosophy begins with the Spanish and Portuguese discovery and colonization of the New World" (462).

2. Gracia (2008b) writes that Latin American philosophy is "the philosophy of an ethnos, and insofar as it is so, and members of ethne do not necessarily share features in common, then what the philosophy of a particular ethnos is exactly will not require any features in common with other philosophies outside the ethnos or even within the ethnos throughout its history. This, I claim, is the best way of understanding the unity of Latin American philosophy" (140).

15. LATINO AND LATIN AMERICAN PHILOSOPHY

MARÍA CRISTINA GONZÁLEZ AND NORA STIGOL

In *Latinos in America* (2008b), Jorge J. E. Gracia, a philosopher with Latino roots, longtime member of the academic professional community, and resident of the United States, expresses concerns involving three queries: What is it to be Latino? What is the place of Latinos in America?[1] And how do Latinos think about themselves and their identity? These questions constitute the core of the so-called Latino challenge. In his response, he develops and uses a theoretical tool to identify Latinos that he dubs the Familial-Historical View. He examines various conspicuously controversial issues related to Latino identity such as their linguistic rights, the advantages and disadvantages of affirmative action for Latinos, and the place of Latinos in the marketplace within the field of professional philosophy. Finally, in the longest section of the book, he performs an in-depth examination of Latino philosophy. This panorama includes a wide range of ideas that Gracia has discussed on other occasions; he revisits and combines them in an overall stance while criticizing alternative theses about particular issues and responding to his critics.

In view of the broad scope of the enterprise, we shall restrict ourselves to highlighting our overlapping concerns, emphasizing some issues that we feel are too succinctly discussed and raising some doubts about the possible consequences of the author's theses when certain issues are overlooked.

Let us start with the notion of Latino identity. In the face of two alternatives, essentialism-realism versus non–essentialism-eliminativism-conceptualism, Gracia chooses a (nominalist) stance reminiscent of Wittgenstein (1953:par. 66). Why does he reject the other two alternatives (Gracia 2008b:30)? The first, because it has lost all credibility; the second, because it is unable to solve the problem of individuation.

From the rejection of the approach that holds that it is necessary to have a property or a set of properties to identify denoted entities, it does not follow that Latinos cannot be identified. Lack of an essence does not entail lack of identity (Gracia 2008b:21). Latinos share "a certain family resemblance." Gracia applies Wittgenstein's metaphor, whereby instead of asking what may be the common feature among individuals whom we call or classify as Latinos, it may be more fruitful to hold that they simply share a "certain family resemblance." The task, in Wittgenstein's words, is to find out this "complex network of overlapping and crisscrossing similarities: sometimes overall similarities, sometimes similarities in details" in this particular case. Wittgenstein's metaphor is particularly appropriate here, even more so than when applied to games, because Latinos are actually a family, although not a genetically based one. Indeed, a married couple share no genetic traits but are nonetheless the cornerstone of a family (Gracia 2000c:50).

The main tenet of Gracia's (2008b:16–19) Familial-Historical View is that Latinos constitute an ethnic group. Ethnicity, which should not be confused with nationality or race, has to do with relations of various sorts—historical and familial, though not in terms of genetic relationships—that contingently tie people.

Although Gracia's strategy is very interesting, it encounters a few difficulties. To begin with, we face some trouble if we apply the thesis to Latinos who live in different regions; in our case, Argentina. It is no easy task to discern in which familial-historical network each person should be placed since there is an intertwining of histories and families that makes it difficult to recognize a peculiar Latino American. The offspring of Spanish, Italian, Russian, and Swedish parents and grandparents—who constitute the majority of the population—seem to be immersed in at least more than one familial-historical network.

Having said that, it is possible to meet this objection if we remember that the original colonization—of a much extended territory, populated by various ethnic groups with very different cultures and languages, with no interconnections—was Spanish and their language was Spanish. Consequently, language—in addition to culture and educational tradition, despite later influences during the eighteenth and nineteenth centuries—seems to be the main feature of Latinos living in Argentina. This applies to Uruguay too and probably to Chile as well. This trait marks an important difference between being Latino in the United States and being Latino in Argentina or Uruguay, where the official language has been Spanish over the past five centuries up to the present.

A second difficulty is related to the origins and limits of Latin American history. When did it begin? No doubt, the discovery of the American continent and the colonial processes are part of the familial-historical network; in fact, they are its starting point. But will this network include Napoléon's invasion of Italy, Egypt, or Russia? Are there no historical links between these events and historical events in the Americas? What about the Russian Revolution of 1917? What about harassment of Jews? What about World War II? These events sent substantial migratory tides to Argentina, for instance. If history is viewed holistically, how can it be split into particular histories to be included in the Familial-Historical View in the case of Latinos outside the United States, at least in some countries? Are Mexican history and Latinos in Mexico more closely linked to U.S. history and Latinos in the United States than to the history of Uruguay and Latinos in Uruguay?

A third controversial issue is related to the identity criteria suggested by Gracia. We believe that there are dissimilar levels of analysis or different problems to be considered. First, there is the issue of the identity of an ethnic group in a broad sense of the term: Latinos, in general, inside and outside the United States. Gracia (2008) does not see "clear ethnic boundaries between the categories of Latinos in the United States and Latinos in Latin America" (xiii). Second, there is a narrower problem: the identity of a social group that shares and coexists in place and time with other social groups, giving rise to discriminatory attitudes and behavior. This is the case with Latinos in the United States. In fact, their social and cultural circumstances are very different from those of Latinos in the rest of the Americas. Indeed, in the United States Latinos have experienced extraordinary growth in the past few years, constituting now the largest minority group in the country and being perceived as a threat to various aspects of the life of the American nation (vii). This is not the case in Argentina, Uruguay, or Chile. In these countries, there seems not to be such a thing as a Latino national challenge, because all of us, at least the absolute majority, are Latinos, speak Spanish, and do not suffer discrimination, except in the case of philosophers or scientists. Indeed, there are some interesting similarities between these two professions, although this is not the place to explore them.

Fourth, an even more specific question to be asked—and in our opinion, the most relevant in this context—concerns the identity of a social group whose members not only belong to the same ethnic group, and therefore belong in the same familial-historical network, but also share the same professional activity and belong to the same professional community, that is, they are Latinos and philosophers. The question is: What characterizes the activities of this group not as philosophy but as Latin American philosophy? We believe that the variables taken into account by the Familial-Historical View are not sufficient to explain these activities as they are developed within different communities. Other factors play essential roles: gender, university studies, and academic connections.

The most significant issue for Latino philosophers who do not live in the United States is not their Latino identity but their philosophical and professional identities. Indeed, an appropriate identification may possibly explain their particular situation at present, because it is probably shared by most Latino philosophers outside the United States. In short, there are two different situations: Latino philosophers in the United States and Latino philosophers outside the United States.

With respect to this point, we note that Gracia has scarcely considered the relationship between ethnic identities in general and communities. This is a flaw in his approach in that, when he analyzes the American philosophical community—his most significant reference to communities—he does not appeal to the category of ethnicity that is otherwise so important for him in the case of Latino identity (Gracia 2008b:chap. 4). In chapter 7, section VIII, he applies the Familial-Historical View to American philosophy also, which he labels from then on, and with good reasons, "Anglo philosophy," stressing the parallelism with Latino philosophy. This parallelism becomes apparent in view of the restricted sense of 'philosophy' he is concerned with—as a professional enterprise—and 'philosopher'—as a person who earns or tries to earn his/her living through this labor (79).

Gracia's analysis of the American philosophical community includes the notions of family and groups, but the historical perspective is absent. So an uninformed reader may be led to believe that the philosophers' profession in the United States has no history, at least in an interesting sense, as seems also to be the case with Latino philosophy. It is true that he mentions genealogical links, but he appears to limit them to current or recent ones.

In our opinion, there is a substantive difference here. We believe that once historians of philosophy in the United States and in Latin America have identified the canon—our use of the word is slightly different from Gracia's (more on that later)—it will be worthwhile to see how the two communities relate to it. Before going into that, however, let us examine Gracia's notion of ethnic philosophy.

Let us grant his proposal on Latino philosophy (Gracia 2008b:130), and also his very persuasive analysis of internal and external factors at play in the universal, cultural, and critical perspectives in which he classifies authors who try to explain this category (they have all failed). So what is Gracia's concept of Latino philosophy as an ethnic philosophy? According to him, an ethnic philosophy is the philosophy of an ethnos, once again returning to his strategy: the Familial-Historical View.

He claims that it is impossible to find a common trait throughout the history of Latino philosophy (no themes, no topics, no method, and no language), but in our view he fails to mention a very important attribute. He makes no reference to the way Latino American philosophical communities, in the United States and in the Americas, practice philosophy as a profession, as either researchers or teachers of philosophy, and in particular to the training of new philosophers. His sole remark is the following: "The unity of this philosophy, just like that of the Latino ethnos, has to do with contextual historical relations and these also help to distinguish it from other philosophies in context" (Gracia 2008b:140). His mention of "contextual historical relations" deserves careful consideration.

Once his premises are granted, Gracia's (2008b) statement is true: "Latino philosophy is the philosophy the Latino ethnos has developed in the circumstances in which the members of the ethnos have found themselves throughout history" (141). And "what Latino philosophy is, when it is understood ethnically, can be asked only in the context of the Latino ethnos" (141). Notwithstanding, it is necessary to include what Latino philosophers do qua philosophers within their own philosophical communities, that is, the problems, theses, and arguments they use, in short, the canon. We believe that it is necessary to distinguish between what Latino philosophers do in the United States and what other Latino philosophers do wherever they live and work outside the United States. They constitute two different communities, which are dissimilar in some peculiar ways—as we shall try to show in the following on the basis of our own experience. It is crucial to identify these features. Rather than on their written work, it is on their practices as philosophers, inside their communities, and the communities themselves, that we should focus if we wish to account for the "complex network of overlapping and crisscrossing similarities," the Wittgenstein-style family resemblance.

Before stating our differences with Gracia's perspective, we would like to refer to Gracia's concept of a canon in order to compare it with another one that we consider more suitable. Incidentally, concern for the philosophical canon was not usual until recent times, but in spite of the relevance of this matter, we have no space to explore it here.

Gracia (2008b) uses a notion of philosophical canon that describes it as "a group of philosophers and their writings that are the subject of repeated study and discussion both philosophically and historically. . . . The authors and texts which make up the canonical list are regarded as having produced something that has value beyond the immediate boundaries of their existence" (159). He distinguishes between general and specific canons and he formulates criteria for the inclusion of philosophers and works in the canons. Thus, for instance, inclusion in histories of philosophy, reference books, philosophical anthologies, and the philosophy curriculum—the most significant place in his view—is one of the tokens of membership in the canon.

The first point to note here is that, if we follow Gracia's definition, the canon is not identical in U.S. colleges and in Argentinean universities, for instance. In our country, at least over the past fifty years, the philosophical canon has included Latino American philosophy in its syllabus. Courses have various denominations: Latino American and Argentinean Thought (*Pensamiento Latinoamericano y Argentino*), Latino American Philosophy (*Filosofía Latinoamericana*), or History of Social, Political, and Philosophical Ideas in Argentina and Latin America (*Historia de las Ideas Sociales, Políticas y Filosóficas en Argentina y América Latina*; cf. curricula at the Universidad de Buenos Aires, the Universidad Nacional de Córdoba, and the Universidad Nacional de Tucumán). We must note that, due to political circumstances that impacted the life and syllabi of universities, implementation has lacked strict quality controls and some courses have occasionally been taught by nonqualified professionals. Consequently, by taking only one of the standard meanings of 'canon,' other analyses are left out (doctrines, traditions, and associations, as well as communities) that might provide useful connections for understanding the institutionalization and professionalization of Latino philosophers. This is why we prefer a broader meaning—present in ordinary language—to clarify the relationship between those concepts. We believe that this offers a more complete explanation of Latino philosophy, at least outside the United States.

We will follow Eduardo Rabossi's (2008) proposal here. Philosophy as currently conceived and valued was established as a professional field in

the nineteenth century when modern universities and schools of philosophy were founded. It is not necessary to subscribe to Rabossi's historical
hypothesis that its origins are rooted in German idealism. It is the task of
historians of institutions to settle the point. We simply wish to stress a less-
arguable issue: the academic institutionalization that philosophy acquired
in Berlin. This fact is intimately connected to the adoption of the professional canon. Ever since the inception of its institutionalization, philosophy
has been ruled by a canon, as is the medical profession, among others. The
canon is

> a basic precept that stipulates and defines domain, theoretical and prac-
> tical suppositions, peculiar goals, aims, and values. Canons of professions
> underlie the formal requirements for practicing the profession, determine
> the general conception of the discipline, and fix the boundaries of its le-
> gitimate exercise. . . . The canon functions within a background that
> specifies the basic conditions philosophy and philosophizing must
> comply with. (Rabossi 2008:76)

The canon, however, is not to be seen either as a very general philosophical
doctrine or as the archetype of an ideal philosophical doctrine, like a model
to be followed by different particular philosophies because they—present or
past ones—are versions or embodiments of contents that philosophers have
constructed from canonical precepts, prioritizing some of them over others:
"[Canonical precepts] express general aspirations about the existence of a domain, a methodology, and a set of problems, the nature of truths to aim at,
differences to be observed, goals and values to be actualized, and the way to
conceive the autonomy and supremacy of philosophy" (77). This level of gen-
erality allows different traditions or doctrines to be displayed as upgraded
versions of the canon—in either present or past times—such that "different
canonical versions bring about the particular *póleis*, they provide the products that are displayed in the windows of that [world philosophical *polis*]"
(96–97).

Evidence in favor of Rabossi's proposal is mentioned in a document of the
Philosophical Documentation Center, according to which basic areas of specialization are the same not only in the United States and Europe but also in
very remote places, albeit with varying local emphases (*International Directory
of Philosophy and Philosophers*, 2001). This notion of canon allows us to maintain, without contradiction, the existence of philosophical communities

that do not overlap with other professional communities ruled by other canons.

Just as the philosophical canon is actualized in different ways, philosophical communities also materialize and develop under different guises, according to the historical context and geographical location of each. Here is where the external and internal factors admitted by Gracia have a role to play.[2]

If these ideas are adopted, we may ask the following questions: What is the Latino philosophical community outside the United States like? What are its features and dispositions? Do those features and dispositions enable us to note any differences between this community and the community in the United States? From the perspective of the Familial-Historical View applied to the notion of philosophical community, we believe that there are clear features in the Latino philosophical community outside the United States that explain its peculiarity. Furthermore, if these are clearly stated, it may be possible to bring about changes in its current situation.

In the first place, and following the views of Mexican philosopher Guillermo Hurtado Pérez, we believe that the Latino philosophical community outside the United States is not a vigorous one, at least not up to now. As he puts it, "We do not have vigorous philosophical communities. . . . We do not have a true Spanish-speaking philosophical community" (Hurtado Pérez 2003:41). This weakness is not due to the absence of high-quality written results published in specialized books and journals or a lack of professional meetings at different levels (national and regional, or thematic conferences and congresses). Rather, it is due to a simple reason: there is no dialogue among us as a community. There are only monologues and, more precisely, in our view, parallel monologues. As Hurtado notes, "An intellectual community is one of reading and dialogue. More properly: it is a critical community that moves around issues inherited from its own *tradition*." There can be no philosophical community where there is no *memory* of past arguments and discussions or, at the very least, the intention of remembering tomorrow what is being discussed today. Congresses and encyclopedias are not of much use, for they do not encourage and nurture ongoing critical dialogues (43, 44).

Hurtado warns us about the fact that Latin American philosophers do not read one another, do not discuss matters among themselves, and are forever alert to whatever happens in other latitudes. The background of this attitude is likely to be a kind of prejudice strengthened by an inferiority complex experienced by some Latin American philosophers about themselves and their production in Spanish, such that "the fate of the bulk of the philosophical production in Spanish—let us be honest—is to lie under the dust in libraries and bookshops" (Hurtado Pérez 2003:43). Peruvian philosopher Augusto Salazar Bondy (1968) also noted that the Latin American philosophical community has been tinged by this inferiority complex.

This attitude of no dialogue, no confidence in our own work, and no interest in philosophy produced in our environment is precisely the central trait that separates the Latino philosophical communities: the community in the United States and the one outside the United States. Apart from whether or not the U.S. Latino philosophical community is only one—and we believe it is—it is a vigorous community (as Hurtado defines it), based on the concept of canon we adopt, although we acknowledge that there are various traditions in the United States. In fact, philosophy as a discipline, inside and outside the United States, encompasses different traditions, for just as in any other profession, some members exercise power and challenge other members in various ways. This is particularly true of the philosophical community in the United States.

In any case, although establishing this point may require further empirical research, we believe that there is regular reading and discussion of philosophy produced in English. This is the usual practice in most fields and issues within the so-called analytic tradition, for instance. It may be, however, that links between traditions are weak (between the analytic and Continental traditions, for example, assuming we reach a consensus about their identities), but this is a disciplinary anomaly of philosophy and not related to its practice, according to Rabossi. Even a glance at English academic journals proves that reading, discussion, and memory are deeply rooted in philosophical practices.

We have no intention of engaging in a sociological analysis, which is beyond our means and scope; however, our experience in the Latino philosophical community outside the United States, particularly in Argentina, displays other meaningful features that distinguish it from the Latino philosophical community in the United States. Our community has always included and still includes all graduates in philosophy. There is no discrimination based on the fact that they are Latinos, considering all the meanings of this concept, including Gracia's definition. Most members of the community teach philosophy in secondary schools and colleges, and a very small subgroup that has considerably increased over the past twenty years is supported by government research agencies. So discrimination based on Latino origin is obviously absent in Latin American countries. (We are not discussing whether there is any other kind of discrimination, which may eventually affect academic life in general, such as gender discrimination.)

Hurtado Pérez (2003) points out—following Carlos Pereda (1987)—another significant feature that marks a difference between both Latino communities:

> Many Ibero-American philosophers suffer from what Pereda termed *novelty eagerness* . . . this is the vice of those who follow in meticulous and exaggerated style any foreign fashion for the sake of being "up-to-date" and "not left behind." During different periods of our history the careful study of foreign communities responded to the purpose of *modernization* . . . but when modernization lasts too long, it becomes harmful, because it provokes amnesia of the best contents of the inherited tradition and it does not allow the development of a philosophy of our own. . . . It is good to be updated about other communities' developments, but it is also good to be updated regarding *our* own philosophical setting. Is not this the case in vigorous philosophical communities? They cultivate a tradition and pay attention primarily to themselves and only after do they look further away, beyond their boundaries. . . . Behind this unquenchable thirst for novelty, there is a prejudice shared by many Ibero-American philosophers regarding their colleagues. It may be expressed in the following words: *I do not read your production because you do not deserve to be read.* (42–43)

Incidentally, it is worth noting that there are no linguistic barriers among members of this community, as could be the case in the U.S. philosophical communities that do not read Spanish.

The philosophical community in Argentina—and we believe that this applies to other countries in the region—is peripheral, according to Rabossi. As such, it is forever on the alert as to everything that is said and written in the philosophical communities of the most developed countries in the West. Rabossi calls them G4. G4 is a set of nonhomogeneous versions produced by top countries (the United States, Germany, France, and the United Kingdom) that "have traditionally undertaken the self-assumed task of providing the contents and defining the fields of specialization. . . . They govern the world polis and monopolize its supply with canonical versions" (Rabossi 2008:97).

These countries produce and export philosophy, and peripheral philosophical communities adopt one or another version issued from the G4 group. Thus, we find ourselves supporting, participating in, and defending philosophical stances that do not genuinely belong to us. This style of making/ importing philosophy becomes an ersatz of a production authentically our own, which is seen as lacking original proposals.

On the other hand, this situation accounts for the frequent controversy among our philosophers (and among Latino American philosophers at large) about whether there is a vernacular philosophy. Peruvian philosopher Francisco Miró Quesada (1979) underscores this fact: "The mere formulation of the ideal of devising a genuine philosophy means that Latino American thinkers foster doubts about their capacity to achieve it. . . . This awareness has two parallel meanings: that we feel the need to formulate a genuine philosophy and that we are anxious about lacking the capacity to do so" (167). Needless to say, the peripheral location of Latino philosophical communities outside the United States is not shared by the Latino philosophical community in the United States. From what has been said it follows that the initiatives proposed by Gracia (2008b:174) to incorporate Latino philosophy in the philosophical canon, as he understands it, in the U.S. philosophical community may be a valid tool to change the situation of Latino philosophers there, and, as such, they merit attention. But they are insufficient to change the peripheral situation of Latino philosophers outside the United States.

Once again, we can pinpoint differences between both communities. Rabossi and Hurtado as Latino philosophers living and working outside the United States, as peripheral philosophers, focus their concern on Latino communities outside the United States. Both maintain the need to encourage the possibility of change. Rabossi (2008) holds that this change has to be approached by "asking what attitudes are to be promoted in order to bring about the conditions for a desirable philosophical practice" (105–6). And he posits a list of conditions. He includes, for instance, living philosophical problems as genuine ones because imported problems are not authentic issues; improving regional exchange; promoting research lines that will generate traditions; clarifying the role of philosophers in public spheres; reading and discussing with a critical approach our own philosophical ancestors; reflecting about the inheritance received, and so forth. And Hurtado Pérez (2003) writes along a similar line:

> It would be advisable to set aside the concept of authenticity, it would be advisable to abandon the obsession with the issue of originality—much the worse for wear and twisting—which is always a relative question and

not the sole virtue of good philosophy. . . . I think we should begin to worry instead about simple tasks such as *reading and discussing* one another's work, and other qualities will eventually come along. (42)

The problems that Latino philosophers face in Latin America are very different from those faced by Latino philosophers in the United States. In the case of the former, the challenge consists in building a vigorous community to cross from the periphery to the center—whatever the center should be. For the latter, the challenge is to be a nondiscriminated member in an already vigorous professional community.

Our differences with some of Gracia's theses should not conceal our main agreement with the author: the need to carry out an analysis of Latino philosophers inside and outside the United States. This analysis requires considering other issues that include metaphilosophical categories, such as the profession of philosophy, the training of professional philosophers, the philosophical canon, the teaching of philosophy outside the profession, and the relationship between philosophy and its history. The debate is open; Gracia's book makes it possible in a wide sense.

NOTES

1. Throughout the book, Gracia uses 'America' in two senses: (1) the United States of America and (2) the Americas.
2. We have offered some clarifications regarding Rabossi's (2008) proposal concerning the notions of canon and community in González and Stigol (2008).

16. AFFIRMATIVE ACTION FOR LATINOS

HOWARD MCGARY

Jorge J. E. Gracia's *Latinos in America* is a clear and analytical account of Latino identity, the situation of Latinos in American life, and how Latinos see themselves. Using the skills characteristic of the analytical philosopher, Gracia tackles each of these issues with great sensitivity to the culture dimensions of the thorny philosophical problems that he encounters. In the first part of the book, he evaluates the two labels 'Hispanic identity' and 'Latino identity.' With great care, he explores the very idea of identities, general and particular. He points to the difficulties associated with lumping Latinos together under one label. In an extremely thoughtful way, he illustrates how attempts to find a general label depend upon stereotypes, and why employing stereotypes is a harmful way to build collective identities. Gracia is well aware that this need to have labels to describe so-called general identities goes in more than one direction. For Gracia, Latinos are just as guilty as other ethnic groups in this stereotypical process of constructing general labels. In part II, Gracia tackles questions that are extremely important to philosophers who are interested in normative philosophy. Here he wrestles with the justness of the marketplace for Latinos, the policy of affirmative action, and language rights. Each of these issues can be used to test the major conceptions of justice and rights that philosophers employ today. Finally, in part III, he situates Latino understandings of who they are within the boundaries of Latino philosophy understood in the context of American and world philosophies.

I have learned a great deal from each part of this book. Although each part explores issues that can stand alone, a full appreciation of the book depends upon seeing the relationship among all three parts of the book. Having said this, with caution, I wish to focus on one aspect of part II of Gracia's valuable text: his discussion of affirmative action for Latinos. Gracia warns us that there has been mistrust, jealousy, and other negative reactions to members of different identities who are perceived to be competitors for scarce resources, but I know that he is also aware of the positive reactions and feelings of solidarity that members of these groups have shared in their efforts to address common concerns. The negative reactions are regrettable but understandable given the dominant narrative in American society of what it means to be an authentic and deserving American. Having said this, Gracia is certainly correct that Latinos and other (ethnic) groups see the policy of affirmative action in America for members of certain designated groups as a zero-sum game. Given this perception, the common misperception is that the policy cannot prove to be beneficial to members of each group that believes itself to be a proper beneficiary.

In the section "Affirmative Action: Meaning and Justification," Gracia (2008b) tells us,

> [First,] Latinos are recognizable as a group and distinguishable from other groups at particular times and places and . . . this is sufficient to implement affirmative action policies. Second, affirmative action aims to ensure equal opportunity to members of groups which have suffered discrimination on the basis of gender, race, or ethnicity, to provide reparation for past wrongs to members of these groups, and to promote the participation of these groups in the political and cultural life of the nation. Third, affirmative action for Latinos considered as a group is justified on the basis of participation in the life of the nation, rather than on the basis of equal opportunity or reparation. (98)

I understand Gracia's sentiments for wanting to limit the types of justifications that can be used to legitimate the use of affirmative action policies for Latinos as a group given the diverse nature of the group. However, I don't believe that the justification that he does endorse, participation in the life of the nation, can be understood independently of the two justifications he rejects. Gracia tell us that the participation in the life of the nation justification can be understood as either justice or utility, but, unfortunately, his explication of why this is so is not rich enough to provide us with an adequate understanding of what he has in mind.

First, it is important to note that utilitarians don't accept the distinction that rights-based theorists have historically drawn between justice and utility. Rights theorists reject the derivate account of rights offered by utilitarians. John Stuart Mill's (2005:chap. 5) classic defense of the principle of utility understands justice in terms of utility. For Mill, it does not make sense to have a conception of justice that does not promote social utility; a society operating with such a conception of justice would not remain stable over time.

Gracia believes that participation in the life of the nation is a good that cannot be understood as equal opportunity or reparation, but if not, what is the nature of this good? Maybe the good that Gracia has in mind is "diversity." But why is diversity a good? It certainly does not seem to be intrinsically valuable. If it is a moral or social good, then it appears to be instrumentally valuable for achieving some higher end. The higher good that Gracia seems to have in mind is utility. The idea is that Latinos, as a group, have so much to offer to the life of the nation that their inclusion is warranted because failing to do so would create disutility. So, on this rationale, we are warranted in providing affirmative action to Latinos in order to achieve a kind of diversity that enhances social utility. Is this always true? It seems to depend upon our definition of affirmative action.

If by 'affirmative action' we mean choosing the candidate who is equally qualified or slightly less qualified than the candidate who does not promote diversity, then maybe it is reasonable to think that including Latinos would serve the ends of affirmative action as diversity. However, if the Latino candidate is qualified but considerably less qualified than other candidates in the pool, then one might question whether such a policy would promote social utility. This justification will require empirical evidence to establish that the cultural and political benefits of including Latinos as a homogeneous group in the pool outweighs the disadvantages of not doing so. Since Latinos are such a significant percentage of the American population, this fact gives us good reason to think that including Latinos would promote diversity in a way that promotes social utility, but we still must do the calculations.

But maybe we should not understand "participation in the life of the nation" in utilitarian terms. Remember Gracia also says that the justification can be understood in terms of justice, but unfortunately philosophers have understood justice in a variety of different ways. Libertarians like Robert Nozick (1975) have understood it in terms of natural rights, where the natural right to one's private property and individual liberty are seen as fundamental. In this account, we are not to judge the justness of a distribution or state of affairs in terms of some societal goal such as diversity, equality, or utility but, rather, in terms of how it squares with the natural rights of those involved. In this reading of justice, "participation in the life of the nation" would not satisfy the constraints of justice.

Fortunately, the libertarian account of justice is only one of the possible ways to describe what justice consists in. Egalitarians, for example, believe that justice requires that we achieve a level of equality in the distribution of goods and opportunities in society, and some egalitarians are more radical in their beliefs about how much equality is needed to satisfy the requirements of justice. It would be helpful to know whether Gracia has an egalitarian understanding of justice in mind when he interprets what it means for Latinos to justly participate in the life of the nation. Since most liberal egalitarian conceptions of justice focus on individuals or on what John Rawls (1971) calls representative individuals, they would be very cautious about giving a preference to a large, diverse group like Latinos if this meant the exclusion of individuals or smaller groups that desire cultural or political participation.

Perhaps Gracia understands justice in terms of needs. The idea of just distribution is one that requires that all involved have their needs satisfied. The issue then becomes: Is cultural and political participation a need that must be satisfied by the just society? The answer to this question is not obviously clear. It seems that a just society might be willing to exclude the participation of Latinos in cultural and political institutions if doing so did not meet some more pressing demand such as ensuring equality of opportunity or rectifying some serious injustice.

I have been a strong supporter of carefully crafted affirmative action policies, but I don't believe that we can justify such policies on purely forward-looking grounds. (For a discussion of the forward-looking and backward-looking justifications of affirmative action, see McGary 1999:130–38.) We need backward-looking justifications that look at a history of transgressions to determine why a preference should be given to members of a group who are better off than members of groups who are excluded by the policy. I know that my way of viewing things requires an adequate theory of collective responsibility, but this is as it should be. We cannot square an affirmative action policy in a liberal society that gives serious weight to individual rights, and the belief that people should be judged by their conduct rather than who they are, without explaining why a member of group G should be required to bear the burden of a social policy that gives benefits to some members of G who are better off than others from the excluded group. I would love to hear more from Gracia on these issues.

17. HISPANICS/LATINOS AND PHILOSOPHY

a response

JORGE J. E. GRACIA

The existence and character of a Latin or Hispanic American philosophy has been in one way or another a topic of discussion in Latin America for a good part of its history and has been a debated and controversial topic for nearly a century. It should not be surprising, then, that with the growth of the Hispanic/Latino population in the United States, and the increasing number of Hispanic/Latino philosophers, this topic has been taken up, mutatis mutandis, in this country.

For the past forty years I have participated in these discussions in Latin America and more recently in the United States, advocating views that have elicited responses from many of those interested in these topics. The topics have varied and often reflect the U.S. context that prompted them. Part II of this volume deals with some of these topics related to theses I had defended in *Hispanic/Latino Identity*. Among these topics are the role of Hispanic/Latino philosophy in American philosophy, the conception of Hispanic/Latino philosophy, and the consequences of the perception of Hispanics/Latinos and their philosophy as foreign and their place in American philosophy. In *Latinos in America* I developed further my views on these and related topics, which have also elicited commentary and disagreement among those interested in these topics not just in the United States but also in Latin America. Among the new theses I proposed were the notion of ethnic philosophy, the use of the label 'Latino philosophy' to refer to the philosophy produced both in Latin America and in the United States, the understanding of this philosophy as an ethnic philosophy, and linguistic rights and affirmative action for Latinos. This prompted a series of exchanges around various topics that are reproduced here. I gather the discussion into five rubrics, some of them subdivided into more pointed issues. Here are the overall topics:

- Hispanics versus Latinos
- Latino philosophy as ethnic philosophy
- Problems with the notion of Latino philosophy
- Latinos and linguistic rights
- Latinos and affirmative action

I begin with the controversy surrounding the use of the labels 'Hispanics' versus 'Latinos,' which I also addressed, although in a different context, in *Hispanic/Latino Identity*. The fact that I have added some dimensions to the original position I took in the earlier book and that in *Latinos in America* I speak about Latinos rather than Hispanics make it a good point of departure. I begin with the objections raised by Renzo Llorente and follow with those voiced by María Cristina González and Nora Stigol.

HISPANICS VERSUS LATINOS

Llorente's objections against my understanding and use of the terms 'Hispanics' and 'Latinos' fall into two categories. The first questions the consistency of my view of the identity of the members of this group, whether we are speaking of Hispanics or Latinos. The second has to do with the use of the labels. Let me begin with the first set of difficulties. They can be summarized in one general argument: it is not clear whether in *Latinos in America* (2008b), I hold the same view concerning Hispanics and Latinos that I adopted in *Hispanic/Latino Identity* (2000c). According to Llorente, the reason is that in the earlier work I treated Hispanics as a larger ethnic group of which Latinos is a smaller ethnic subgroup and in general argued against a cultural conception of ethnicity, whereas in the later book I point to culture as a factor to be reckoned with in the choice of label to use.

My answer to this criticism is that the views I present in the two books are not different and that what I say in them is consistent. Two key points need to be kept in mind to understand this, although Llorente neglects to consider them and this might be the reason for his discomfort. The first is the distinction between ethnos and ethnicity; the second involves the particular conceptions that I have proposed of them. An ethnos is a group of people;

ethnicity is a second-order property shared by members of an ethnos that is in turn based on various first-order properties. On the one hand, we have a group of people, say Latinos, and on the other we have the second-order property of being Latino shared by Latinos, which is itself based on first-order properties such as genealogy, location, language, and so on. The second point is that in my view the first-order properties that constitute the basis of the second-order properties of ethne depend on the familial-historical complexes of properties of particular ethne in particular contexts.

This means that when we think of Hispanics and Latinos as ethne, there is no difficulty in thinking of one of them, say Hispanics, as encompassing the other, Latinos, so that every Latino is Hispanic but not every Hispanic is Latino. Indeed, as Llorente points out, this is very much the way "Jew" and "Ashkenazi" function, where the second is a subgroup of the first.

Moreover, that members of ethnic groups share second-order properties that are themselves based on variable lists of first-order properties means that the first-order properties that justify ethnic labels such as 'Latino' may not be the same at different times and places, and even more likely so when we are dealing with subgroups within larger groups such as Hispanics. Hence, there is nothing wrong with my emphasis on culture in certain contexts and not in others when I speak of Hispanics or Latinos, or with emphasizing culture when I speak about Hispanics and emphasizing it less or not at all when I speak about Latinos. In some cases I am speaking about ethne and in others about ethnicity, and culture itself is a complex set of first-order properties that support second-order properties. This is why there is no tension between what I say in *Hispanic/Latino Identity* and *Latinos in America*.

Beyond the charge of theoretical inconsistency, Llorente also objects to my use of the labels 'Hispanic' and 'Latino.' The difficulties he voices can be summarized in six arguments:

1. In *Hispanic/Latino Identity* I defend the use of 'Hispanic' over 'Latino,' but in *Latinos in America* I defend 'Latino' over 'Hispanic.' So my position has changed and is inconsistent.

2. If we take seriously the understanding of Hispanics and Latinos as ethnic groups, one of which is included in the other, then the question of which label, 'Hispanic' or 'Latino,' is appropriate makes no sense, for the labels name different things.

3. In *Latinos in America* I argue against Linda M. Alcoff's defense of the label 'Latino' in terms of its connotation of colonialism, but I am

inconsistent in that I endorse the political advantages of the use of 'Latino' and at one point even refer to colonialism to justify it.

4. I do not provide a rationale why the regional connotation of 'Latino' is politically significant.

5. The connotations of 'Latino' in Latin America are not the same as in the United States, lacking a deprecatory character, and so the political usefulness of 'Latino' may be restricted to the United States.

6. The use of the label 'Latinos' should be reserved for Latin Americans who have emigrated to a non–Latin American country and for their descendants, in accordance with the current practice in Latin America of referring to populations by their national labels (e.g., Mexican) rather than by a more general label (e.g., Latino).

My answer to the first argument (1) is that I have not changed my view about the value of the labels 'Hispanic' and 'Latino' from book to book insofar as in neither book do I deny what I say about the labels mentioned in the other book. The advantages and disadvantages I pointed out about the use of 'Hispanic' and 'Latino' in the first book still hold, although in the second book I recognize additional advantages to the use of 'Latino' and disadvantages to the use of 'Hispanic.' In neither book do I completely reject a label in favor of the other. Indeed, I explicitly recognize that, as historiographical and social labels, these terms carry connotations some of which are good and some of which are bad and therefore their informative value may differ depending on circumstances and aims. For example, 'Hispanic' works better when one tries to explain certain phenomena in the history of philosophy and 'Latino' works better when one tries to understand certain social and political realities. The effectiveness of their use is contextual.

To this I would like to add that another factor that needs to be taken into account in the evaluation of my position, and that Llorente seems to neglect, involves the context and times in which the two books were written. They were written almost ten years apart, in different contexts, and with different aims. Indeed, the titles already point to a major difference. One is titled *Hispanic/Latino Identity* and the other *Latinos in America*. It should be obvious that this is significant. The second book represents a deeper understanding of what it means to be Latino in the United States, rather than a rejection of what it means to be Hispanic.

With respect to the second argument (2), I need only point out that the discussion of the merits of the use of 'Hispanic' or 'Latino' is justified in two ways. First, the question of their relative merits is not of my own making; it is a question that points to a controversial issue raised in the literature. I address it because it is there, having been addressed by others. Second, my answer clarifies the way in which the question makes sense and in which senses it does not, by distinguishing between ethnos and ethnicity, and by providing views of these. Once the question is clarified, it becomes clear also how and why the terms 'Hispanic' and 'Latino' are used as well as their advantages and disadvantages. 'Hispanic' refers to a larger, more encompassing group than 'Latino,' and it has cultural connotations that are stronger than those of 'Latino,' whereas 'Latino' is a narrower label and has political and social connotations that 'Hispanic' seems to lack. The different connotations of the terms prove helpful in different ways. Furthermore, what is often at stake in the controversies surrounding the use of these terms has to do with the particular populations picked out by the terms. The question involves which label is more appropriate in order to refer to a particular population in a certain context and for specific purposes. In some cases, 'Hispanic' works better in a cultural context that extends beyond that of the narrower 'Latino' label. But in other contexts, 'Latino' might work better precisely because it is narrower and has a political connotation.

With respect to the third argument (3), concerned with colonialism, although I argue against Alcoff's use of the term 'colonialism,' my own use of it is not in conflict with my criticism of Alcoff's usage. My objection against Alcoff is that she stretches the meaning of the term so as to include the present relation of the United States to Latin America, and that relation, whatever it may be, is not colonial strictly speaking. But certainly we cannot deny that Latin America was a colony of European powers, and that Latin Americans were subjected to a colonial political system for centuries. There is nothing wrong, then, with rejecting Alcoff's argument and understanding of 'Latino' and at the same time recognizing both the role that colonialism has played in Latin America and the connotation that the term 'Latino' and its derivatives have in relation to this role. The label is helpful insofar as it brings up an important dimension of the history of a particular population some of whose consequences some members of the population are still suffering. Besides, it helps us focus on the divide between Latin America and Anglo-America, which has informed most of Latin American history.

The fourth criticism (4) charges that I do not provide evidence for the political significance of the regional use of 'Latino.' However, I believe that I should be excused from providing it for two reasons. One is that others have already provided such evidence. Indeed, if anything, this seems to be standard with many philosophers who think about these matters, and there is plenty of support in the sociological and anthropological literature in addition (e.g., Alcoff, I:2; Mendieta, II:11). Another is that providing such evidence would have taken me far away from philosophy. Indeed, this is the sort of thing best done in other disciplines, because it is not the business of philosophy to gather empirical data.

The last two objections (5 and 6) raised by Llorente in this context seem to beg the question. To say that the term 'Latino' does not have deprecatory connotations in Latin America and that labels such as 'Hispanic philosophy' and 'Latin American philosophy' are better than 'Latino philosophy' because the last one is a new term I have introduced in the controversy surrounding Latin American philosophy constitute not arguments but merely disagreements with my view. If Llorente wishes to do more than disagree with my position in these matters, he should examine the arguments I give in favor of the use of 'Latino' and 'Latino philosophy,' rather than assert that my view does not work. And, indeed, he has done this, although only *in part*, in other sections of his commentary, to which I turn later.

Since we are dealing with the question of 'Hispanic' versus 'Latino,' it is appropriate that I go back to a criticism that Lawrence Blum (I:4) formulated. There he expresses some discomfort with my defense in *Hispanic/Latino Identity* of the use of 'Hispanic' instead of, or in addition to, 'Latino.' Why do we need this term at all? He seems to think that the only reason I have in mind is that it is more inclusive—it includes more than 'Latino.' And thus he asks, Why is inclusiveness a virtue?

My argument in favor of the use of 'Hispanic' is rather extensive and includes many reasons. I have discussed its virtues both in *Hispanic/Latino Identity* and, more recently, in *Latinos in America*. The gist of these arguments is not that 'Hispanic' is more inclusive than 'Latino' but that, unlike 'Latino,' the term has cultural connotations that include the cultures of Iberia and Latin America and thus allows us to do justice to the factual cultural influences between the two, something that 'Latino' does not do as well. 'Latino' is not only restricted to Latin America and Latinos in the United States but also seems to have a primarily sociopolitical connotation. Here is an example: if we use 'Latino' in the context of the history of philosophy, the connection of Latin American philosophy to Iberian philosophy can be overlooked altogether, but if we use 'Hispanic,' that connection becomes explicit. It is not just a matter of inclusiveness but also of the kind of historical and cultural inclusiveness that allows for an understanding of facts that otherwise would be difficult to understand. In *Hispanic/Latino Identity*, I was particularly concerned with the understanding of philosophical traditions, not with sociopolitics, and that is a good reason to use 'Hispanic.'

Now let me take up the question of the effective boundaries for the Latino ethnos, an issue raised by González and Stigol in their commentary. The arguments they develop are deployed against not only my view of the Latino ethnos but also that of Latino philosophy. Here I deal exclusively with their objections to my view of Latino ethnicity, leaving objections against the notion of a Latino philosopher for later.

The position I favor concerning ethnicity in general and Latino ethnicity in particular prompts González and Stigol to voice two difficulties that, for them, have to do with the unity and boundaries of the Latino ethnos. The first questions whether it is possible to explain adequately the unity of Latinos throughout the Americas. Indeed, they find that the different historical and familial origins of Latinos in various places—for example, Spanish, Italian, Russian, and so on—cannot give rise to anything peculiar that would justify an overall Latino identity.

As we have seen, this objection has been raised by others in different forms, often in the context of a discussion of the value of using 'Hispanic' rather than 'Latino,' and I have addressed it already, so I abstain from taking it up in detail here (Bernstein, II:7; Gooding-Williams, II:8; Gracia, II:12). Nonetheless, I should point out that this criticism begs the question insofar as it rejects my view by claiming that it cannot do precisely what I say should not be done. My position is that the unity of an ethnos, including the Latino ethnos, is not to be explained in terms of properties or "peculiar features," as González and Stigol want. So, it is not surprising that my theory does not identify such properties or features, but it does not follow from this that my view cannot account for the unity of the Latino ethnos. According to my position, the unity of an ethnos is explained not through properties common to all members of the ethnos but rather in terms of a familial relationship based on historical processes. As in a family, in which members have no properties common to all of them but have properties common to some of them, not all members of an ethnos need have properties in common; it is enough for their ethnic identity and membership that every member of the ethnos have some features in common with some other members at certain times and places that result from a history.

The second difficulty González and Stigol voiced involves the question of boundaries. What counts as part of the historical family that I claim an ethnos is, and what does not? In the case of Latinos: pre-Columbian history? The assassination of Atahualpa? Napoléon's invasion of Italy? It is not clear, according to González and Stigol.

Again, this criticism has already been raised before by others and in various forms, and I have addressed it as well, so I do not dwell on it at any length here (Bernstein, II:7; Gooding-Williams, II:8; Pappas, II:9; Stavans, II:10, in particular; Gracia, II:12.) But let me at least repeat that it is a characteristic of social groups, such as families, to have flexible boundaries. Indeed, we could raise all sorts of questions about the particular families to which González and Stigol belong. We can talk about their brothers and sisters, in-laws, distant relatives, cousins thrice removed, adopted siblings, and so on, and question which of these do, and which do not, belong to their families. Does this mean that the notion of a family in general, and of the families of González and Stigol in particular, is useless or that it does not serve a function? Clearly not. Indeed, I am sure that González and Stigol would vehemently argue that they have families, even if in fact disagreements may surface about whether particular persons belong or do not belong to them. And the same applies to ethne in general and the Latino ethnos in particular.

This criticism is, like the first, based on an assumption concerning the nature of ethnic groups, namely, that contrary to the evidence, they have rigid and well-demarcated boundaries. But it is not only the notions of ethnos and family that have flexible and undefined boundaries. Many of our most common conceptions do, and yet they are not unacceptable because of that, as I explain earlier in this volume (Gracia, II:12). Many of our categories have some things that are clearly members of it, some things that are clearly not members of it, and some things whose membership is rather unclear. And this is what happens with ethne.

LATINO PHILOSOPHY AS ETHNIC PHILOSOPHY

Susana Nuccetelli's discussion centers on "Latin American philosophy," whereas the discussion to which she refers in *Latinos in America* (Gracia 2008b) is about "Latino philosophy." The difference between Latin American philosophy and Latino philosophy, as I propose, is that the first consists in the philosophy from Latin America, but the second consists in both the philosophy from Latin America and the philosophy developed by Latinos who reside in the United States. The difference is important in various ways I explain in *Latinos in America*, but it is not essential to the present discussion of Nuccetelli's objections against my view. So for the sake of simplicity and economy, I ignore the distinction here, although I briefly return to it at the end.

As Nuccetelli indicates, the main thesis of my view is that there are distinct advantages in conceiving Latin American philosophy as an ethnic philosophy. Among these advantages is that many of the works whose inclusion in it is controversial, and which are often excluded from its canon, may find a place in it (Gracia 2008b:141–43; for issues and positions related to the identity of Latin American philosophy, see also Gracia 2010b:253–68). Nuccetelli's general concern is with the question, "Which works are to count as belonging to the discipline [Latin American philosophy]?" And her general criticism of my position is that my proposal to consider Latin American philosophy as ethnic "falls short" of accommodating "certain nonstandard works" because "in the end it is unclear *which* works are to be included or excluded by it, and how we are to decide this." Nuccetelli's general criticism is cashed out in terms of three specific points:

1. My view fails to resolve the controversial cases that it is intended to resolve.
2. It fails to offer a specific criterion for determining what counts as Latin American philosophy.
3. I fail to apply the general criterion of inclusion that I offer to the particular case of *Popol Vuh*, leaving its status unresolved, when in fact this work satisfies it.

In my response, I begin by taking up each of the three specific points of criticism raised by Nuccetelli and offering my rebuttals. Then I take up the case of *Popol Vuh* and show how the conception of philosophy one adopts, together with the consideration of appropriate evidence, may yield an answer to the question of its place in relation to Latin American philosophy. Finally, I draw some general lessons that can be learned about the nature of Latin American philosophy and its historiography from the exchange between Nuccetelli and me. This ensures that the discussion is not taken just as a defense of my position; my purpose here is not merely apologetic but also, and most important, the advancement of the topic.

Failure to Resolve the Cases for Which
My Theory Is Intended

The first of Nuccetelli's criticisms is that my view does not resolve the cases that it is intended to resolve. This is illustrated with *Popol Vuh*, the Maya narrative of creation, because in the end I do not make a determination on whether it should be counted as part of Latin American philosophy or not. And yet it is this sort of case that to some extent prompted me to develop my theory.

My response to this objection is that my aim in developing the theory was not to establish the canon of Latin American philosophy, or determine whether particular works are to be included in, or excluded from, it. Rather, my aim was, first, and more directly, to propose a conception of Latin American philosophy that would facilitate the discussion and investigation of certain works whose status is controversial; and second, indirectly, my aim was to develop a rationale for the disagreement concerning the status of various works, pointing to ways in which one may explain why they are regarded as part of the canon by some historians, not part of the canon by others, and having an unclear status by still others. Hence, I do not consider the fact that I do not make a claim concerning the status of *Popol Vuh*, and similar works, an effective objection to my view, particularly when I explicitly give the reason why I do not.

Nuccetelli misinterprets my aim if she thinks that my exclusive, or even primary, intention in offering the view of Latin American philosophy as ethnic was to resolve disputed cases or come up with the list of works that should constitute the canon of Latin American philosophy (Gracia 2008b:158–84, 2010a). That would be a proper task for a historian of Latin American philosophy, not for someone concerned with the theoretical issues involved in historiography, as I was, a point I make explicitly (Gracia 2008b:142). Indeed, there is an important difference between the two tasks. The first involves *composing a history* of Latin American philosophy and therefore entails establishing which works are part of its canon and which are not. This would include, for example, determining whether to count *Popol Vuh* in it. This task is fundamentally historical. The second task is *to raise and resolve the theoretical difficulties that arise when one considers the task of composing a history* of Latin American philosophy. This is why it was essential for me to develop an understanding of Latin American philosophy. This task does not belong to history, but rather it is the province of historiography when this is understood as the discipline concerned with the theoretical analysis of the problems posed by the composition of history.

Failure to Offer a Specific Criterion of Inclusion

This leads me to the second criticism that Nuccetelli makes of my view, namely, that I do not offer a specific criterion of inclusion in Latin American philosophy, which, according to her, is something "I owe." Indeed, she adds that the general criterion of inclusion I offer is too broad insofar as it counts as Latin American philosophy any work produced by the Latino ethnos, opening the doors to works that are not philosophy.

My answer to the first part of Nuccetelli's second criticism is that, if what I have just said in the previous section is taken seriously, namely that my task was not to compose a history of Latin American philosophy or determine its canon, then it should not be surprising that I do not offer a specific criterion of inclusion in it. That is something for historians themselves to specify, although I can point out the kinds of issues that trying to do it involve. And this is precisely what I do. I point out that if Latin American philosophy is understood as the philosophy of an ethnos, then one should stay away from trying, as many historians have done and at which they have failed, to come up with a set of properties that fit all Latin American philosophy and can be used as a criterion of inclusion.

The consideration of this failure should lead to a better grasp of what is necessary to write a history of Latin American philosophy. In my view, the key to doing so is a proper understanding of Latin American philosophy, and it is helpful to consider it ethnically. For, as an ethnic product, Latin American philosophy is, like ethne, a changing reality, dependent on context and history. This is as far as the philosophical task of the theoretical historiographer goes. To go beyond this would involve engaging in a different enterprise, the sort of thing that historians, whether of philosophy, culture, or society, do. It is for them to determine what counts as Latin American philosophy if it is understood, as I propose, in ethnic terms. This explains my reluctance to offer specific criteria of inclusion, for qua historiographer, rather than qua historian, it is none of my business to offer such criteria. Indeed, I state explicitly that I do not find this task philosophically interesting, and the reason is that the task is not, properly speaking, philosophical but historical.

My answer to the second part of Nuccetelli's second criticism, that the general criterion of inclusion I offer is too broad insofar as it counts as part of Latin American philosophy any work produced by the Latino ethnos, is based on a misreading of the statement of my claim. I do not hold that a work belongs to an ethnic philosophy just because *the work is the product of the ethnos*. Rather, I hold that a work is classified as part of an ethnic philosophy because *it is judged to satisfy certain criteria of belonging to the philosophy of the ethnos*. Indeed, nowhere do I say anything that would suggest the first.

Nuccetelli's mistake is that she thinks that I regard "being a work of an ethnos" as a sufficient condition of the work's belonging to the philosophy of the ethnos. Thus, she argues that if *Popol Vuh* is a work of the Latino ethnos, it should be part of the philosophy of the Latino ethnos. But this is not what I say. What I say is that "an ethnic philosophy is the philosophy of an ethnos," not that any work belonging to an ethnos also belongs to its philosophy (Gracia 2008b:139). Moreover, the condition this stipulates is necessary, but not sufficient; which means that additional criteria are in order.

In some cases, these sufficient criteria are determined internally by the ethnos, in some they are determined externally by people outside the ethnos, and in still other cases they are determined both internally and externally. In my view the matter depends on how the ethnos has been constituted by history. Indeed, the conditions could vary widely not just from ethnos to ethnos but even throughout the history of the same ethnos. This is not different from what applies to the identity conditions of ethne. For some ethne, a genetic link is sufficient for belonging to the ethnos, but for others a cultural (say, religion) or a geographical tie is sufficient. The mechanisms of such determination will depend on both one or more communities as well as historical and contextual circumstances at play. More on this later, but for the moment what I have said should suffice to indicate why Nuccetelli's criticism against the lack of providing a specific criterion of inclusion in Latin American philosophy fails.

Failure to Apply the General Criterion I Offer to *Popol Vuh*

This takes me to the third criticism voiced by Nuccetelli. This is that, although I offer a general criterion of inclusion in Latin American philosophy, I fail to apply it to the case of *Popol Vuh*, which nicely satisfies it. Nuccetelli questions why I do not count this work as part of Latin American philosophy when it is a work produced by the Maya, who are part of the Latino ethnos. For, she argues, if it is a work produced by the Latino ethnos, it should, according to the general criterion I have provided, count it as part of Latin American philosophy when this philosophy is understood as an ethnic philosophy.

Considering what I have just said, it should be clear why I do not apply the general criterion to *Popol Vuh*. First, as a historiographer, it is none of my business to establish whether this work belongs to Latin American philosophy or not, although as a historian of Latin American philosophy I may have views about it based on the conception of philosophy I may want to use—which explains why I have excluded it in some places because I was working with an externally determined universalist conception of philosophy. And second, the general criterion to which Nuccetelli refers is not in fact a criterion I endorse, whence that *Popol Vuh* is a work produced by the Latino ethnos does not entail that it is part of Latin American philosophy, just as *Martín Fierro* is not. Whether it is or not part of it depends on other factors, not just on the fact that it was produced by this ethnos.

But more than this can be said against Nuccetelli's objection. If we adopt the view of Latin American philosophy as ethnic, then the same general characteristics that apply to ethne apply to Latin American philosophy. Most important among these characteristics for our purposes is that what is considered ethnic identity changes with times and circumstances, and so do what are considered to be ethnic products. As I have argued elsewhere at greater length, criteria of inclusion in ethne are not the same for all ethne, and even for the same ethnos throughout its history (Gracia 2005b:esp. chaps. 3, 6; I:5). Whoever is considered Latino today may not be considered Latino sometime in the future, or may not have been considered Latino at some time in the past. And just as the view of who qualifies as a member of an ethnos changes, so do views about what counts as part of particular ethnic identities and ethnic products. So it makes no sense to try to establish criteria *sub specie aeternitatis* for ethnic identity and ethnic products, including ethnic philosophy. Just as the criteria for being Latino change depending on history and context, so the criteria for Latin American philosophy, when this is understood in ethnic terms, change depending on history and context.

In the case of Latin American philosophy, then, we should not expect to have a canon that will remain the same forever. Canons are cultural constructs and as such are flexible and mutable. The criteria of particular ethnic philosophies, whether Latin American or otherwise, are determined historically and contextually and often include both internal and external factors. Social and cultural historians develop theories about those criteria and the reasons why particular societies may develop them, among other things; they do not develop the criteria themselves. And philosophers develop theories about the nature of philosophy and its kinds, rather than criteria of particular ethnic philosophies.

The Case of *Popol Vuh*

But what do we make of *Popol Vuh*? The question, as noted, is not one that was relevant for the task I set out for myself in *Latinos in America*, but it is nonetheless an interesting and legitimate question if one is concerned with whether to include this work in a discussion of Latin American philosophy in the classroom or in a historical study. And since Nuccetelli wishes me to answer it, let me put on the hat of historian of Latin American philosophy and take this question up here. In my view, and contrary to what Nuccetelli seems to think, the answer is not obvious, even if one adopts a conception of Latin American philosophy as ethnic, although this view of Latin American philosophy helps us to understand better the issues involved in finding an answer.

Before an acceptable answer to this question can be offered, we must be clear concerning the kind of conception of philosophy we are using, for the answer to the question varies depending on it. It is one thing to ask whether *Popol Vuh* is part of Latin American philosophy when this philosophy is conceived in universalistic terms and another when it is conceived as an ethnic philosophy, although Nuccetelli seems to think that the answer in both cases is affirmative.

In the first case, Nuccetelli argues in favor of it because *Popol Vuh* could be taken, as the work of the pre-Socratics is, as a kind of protophilosophy. Just as the work of Thales and Parmenides, for example, led to the well-developed philosophy of Socrates and other Greek philosophers, and is therefore considered part of Greek philosophy, *Popol Vuh* can be taken as a protophilosophy to the well-developed philosophy of Bartolomé de Las Casas and those who followed after him and therefore should be considered part of Latin American philosophy.

Contrary to what Nuccetelli believes, however, the question of whether *Popol Vuh* is a kind of protophilosophy to Latin American philosophy, if one holds a universalistic conception of philosophy, is not so clear, and there can be justifiable disagreement with respect to it. For example, one could argue that the work of the pre-Socratics constitutes a major break from the religious and mythical works that preceded them, and in this sense it is closer to later Greek philosophy than to religion. The pre-Socratics were not concerned primarily with the "creation" of the universe, nor did they provide theories about the origin of the universe in terms of the wills of gods. Their inquiry was intended fundamentally to explain why things happen as they do, and their answers were in terms of natural causes, elements, and principles of intelligibility, such as attraction, atoms, and the Logos, that explained how they happen as they do. This is quite different from questions concerning the creation of the world, as explored in religious cosmologies included in mythical works such as *Popol Vuh*, and the answers given to them, which involve divine and supernatural beings. Just for these reasons one could very well conclude that *Popol Vuh*, in contrast with the work of the pre-Socratics, cannot be considered protophilosophical. Naturally, the point is arguable, but that is not relevant for my purposes or Nuccetelli's argument. What is relevant to both is that the case for this work as protophilosophical is not as clear or easy to resolve as Nuccetelli claims when we are working with a universalistic conception of philosophy.

But now let us look at the situation when we adopt the view of Latin American philosophy as ethnic. Is it clear that in this case, as Nuccetelli argues, *Popol Vuh* should be considered part of the Latin American philosophical canon? One of the reasons why Nuccetelli is mistaken in this regard is that, contrary to her opinion, one could legitimately question the degree to which the Maya are part of the Latino ethnos. Not that I would like to do so—in fact I think that it makes sense to consider them as part of it. But not everyone might agree. For example, for those who view mestizos in Latin America as properly constituting the Latino ethnos, the pre-Colombian, uncontaminated, and presumably unmixed Maya should be considered a different ethnos. Indeed, many authors pit these two groups of people against each other rather than viewing the Latino ethnos as encompassing the Maya ethnos. Moreover, the evidence that Nuccetelli provides for counting the Maya as part of the Latino ethnos (i.e., the popularity of some Maya among Latin Americans) is a nonstarter for too many reasons to enumerate here. In short, if the skeptics of Maya Latinity are right, then it is not at all the case that *Popol Vuh* can be counted as a product of the Latino ethnos and therefore part of Latin American philosophy.

The other reason why Nuccetelli is mistaken I have already mentioned: in order to count *Popol Vuh* as part of Latin American philosophy, this work must be considered part of it by those who determine such a status, whether internally, externally, or both. But this requires an investigation into the matter and cannot be taken for granted. This investigation falls under the purview of historians rather than of philosophers.

A comparison of the status of *Popol Vuh* and some of the works that narrate the Hindu myths of creation illustrates how the concept of ethnic philosophy is useful in understanding the status that these works enjoy. On the one hand, there is wide disagreement among historians of Latin American philosophy on whether *Popol Vuh* should be considered part of Latin American philosophy, whereas many of the Hindu narratives are widely accepted both by Indian and Western historians of philosophy as part of Indian philosophy. Something similar occurs with some of the works of Chinese philosophy—they are considered philosophy by both Chinese and Western historians of philosophy. So why the discrepancy? Because the judgment is based on criteria determined largely by the ethnos that produced those works. This is evident in Indian and Chinese philosophy: Indian and Chinese historians of philosophy include these works in the canons of the philosophies they study, even though these works are very different from anything produced in the West and taken to be part of philosophy by Western historians of philosophy.

The situation of *Popol Vuh* in Latin America is different from that of these works because a majority of historians of Latin American philosophy consider themselves part of the Western philosophical tradition and use the criteria prevalent in this tradition to judge inclusion in the Western philosophy canon. If instead of adopting Western criteria, they tried to use criteria developed by Latin American thinkers themselves that reflect the perspective of the Latino ethnos, then they might be more amenable to the inclusion of *Popol Vuh* among works of Latin American philosophy. Perhaps this will happen in the future, but it is certainly not a widespread phenomenon today. In fact, I am pessimistic that it will happen, because of the divided roots of Latin America. It is easy for China and India to develop their own view of what counts as philosophy, independently of the West, and as such remain largely unchallenged in their views because these countries and cultures develop and continue to function largely independently from Western countries and cultures. But Latin America is closely tied to the West. Indeed, it is precisely the mixed character of Latin America, between the West and pre-Columbian America, that has characterized most members of the Latino ethnos and thus also of its ethnic products. And I do not see a future in which this *mestizaje* will become irrelevant or uncontroversial. (For more on this, see Gracia 2000c:chaps. 4, 5.)

In short, the understanding of Latino philosophy as ethnic opens the door for the consideration of works such as *Popol Vuh* to be part of Latin American philosophy, but it does not ensure their inclusion. This is precisely what I argued in *Latinos in America*.

Lessons from the Exchange

In closing I would like to point to some lessons we can learn from the exchange between Nuccetelli and me. First among these is that the notion of ethnic philosophy can help us understand why certain works are included in, or excluded from, the canon of different philosophies, and particularly in the case of Latin American philosophy.

Second, the exchange points to the need to take into account the changing and passing nature of cultural products such as philosophy. It is a mistake to think of philosophical works and views as permanent, obeying laws *sub specie aeternitatis*. Philosophies are cultural products and should be treated as such, even though the understanding philosophers seek may transcend particular times and places.

Third, it is helpful, in the discussion of such phenomena as Latin American philosophy, to keep questions of history separate from questions of historiography. The inquiries are different, their objects are different, and so are their methodologies and the roles of the inquirers.

Finally, although not explicitly discussed here, it is beneficial to introduce the notion of a Latino philosophy to which I referred at the beginning rather than to use the notion of Latin American philosophy, because this allows us to include in it both the philosophy of Latinos in Latin America and the philosophy of Latinos in the United States and elsewhere. Indeed, if it makes sense to speak of a Latino ethnos, it should also make sense to speak of a Latino philosophy. Moreover, this should not be taken as undermining the talk of Hispanics and Hispanic philosophy when the first includes people from the Iberian Peninsula and the second includes the philosophy of Latinos and Iberians, as I have argued elsewhere (esp. Gracia 2000c, 2008b:chap. 3).

So much, then, for the objections brought up by Nuccetelli about the notion of Hispanic/Latino philosophy as an ethnic philosophy. This, however, does not exhaust the topic, as is clear from the questions raised by Eduardo Mendieta (II:11) and my response to them (II:12), and from the other objections raised to my views in this part of the book, to which I now turn.

PROBLEMS WITH THE NOTION
OF LATINO PHILOSOPHY

Llorente's difficulties with the conception of Latino philosophy I propose can be summarized in three arguments:

1. I do not properly acknowledge that my proposal of using the term 'Latino philosophy' involves terminological revisionism.
2. I argue that ethne have a role to play in what is to be considered philosophy for them, but then I inconsistently turn around and propose a view of philosophy that is not ethnic, as "a view of the world or any of its parts that seeks to be accurate, consistent, comprehensive, and supported by sound evidence."
3. Because Latino philosophy has a backward and marginal connotation, we should, contrary to what I argue, choose a label such as 'Hispanic philosophy' or 'Latin American philosophy,' as I suggested in *Hispanic/Latino Identity*, that does not have such connotations and abandon the label 'Latino philosophy.'

My response to the first of these arguments is that, contrary to Llorente's charge, I explicitly and repeatedly make clear that my use of the label 'Latino philosophy' is revisionist, although I do not use the term 'revisionist' to describe it, and that such a revision of the way we speak is warranted by the advantages I point out in *Latinos in America*. Indeed, I do this with various expressions and terms, including 'America,' 'Latino,' and 'American philosophy,' as I did so with 'Hispanic' and 'Hispanic philosophy' in *Hispanic/ Latino Identity*. My point is precisely that, unless we adopt terms such as 'Latino philosophy' and 'Hispanic philosophy,' we leave out of consideration all kinds of phenomena that are important for understanding the history of philosophy. The discussion I (I:5) have with K. Anthony Appiah (I:3) attests quite clearly to the fact that I believe that all philosophy is revisionary (or revisionist, as Llorente calls it). If philosophy were not revisionary, what would be the point of it? And the same applies to science by the way. Galileo's theory of the heavens was certainly a revision, and a radical one at that, of Ptolemy's view.

My response to the second argument is that my proposal concerning philosophy as "a view of the world . . ." is not intended as a dogmatic definition of the discipline. It is rather a broad and loose conception, presumably acceptable to most philosophers, and heuristically intended, that allows us to carry on a discussion. Its use still permits me to say, without contradiction, that ethne can introduce requirements for what they believe philosophy to be. Just consider for a moment other large philosophical labels like 'Chinese philosophy' and 'Indian philosophy.' Both fit loosely within the description I have provided, but I think that it is easily recognizable that there is much in Chinese philosophy that would not be considered philosophy by Indian or Western standards, and in Indian philosophy that would not fit Chinese or Western standards, and so on.

Let me add in passing that the character of a philosophy—its properties if you will—is not what turns it into an ethnic philosophy. Llorente assumes this is so because he is still working with a notion of ethnic as involving a set of particular properties, and probably idiosyncratic. But my view about what makes philosophy ethnic has little to do with that, as I have stated and explained repeatedly (Gracia, I:5; 2008b:7).

Finally, against the third argument let me suggest that it is a very bad idea to abandon labels that have some historical grounding or conceptual advantages because some of their connotations may be negative. I have in fact made this case in various places (e.g., Gracia 2008b:3). Should blacks reject the label 'black' because of what it connotes in the minds of some people? Should Jews reject the label 'Jew' because of similar reasons? I do not think so, and likewise, we should not reject 'Latino' because in the minds of some, or even a majority, the label has deprecatory connotations. Our task should be to educate people rather than to leave prejudice unchallenged.

Like Llorente, González and Stigol object to my proposed conception of Latino philosophy, but their arguments differ from those formulated by Llorente. They articulate three objections to my view that may be gathered under a category that is the source of much of the concern González and Stigol voice against my position. Moreover, it is here that they address a dimension of our topic that I have not discussed before anywhere and, therefore, need to address more fully. The overall category has to do with the identity criteria for ethnic groups in general and for Latinos in particular. This is then applied in three different contexts, although I take up only the third of these because most of their discussion revolves around it, namely, the identity of Latino philosophers.

González and Stigol argue that my account of the identity of Latino philosophers is inadequate for a variety of reasons. The issue, as they point out, is "the identity of a social group whose members not only belong to the same ethnic group, . . . but also share the same professional activity and belong to the same professional community, that is . . . Latinos and philosophers." And they ask, "What characterizes the activities of this group not as philosophy but as Latin American philosophy?" Their criticism is that the Familial-Historical View I use to account for the identity of this group does not include a sufficient number of variables to be adequate. Such factors as gender, university studies, and academic connections, among others, are left out. This is the overall thrust of the objection, which is subsequently developed in further detail. Let me offer a general answer to the overall formulation first and then turn to the details.

The general objection seems to have two parts. The first criticizes my view because it does not adequately identify what characterizes Latin American philosophy or the Latin American philosophical community. The second criticizes my view because it does not take into account certain factors, such as gender, curricula, and professional relations, that are important for understanding the Latin American philosophical community.

My response to the first part is that the objection begs the question insofar as it asks for precisely what I have pointed out should not be asked. (This is a similar move to the one they make in the objection they raise about the unity and boundaries of an ethnos I discussed earlier.) My view does not identify what characterizes Latin American philosophers because Latin American philosophers, just like the members of my family, have no property that characterizes all of them at all times and places, even if they have all sorts of properties that characterize some of them at some times or places. Indeed, consider such examples as Las Casas, Sor Juana, Mariátegui, Ingenieros, and Frondizi. Many efforts have been undertaken to find such common properties, and so far they have failed. In my view, this search should be abandoned because it is based on a misunderstanding of the familial-historical character of ethne and their cultural products.

To the second part of the general objection I respond that, contrary to what González and Stigol claim, my view *does* take into account implicitly, if not as explicitly as they would like, such variegated factors as gender and professional relations, by acknowledging that Latin American philosophers are tied historically in a variety of ways and that history is the foundation of their ethnicity. History is a complex phenomenon and includes all the phenomena to which González and Stigol refer. Historical figures have genders, engage in academic activities, are members of professional associations, and so on. History functions as an umbrella that covers the complexity and contextual character of the situation. Moreover, I point out that it is precisely that history and contextual character that give rise to the properties that tie members of these groups and separate them from others in particular times and places. What links González and Stigol to Argentinean philosophy, for example? They are Argentinean nationals, were associates of Eduardo Rabossi, are members of the Sociedad Argentina de Análisis Filosófico, have the privilege of residing in Buenos Aires, and so on. Of course, they are also women, and this means that, independently of philosophy, they have also a tie to other women who probably feel oppressed by the machismo of Argentinean men, and so on.

This is my answer to the two parts of the general formulation of the objection. Now let me turn to the details, where probably the devil is hiding. Although González and Stigol bring up various concerns as they make their case, there is a central point they stress. This is that in my discussion of Latino philosophy I put too much emphasis on the overall category and neglect to take into account that Latino philosophers break down into two communities that are quite different in various and important aspects. My account makes no reference to significant aspects of these communities that involve the way philosophers practice their profession and are trained, and this is what causes me to ignore their differences. Some of the most important of these aspects are the following:

1. Latino philosophers have different histories.
2. The Latino philosophical community in Latin America lacks the vigor that the U.S. Latino community has.
3. Latino philosophers in Latin America do not engage in dialogue among themselves in the way Latino philosophers in the United States do.
4. Latino philosophers in Latin America do not suffer discrimination as Latino philosophers in the United States do.
5. Eagerness for novelty and a sense of being peripheral characterizes Latino philosophers in Latin America but not Latino philosophers in the United States.
6. Latino philosophers in Latin America tend to take stances that are inauthentic, whereas Latino philosophers in the United States do not.

González and Stigol base their argument on evidence that has been developed by well-known Latin American philosophers who have reflected on the nature and character of Latin American philosophy. Indeed, the points they bring up are frequently cited in the literature, and this gives weight to their case. And I should add at the outset that I think some of them have merit, a fact I have recognized elsewhere going back several years. So my strategy will not be to claim that the six aspects of Latin American philosophy that, according to González and Stigol, differentiate between various communities of Latin American philosophers are spurious, but rather to challenge that they (1) hold across the board, (2) distinguish Latino philosophers who work in Latin America from Latino philosophers working in the United States, and (3) cannot be accommodated within my view.

Let me begin with the first challenge, namely, that the features to which González and Stigol refer do not hold across the board. By this I mean that they do not apply to all the members of the two groups to which they refer. I think that it could be easily shown that not all Latino philosophers in Latin America fail to engage in dialogue (characteristic 3), are consumed by the pursuit of novelty (characteristic 5), or produce inauthentic philosophy (characteristic 6).

One can easily claim, for example (Gracia and Vargas 2013), that in colonial philosophy in Latin America, for instance, there was limited dialogue among philosophers—recall that geographical distances were enormous and isolation was pervasive—but can we really claim the same today, when the exchanges between philosophers in Latin America have become frequent? Consider the number of philosophers today who publish, travel, and work in countries other than their own and the numerous congresses and visiting appointments that are held every year in such distant places as Mexico and Argentina. And this process of dialogue and exchange is growing exponentially as time passes and distances become shorter because of increased transportation facilities.

As to the attitude that González and Stigol call, following Carlos Pereda, novelty eagerness, one could easily point out that this does not apply to every Latin American philosopher. Many of them have in fact explicitly rejected such an attitude, including some of the authors González and Stigol cite, and some have gone in search of ideas rooted in the Latin American experience. Indeed, one of the currents most popular in philosophy in Latin America, the so-called philosophy of liberation, claims just that. Now, some critics of it have argued that the philosophy of liberation is in fact a copy of other philosophies (e.g., European Continental philosophy), or that it is no philosophy at all (because of its unintelligibility, ideological character, and lack of rigor). But these responses constitute contentious ways of establishing their point, and probably beg the question.

Finally, with respect to authenticity, in the sense that Latino philosophers in Latin America lack novelty, I think that we need to tread carefully. The aim of philosophy generally, at least for those philosophers who think of themselves as having much in common with scientists, is not novelty but truth. And if someone else has found truth, then why should philosophy try to go in a different direction? Indeed, Guillermo Hurtado Pérez warns of the dangers of a philosophical search for novelty in one of the texts González and Stigol cite. The romantic idea that philosophy is a matter of personal or social expression and identity is just one among many views of philosophy, and to apply it to all philosophy carried out in Latin America seems rather parochial. It certainly applies to the disciples of José Ortega y Gasset, for example, but it would be difficult to argue it applies to sixteenth-century scholastics or nineteenth-century positivists.

Now let me turn to the second challenge, namely, that the characteristics González and Stigol single out as distinguishing Latino philosophers in the United States and in Latin America do not in fact distinguish them. Again, for the sake of parsimony, let me refer to just three they mention: philosophers in Latin America and the United States have different histories, philosophers in Latin America do not engage in dialogue, whereas Latino philosophers in the United States do, and Latino philosophers in the United States suffer discrimination, whereas Latino philosophers in Latin America do not.

Consider the claim that the history of Latino philosophers in the United States is different from the history of Latino philosophers in Latin America. Although this applies to many of them, it does not seem to apply neatly to all Latino philosophers. Many Latinos working in philosophy in the United States actually come from Latin America and maintain strong ties to their countries of origin. Risieri Frondizi and Héctor-Neri Castañeda are two from a previous generation to which this applies. But of the ones active today, I need mention only Eduardo Mendieta, Nuccetelli, and me. Yes, our individual histories are different, but so are the histories of González, Stigol, and Pereda. Our histories integrate much from Latin America, and in this they are similar. I do not think that it is right to ignore these facts. The boundaries between Latino philosophers working in the United States and Latino philosophers working in Latin America would not appear to be as sharp as González and Stigol would have us believe.

The point about dialogue does not work either. One reason is that dialogue among Latino philosophers in the United States is rather a recent phenomenon. Indeed, a student of mine, Ernesto Rosen Velásquez (2009), wrote a dissertation that consists in mapping out the history of the discussion of Latino identity among Latino philosophers in the United States. This discussion, which is a paradigm of dialogue among half a dozen prominent Latino philosophers, dates back only from a few years ago. Now, Latino philosophers in Latin America have been engaged in dialogue concerning various issues for decades. Consider, for example, the discussion that began in the 1940s about the nature of Latin American philosophy between Leopoldo Zea and Risieri Frondizi, to which practically every Latino philosopher has contributed, including González and Stigol with their contribution to this volume.

Finally, concerning the issue of discrimination, I would like to note that not all Latino philosophers in the United States suffer discrimination, a fact that González and Stigol recognize. Indeed, it would be difficult to argue that they do considering that two recent past presidents of the Eastern Division of the American Philosophical Association are Latino and I have served as a member of the Nominating and Executive Committees and as chair of the Program Committee, as well as in various other functions. The object of discrimination is not Latino philosophers but, rather, Latino philosophy. Latino philosophers suffer discrimination primarily insofar as they do Latino philosophy, and particularly when they do it exclusively.

Now let me turn to the third challenge, namely, that the characteristics mentioned by González and Stigol cannot be easily accommodated within my theory. A salient point of my view is precisely that Latino philosophy is a useful category to understand something about the history of philosophy, but that in order to do so, one has to grasp it in familial-historical terms. To do this is to understand that this philosophy is tied by different relations among peoples from different places. And these relations involve all sorts of things, including personal histories, professional alliances, institutional realities, education, and so on. We need to begin by speaking about a category of Latinos, people who in some ways are tied in ways that Anglos are not. And then we need to think about what they do when they do philosophy as well as what they think about it. Then we should be able to realize that the resulting picture is not neat and clear but messy and confusing. But this is in fact the way things are, even if they are not the way some would like them to be. Frankly, from a personal point of view, I am quite happy with the mess.

LATINOS AND LINGUISTIC RIGHTS

Llorente agrees with the case I build against the English First position defended by Thomas Pogge with respect to the teaching of English in schools, but he objects to my treatment for one reason, which can be put as follows: although I acknowledge at the end of the chapter that Pogge's position may be motivated by a wrong sense of ethnic nationalism, I do not go beyond it. In this he believes my treatment is misguided, for it addresses the wrong problem. The real problem that I should address, according to Llorente, is the "nativist or nationalist assumptions" behind the way linguistic rights are treated, and not the kind of argument proposed by Pogge.

At the end of his comments he suggests that, precisely because of the currency of these nativist and nationalist assumptions my claim that Latinos do not pose a threat to other social groups in the United States is also misguided. The reason in his view is that I do not clarify that they are perceived to pose such a threat, and with some reason.

My answer to the first part of this criticism is that I entirely agree with Llorente in his concern with the nativism and nationalism that seem to be behind much of the discussion of linguistic rights. I also agree that this is an area that should be discussed and brought out into the open by philosophers and nonphilosophers alike. However, I disagree with him in that I do not believe that every discussion of linguistic rights needs to do this. I chose to do instead what seems an equally pressing matter, namely, addressing a kind of argument that carries considerable weight in mainstream philosophical circles today and a version of it presented by a leading exponent of liberalism, which is a favorite political philosophy in the United States. The argument I criticize does not clearly have as premises the kinds of nativism and nationalism of which Llorente speaks, and to which I refer in different language at the end of the chapter. This is the reason that I only mention it as a suggestion at the end, precisely to entice readers, such as Llorente, to take up the gauntlet. In short, I do not think that my strategy is misguided. Indeed, it seems to have been quite effective, convincing Llorente that Pogge's argument is unsound, and prompting him to raise questions that lead in the direction I suggest.

Finally, to the matter of the Latino threat Llorente wants to reinstate, I answer that he has misunderstood my claim. Obviously some social groups in the United States feel threatened by the growing influence and empowerment of Latinos. My point is not to deny this but rather to point out that such feelings are based on a confused conception of ethnicity. Once the confusion is clarified, then it is possible to understand and address these fears.

LATINOS AND AFFIRMATIVE ACTION

Howard McGary's discussion of *Latinos in America* centers on the chapter in which I present my view of affirmative action. He rehearses three strategies I discuss as possible justifications for affirmative action, the first two of which I accept and the third of which I reject. According to the first, affirmative action is justifiable in terms of utility, that is, in terms of the benefits that it produces. According to the second, affirmative action is justified because without it we cannot meet the requirements of justice. And according to the third, affirmative action is justified because it rectifies past wrongs committed against groups of people who suffered discrimination and abuse in the past. According to McGary, the first two strategies are forward-looking ones, whereas the third is backward looking: in the first two affirmative action is justified because of what it can do in the future, whereas in the third, affirmative action is justified because it rectifies past wrongs. McGary's main criticism is that it is a mistake to dismiss the backward-looking strategy in favor of the two forward-looking strategies, because the forward-looking strategies do not provide proper justification for favoring one social group over another. In his view, this can be done only when one looks back to the transgressions committed against the groups for which affirmative action is intended.

I would like to make three points in response to McGary's criticism. The first is that the distinction between forward- and backward-looking strategies is not as clear as he seems to think, whether one looks at the distinction from the so-called forward-looking strategy or from the backward-looking strategy. The backward-looking strategy's aim is precisely to correct *in the present and for the future* whatever abuses were committed in the past. So, although the strategy looks back to past abuses, it also looks forward to a future in which such abuses are both corrected and not committed. The two forward-looking strategies aim to maximize justice and the benefits of a society in which presumably such maximization was and still is not present— it makes no sense to think about a better future, in terms of utility or justice, without a reference to a worse present and past. So, although the two "forward-looking" strategies may look forward, they do so based on a perspective that extends to the past. In short, we cannot distinguish the two types of strategies in the way that McGary has. The difference between them is not in being backward- and forward-looking but in being concerned with maximizing benefits, implementing justice, and avoiding abuses on the one hand and addressing past transgressions on the other.

This brings me to another important difference between the first two strategies and the third. This is that the object of the first two is society at large, even if they entail that some benefits will go to people who did not have them before. The utility and justice involved are not utility and justice *for some* but utility and justice *for all*, which requires, of course, utility and justice for each of the groups and individuals who constitute the society. But the third justification involves only the group that suffered abuses, and this opens the door to group resentment and conflict, thus defeating the whole enterprise. The aim of affirmative action for Latinos is not the well-being of Latinos per se, according to the first two strategies, but the well-being of the nation, which in turn entails certain measures for dealing with Latinos when they are not treated as other members of society. It is not, as affirmative action for Latinos based on past wrongs would be, aimed exclusively at the benefit of Latinos.

The second point I would like to make is that in fact I do not reject the past-wrongs strategy in all cases. I agree that in cases where groups of people have been systematically abused, reparations are in order and these reparations could be considered part of an affirmative action policy. So I cannot be taken as rejecting completely the past-wrongs strategy.

This leads to the third point I wish to make in my response to McGary, namely that my argument against the past-wrongs strategy refers to the particular case of Latinos. Latinos constitute a pan-ethnic group, containing many subethne within it, and it is very difficult to establish that they as a whole have had to suffer abuses because of their ethnicity. This does not mean that certain subgroups of Latinos in certain places have not had to suffer those abuses. There is well-established evidence that they have. But not all Latinos or subgroups of Latinos have had the same experience. We have to distinguish between Cubans and Puerto Ricans, Mexicans and Argentineans, and so on. Moreover, some of the discrimination and abuse that some of these groups have suffered had to do with race rather than ethnicity, or even with nationality. It is very hard, then, to make a case for affirmative action for Latinos as a whole on the basis of past wrongs committed against them.

Now, if we cannot adopt the justification of affirmative action for Latinos on the basis of past wrongs, do we have to abandon the idea of affirmative action for them? Not, in my view, if we conceive the justification of affirmative action in the terms that I set out in *Latinos in America*, namely, in terms of participation in the life of the nation. But McGary rightly asks about the nature of this good. His point is that I do not make clear whether it is a matter of diversity, utility, justice conceived in terms of natural rights, equality, or needs. And he is right to the extent that I do not present my position in these terms. Of course, settling a matter that has been controversial since the very beginning of philosophy would be impossible in a few words, which is all that is possible here. Still, to oblige him, let me add that my view does not neatly fit into any one of these theoretical categories, as he seems to think that it should. Perhaps the best way to approach it is to go back to the Platonic conception of justice as "giving each his due" and modify it with an Aristotelian touch as follows: giving each his/her due opportunity to flourish as a human being. This conception involves equality, justice, utility, and the other criteria mentioned earlier, for surely a nation in which everyone is given his/her due opportunity to grow and develop to the level of his/her capabilities will be a society in which the good of each member of the nation and of the nation as a whole will be maximized to the fullest possible extent.

CLOSING THOUGHTS

JORGE J. E. GRACIA

Dialogue is of the essence in philosophy. In the West, philosophy began in Greece, and it was the Greek commitment to dialogue that gave it birth. We have the finest example of philosophizing in the dialogues of Plato, where a teacher, Socrates, engages young minds in the pursuit of a solution to a problem. And yet seldom does a Platonic dialogue end with an answer to the problem posed in it, for the essence of dialogue is to remain open; what counts is the inquiry, not the solution. Enlightenment results from a deeper understanding of a question explored, not from an answer reached. Answers tend to be final, dogmatic even; they often end conversations and inquiry, and they tend to be contextual and therefore limited by the circumstances. But a dialogue ends as it begins, open to further inquiry, change, and growth, although with a deeper grasp of the terms under discussion.

This is significant because it indicates that knowledge is always in the process of revision and understanding is progressive; they never advance in the way in which we assume that they should. To be a philosopher is to engage in this endless pursuit and always end up wanting. There is no philosophical view or philosophical claim that has ever gone unchallenged, is universally accepted, or is found completely satisfactory. So why do philosophers continue in a quest that appears to have no end? It is difficult to be a philosopher. And not just difficult, it can be devastating precisely because, although as young philosophers we tend to want answers and desperately seek them, with time we realize that our quest will always remain unfinished. Only when we understand that it is not the end we crave but the road toward it do we grasp the nature of our discipline, becoming true practitioners of it. Philosophy is ultimately a Faustian enterprise.

Socrates is without a doubt the epitome of the philosopher, and his life is the paradigm of the philosophical life. What did he do? He was a sort of bum. His wife supported him, and he spent his time talking to young men, challenging their views about the world and themselves in any ways he could, demolishing the dogmatic structures that had been passed on to them by their parents, ancestors, and society at large. I hate to think what his wife said to him when he got home after a day of leisure while she was laboring as a midwife. And I am sure she did not appreciate that he would say to her that he was also a kind of midwife, although not of babies, but of ideas! After all, where was the fee?

No wonder Socrates was ultimately condemned to death for corrupting the youth of Athens. Surely it is true that he was corrupting the youth by making them realize that what they thought they knew they did not know. This revolutionary, even subversive, idea became a mantra: I know only that I know nothing. So, we may ask, why engage in these dialogues? And does not the philosophical enterprise, as so many have argued, undermine the very bases of society? Does it not dynamite the foundations of religion, morality, and science?

The answer to the last two questions is the same: yes, of course it does. This is why not only Socrates but also other philosophers have been ridiculed and subjected to abuse by the Social Establishment for their views. We need only think of Averroës, the greatest Islamic philosopher of all times, and Abelard, one of the shining lights of medieval thought. Both suffered dearly for being philosophers and living the philosophical life. It is unfortunate that the critics of philosophy do not realize that, even if philosophy may not provide answers, it makes progress in other ways. For one thing, it makes us realize the unsupported evidence we have for views we regard as sacred cows. Getting rid of false beliefs and realizing the weak bases on which we hold them constitute, without a doubt, great improvement and advance. It is better to see, even if what we see is that we are perched on a rope over a precipice, than not to see at all and continue walking blindly, not realizing where we are. The danger is that by seeing we will become afraid, mutable, and more likely fall into the abyss, but do we really want to save ourselves through ignorance? Is it not better to die knowing than to live blindly? Yes. Why? Because it is in our nature to know. As Aristotle so perspicaciously pointed out, curiosity defines who we are, separating us from the rest of nature. We are knowing animals and to shut ourselves in ignorance turns us not just into mere animals—they cannot do otherwise—but into something much worse. Dogmatic ignorance yields monsters.

A critical dimension is essential to philosophy and clearly flourishes in dialogue. A dialogue is a way of opening us to others, to engage perspectives new to us, and to encounter previously unsuspected challenges. Inbreeding leads to deception. We need other people, their views, and their help. Confrontation with them makes us human. Often I see people engaged in conversations that amount to nothing more than monologues. This is not dialogue; true dialogue involves an exchange, an engagement with the other. Nor can we have a dialogue if what we say is not open to change. Dialogue requires that the participating parties be willing to consider the views of the interlocutors and, more than that, to change their own positions when presented with better ones.

Unfortunately, most of us live in dogmatic cages, conceptual structures we are not able, or want, to escape. It is so comfortable to continue believing what we believe! This applies to religious beliefs, scientific theories, and philosophical views. It applies even to our intercourse with our social groups, friends, and family. For those of us who function in the world of ideas, it applies to the disciplines of learning we practice. We feel comfortable when we hear what we are used to hearing. Why should I, a philosopher, engage an artist, or a literary writer, or a physicist, in dialogue? After all, it is easier to stay with those who think like I do, who share my assumptions and prejudices. We need them because it is in dialogue with them that we can more easily realize how silly and wrongheaded some of our views are.

Perhaps the dependence of philosophy on dialogue and criticism is in part the result of the fact that philosophy is not an empirical study and it is often influenced by subjective biases and prejudices. As philosophers we need to be confronted by other perspectives; we need to face sharp criticisms; and we need to consider tough objections to the views that we value deeply in order to eliminate as many of those biases and prejudices as possible. The process is infinite, as Jorge Luis Borges would say, because there is always some way in which even a relatively good philosophical view can be improved.

The opportunity to have my work subjected to serious criticism by other philosophers who have given careful thought to it and who have in many ways helped shape current discussions of the topics examined in this book has been an extraordinary opportunity. I am particularly honored to have a truly outstanding roster of distinguished minds be my critics. Their comments and concerns are especially significant because most of them work within traditions that are different from mine and reflect points of view different from those I tend to favor. I often recall that John Stuart Mill was right when he pointed out the need for us to pay attention to those with whom we disagree rather than to those who share our intellectual heritage. Moreover, I appreciate that my critics have pulled no punches, because truth tolerates no compromise. Still, I also value that they have been fair, courteous, and generous.

More important still, the criticisms contained in this volume have helped me understand many things I did not see clearly before. I have learned many important lessons from my critics, and I hope the discussion of my views has helped them as well to delve more deeply into the murky issues of race, ethnicity, and Hispanic/Latino identity. Indeed, I have conceived my task here not so much as apologetic, with the aim of criticizing my critics in order to save my intellectual hide, but rather as an attempt to extend our collective grasp of the philosophical problems they raise.

The issues posed by my critics are complex and rich, whereas my space to respond has been limited, so I have had to focus on and select those aspects of their criticisms that seem to me more substantial and challenging and that in my opinion address current and pressing philosophical problems. This entailed leaving untouched many controversial topics I discuss and theses I defend in my work. But readers who feel left out because they suspect the critics that have contributed to this volume may have exhausted the areas that I have addressed in my writings, or they have been too generous in their criticisms, should take heart, for there is plenty left in my views for them to criticize.

In sum, I wish to thank the contributors to this volume for giving me this opportunity to clarify many aspects of my views that I may have left unclear and to dwell further in areas of great interest to me. I am sure they will not be entirely satisfied with my rejoinders. Indeed, I am far from being satisfied myself. Still, I hope to have given them, and the readers of this book, some food for thought, and perhaps to have opened the doors to further discussion and dialogue. Apart from having thoroughly enjoyed reading the comments of my critics, I have appreciated their kind words about my work, their professionalism, and philosophical depth, which have renewed my respect for their obvious commitment to truth and fairness. I want to express my sincere thanks to them for having taken the time to prepare their comments with the obvious care that they have. Finally, let me acknowledge my great debt to my former student and friend, Iván Jaksić, for undertaking the cumbersome and time-consuming task of compiling these exchanges. Very few mentors have been as lucky as I have been in having someone like him as a student and friend.

APPENDIX

ORIGINAL PANELS AND DISCUSSIONS

American Philosophical Association author-meets-critics panel organized by Linda M. Alcoff at the Eastern Division meetings in December 1999 to discuss Gracia's *Hispanic/Latino Identity.* Participants: Linda M. Alcoff, Anne Freire Ashbaugh, Richard J. Bernstein, J. L. A. García, Robert Gooding-Williams, Eduardo Mendieta, and Gregory Pappas.

American Philosophical Association author-meets-critics panel organized by Elizabeth Millán at the Eastern Division meetings in December 2006 to discuss Gracia's *Surviving Race, Ethnicity, and Nationality.* Participants: Linda M. Alcoff and Lucius T. Outlaw Jr.

American Philosophical Association author-meets-critics panel organized by Susana Nuccetelli at the Eastern Division meetings in December 2008 to discuss Gracia's *Latinos in America.* Participants: María Cristina González, Renzo Llorente, Howard McGary, and Nora Stigol.

The University at Buffalo Humanities Institute Distinguished Scholar Session to discuss Gracia's work on the interpretation of race, literature, and art organized by Erik Seeman in September 2012. Participants: K. Anthony Appiah and Ilan Stavans.

REFERENCES

Alcoff, Linda M. 2008. "Mapping the Boundaries of Race, Ethnicity, and Nationality: A Commentary on Jorge Gracia's *Surviving Race, Ethnicity, and Nationality*."
International Philosophical Quarterly 48, no. 2:213–38.

——. 2007. "Comparative Race, Comparative Racisms." In *Race or Ethnicity? On
Black and Latino Identity*, edited by Jorge J. E. Gracia, 170–88. Ithaca, N.Y.: Cornell University Press.

——. 2006. *Visible Identities: Race, Gender and the Self.* Oxford: Oxford University
Press.

——. 2005a. "Latino Oppression." *Journal of Social Philosophy* 36, no. 4:536–45.

——. 2005b. "Latino vs. Hispanic: The Politics of Ethnic Names." *Philosophy and
Social Criticism* 31, no. 4:395–408.

——. 2005c. "A Response to Gracia." *Philosophy and Social Criticism* 31, no. 4:419–22.

——. 2000. "Is Latina/o Identity a Racial Identity?" In *Hispanics/Latinos in the United
States: Ethnicity, Race, and Rights*, edited by Jorge J. E. Gracia and Pablo De Greiff,
23–44. New York: Routledge.

——. 1995. "Mestizo Identity." In *The Idea of Race*, edited by Robert Bernasconi and
Tommy L. Lott, 139–60. Indianapolis: Hackett.

Andreasen, Robin. 1998. "A New Perspective on the Race Debate." *British Journal for
the Philosophy of Science* 49, no. 2:199–225.

Appiah, K. Anthony. 2004. *The Ethics of Identity.* Princeton, N.J.: Princeton University Press.

——. 2000. "The Uncompleted Argument: Du Bois and the Illusion of Race." In *The
Idea of Race*, edited by Robert Bernasconi and Tommy L. Lott, 118–35. Indianapolis:
Hackett.

——. 1996. "Race, Culture, Identity: Misunderstood Connections." In *Color Conscious*, by K. Anthony Appiah and Amy Gutmann, 30–150. Princeton, N.J.: Princeton University Press.

——. 1992. *In My Father's House: Africa in the Philosophy of Culture*. Oxford: Oxford University Press.

Appiah, Kwame Anthony, and Henry Louis Gates Jr., eds. 1995. *Identities*. Chicago: University of Chicago Press.

Bambrough, Renford. 1960–1961. "Universals and Family Resemblances." *Proceedings of the Aristotelian Society* 61:207–22.

Barth, Fredrik. 1969. *Ethnic Groups and Boundaries: The Social Organization of Culture Difference*. Long Grove, Ill.: Waveland Press.

Bernasconi, Robert, ed. 2001a. *Race*. Malden, Mass.: Blackwell.

——. 2001b. "Who Invented the Concept of Race? Kant's Role in the Enlightenment Construction of Race." In *Race*, edited by Robert Bernasconi, 11–36. Malden, Mass.: Blackwell.

Bernasconi, Robert, and Tommy L. Lott, eds. 2000. *The Idea of Race*. Indianapolis: Hackett.

Bernstein, Richard J. 2001. "Comment on *Hispanic/Latino Identity* by J. J. E. Gracia." *Philosophy and Social Criticism* 27, no. 2:44–50.

Beverly, John, José Oviedo, and Michael Aronna, eds. 1995. *The Postmodernism Debate in Latin America*. Durham, N.C.: Duke University Press.

Blum, Lawrence. 2010. "Latinos on Race and Ethnicity: Alcoff, Corlett, and Gracia." In *A Companion to Latin American Philosophy*, edited by Susana Nuccetelli, Ofelia Schutte, and Otávio Bueno, 269–82. Malden, Mass.: Blackwell.

——. 2002. *"I'm Not a Racist, But . . .": The Moral Quandary of Race* Ithaca, N.Y.: Cornell University Press.

——. 1999. "Ethnicity, Identity, and Community." In *Justice and Caring: The Search for Common Ground in Education*, edited by Michael S. Katz, Nel Noddings, and Kenneth A. Strike, 127–45. New York: Teachers College Press.

Boxill, Bernard, ed. 2001. *Race and Racism*. Oxford: Oxford University Press.

——. 1984. *Blacks and Social Justice*. Totowa, N.J.: Rowman and Littlefield.

Castro-Gómez, Santiago. 1996. *Crítica de la razón latinoamericana*. Barcelona: Puvill Libros.

Collin, Finn. 1997. *Social Reality*. London: Routledge.

Corlett, J. Angelo. 2003. *Race, Racism, and Reparations*. Ithaca, N.Y.: Cornell University Press.

——. 2001. "Latino/a Identity." *APA Newsletter on Hispanic/Latino Issues in Philosophy* 1, no. 1:97–104.

——. 1999. "Latino Identity." *Public Affairs Quarterly* 13, no. 3:273–95.

Craig, Edward, ed. 1998. *Routledge Encyclopedia of Philosophy*. London: Routledge.

Crummell, Alexander. 1966. "The Problem of Race in America." In *Negro Social and Political Thought, 1850–1920*, edited by Howard Brotz, 180–90. New York: Basic Books.

Du Bois, W. E. B. 1897. *The Conservation of Races*. American Negro Academy Occasional Papers, no. 2. In *W. E. B. Du Bois Speaks: Speeches and Addresses, 1890–1919*, edited by Philip S. Foner. New York: Pathfinders Press, 1970.

Frondizi, Risieri. 1949. "Is There an Ibero-American Philosophy?" *Philosophy and Phenomenological Research* 9, no. 3:345–55.

Frondizi, Risieri, and Jorge J. E. Gracia, eds. (1975) 1981. *El hombre y los valores en la filosofía latinoamericana del siglo XX*. Mexico City: Fondo de Cultura Económica.

García, J. L. A. 2007. "Racial and Ethnic Identity?" In *Race or Ethnicity? On Black and Latino Identity*, edited by Jorge J. E. Gracia, 78–100. Ithaca, N.Y.: Cornell University Press.

——. 2001. "Is Being Hispanic an Identity? Reflections on J. J. E. Gracia's Account." *Philosophy and Social Criticism* 27, no. 2:29–43.

Gilson, G. 2006. "The Project of Exact Philosophy: An Interview with Mario Bunge." *APA Newsletter on Hispanic/Latino Issues in Philosophy* 6, no. 1:8–10.

Goldberg, David Theo. 1993. *Racist Culture: Philosophy and the Politics of Meaning*. Oxford: Blackwell.

González, María Cristina, and Nora Stigol. 2013. "Gracia on Latino and Latin American Philosophy." *Journal of Speculative Philosophy* 27, no. 1:79–90.

——. 2008. "La enseñanza de la filosofía y el canon filosófico." In *Cuestiones filosóficas: Un homenaje a Eduardo Rabossi*, edited by D. Pérez and L. Fernández Moreno, 533–54. Buenos Aires: Editorial Catálogos.

Gooding-Williams, Robert. 2001. "Comment on J. J. E. Gracia's *Hispanic/Latino Identity*." *Philosophy and Social Criticism* 27, no. 2:3–10

Gracia, Jorge J. E. 2014. "The Fundamental Character of Metaphysics." In "Metaphysics," edited by Jorge J. E. Gracia and Javier Cumpa. Special issue, *American Philosophical Quarterly* 51, no. 4:305–18.

——. 2013a. "*Latinos in America*: A Response." *Journal of Speculative Philosophy* 27, no. 1:95–111.

——. 2013b. "What Is Metaphysics?" In *Neo-Aristotelian Perspectives in Metaphysics*, edited by Daniel D. Novotny and Lukáš Novák, 19–41. London: Routledge.

——. 2012. *Painting Borges: Philosophy Interpreting Art Interpreting Literature*. Albany: SUNY Press.

——, ed. 2011. *Forging People: Race, Ethnicity, and Nationality in Hispanic American and Latino/a Thought*. Notre Dame, Ind.: University of Notre Dame Press.

——. 2010a. "Cánones filosóficos y tradiciones filosóficas: El caso de la filosofía latino-americana." *Análisis filosófico* 30, no. 1:17–34.

——. 2010b. "Identity and Latin American Philosophy." In *A Companion to Latin American Philosophy*, edited by Susana Nuccetelli, Ofelia Schutte, and Otávio Bueno, 253–68. Malden, Mass.: Blackwell.

——. 2010c. "Latin American Philosophy as Ethnic Philosophy: A Response to Susana Nuccetelli." *Inter-American Journal of Philosophy* 1, no. 1:44–55.

——. 2008a. "The Foundations of a Philosophy of Race, Ethnicity, and Nationality." *International Philosophical Quarterly* 48, no. 2:246–55.

——. 2008b. *Latinos in America: Philosophy and Social Identity*. Oxford: Blackwell.

——. 2007a. "Individuation of Racial and Ethnic Groups: The Problems of Circularity and Demarcation." In *Race or Ethnicity? On Black and Latino Identity*, edited by Jorge J. E. Gracia, 78–100. Ithaca, N.Y.: Cornell University Press.

——, ed. 2007b. *Race or Ethnicity? On Black and Latino Identity*. Ithaca, N.Y.: Cornell University Press.

——. 2005a. "A Political Argument in Favor of Ethnic Names." *Philosophy and Social Criticism* 31, no. 4:409–17.

——. 2005b. *Surviving Race, Ethnicity, and Nationality: A Challenge for the Twenty-First Century*. Lanham, Md.: Rowman and Littlefield.

——. 2003. *Old Wine in New Skins: The Role of Tradition in Communication, Knowledge, and Group Identity*. Aquinas Lecture 2003. Milwaukee: Marquette University Press.

——. 2001a. *How Can We Know What God Means? The Interpretation of Revelation*. New York: Palgrave Macmillan.

——. 2001b. "Response to the Critics of *Hispanic/Latino Identity*: Tahafut Al-Tahafut." *Philosophy and Social Criticism* 27, no. 2:51–75.

——. 2000a. "Affirmative Action for Hispanics? Yes and No." In *Hispanics/Latinos in the United States: Ethnicity, Race, and Rights*, edited by Jorge J. E. Gracia and Pablo De Greiff, 201–21. New York: Routledge.

——. 2000b. "Borges's 'Pierre Menard': Philosophy or Literature?" *Journal of Aesthetics and Art Criticism* 59, no. 1:45–57.

——. 2000c. *Hispanic/Latino Identity: A Philosophical Perspective*. Malden, Mass.: Blackwell.

——. 2000d. "Sociological Accounts and the History of Philosophy." In *The Sociology of Philosophical Knowledge*, edited by Martin Kush, 193–211. Dordrecht: Kluwer.

——. 1999a. "Ethnic Labels and Philosophy: The Case of Latin-American Philosophy." *Philosophy Today* 43 (suppl.): 42–49.

——. 1999b. *Metaphysics and Its Task: The Search for the Categorical Foundation of Knowledge.* Albany: SUNY Press.

——. 1999c. "Socioculturalismo y antisocioculturalismo en la historiografía filosófica: Un falso dilema." *Concordia* 35:95–110.

——. 1998. *Filosofía hispánica: Concepto, origen y foco historiográfico.* Pamplona: Universidad de Navarra.

——. 1995. *A Theory of Textuality: The Logic and Epistemology.* Albany: SUNY Press.

——. 1993. "Hispanic Philosophy: Its Beginning and Golden Age." *Review of Metaphysics* 46, no. 3:475–502.

——. 1992. *Philosophy and Its History: Issues in Philosophical Historiography.* Albany: SUNY Press.

——. 1988. *Individuality: An Essay on the Foundations of Metaphysics.* Albany: SUNY Press.

——, ed. 1986a. *Latin American Philosophy in the Twentieth Century: Man, Values, and the Search for Philosophical Identity.* Buffalo, N.Y.: Prometheus Books.

——, ed. 1986b. *Risieri Frondizi: Ensayos filosóficos.* Mexico City: Fondo de Cultura Económica.

——. 1984. *Introduction to the Problem of Individuation in the Early Middle Ages.* Munich: Philosophia Verlag; Washington, D.C.: Catholic University of America Press.

——, ed. 1980. *Man and His Conduct: Philosophical Essays in Honor of Risieri Frondizi / El hombre y su conducta: Ensayos filosóficos en honor de Risieri Frondizi.* Rio Piedras: Editorial Universitaria, Universidad de Puerto Rico.

——, ed. 1977. *Francesc Eiximenis: Com usar bé de beure e menjar.* Barcelona: Curial.

——. 1973. "The Convertibility of *Unum* and *Ens* According to Guido Terrena." *Franciscan Studies* 33:143–70.

——. 1970. "Problems of Interpretation in Bradwardine's 'Tractatus de proportionibus.'" *Divus Thomas* 73:175–95.

——. 1969. "The Doctrine of the Possible and Agent Intellects in Gonsalvus Hispanus' Question XIII." *Franciscan Studies* 29:5–36.

Gracia, Jorge J. E., and Douglas Davis. 1989. *The Metaphysics of Good and Evil According to Suárez.* Munich: Philosophia Verlag.

Gracia, Jorge J. E., and Pablo De Greiff, eds. 2000. *Hispanics/Latinos in the United States: Ethnicity, Race, and Rights.* New York: Routledge.

Gracia, Jorge J. E., and Iván Jaksić, eds. 1988. *Filosofía e identidad cultural en América Latina.* Caracas: Monte Ávila Editores. [Manuscript originally completed with copyright in 1983]

Gracia, Jorge J. E., and Elizabeth Millán. 1995. "Latin American Philosophy." In *The Oxford Companion to Philosophy*, edited by Ted Honderich, 462–63. Oxford: Oxford University Press.

Gracia, Jorge J. E., and Elizabeth Millán-Zaibert, eds. 2004. *Latin American Philosophy for the 21st Century: The Human Condition, Values, and the Search for Identity.* Amherst, N.Y.: Prometheus Books.

Gracia, Jorge J. E., Eduardo Rabossi, Enrique Villanueva, and Marcelo Dascal. 1984. *Philosophical Analysis in Latin America.* Dordrecht: Reidel. [*El análisis filosófico en América Latina.* Enlarged ed. Mexico City: Fondo de Cultura Económica, 1985]

Gracia, Jorge J. E., and Manuel Vargas. 2013. "Latin American Philosophy." In *Stanford Encyclopedia of Philosophy*, edited by Edward N. Zalta. http://plato.stanford.edu/entries/latin-american-philosophy/.

Harris, Leonard, ed. 1999. *Racism.* Amherst, N.Y.: Humanity Books.

——. 1984. *Philosophy Born of Struggle: Afro-American Philosophy from 1917.* Dubuque, Iowa: Kendall Hunt.

Haslanger, Sally. 1995. "Ontology and Social Construction." *Philosophical Topics* 23, no. 2:95–125.

Huntington, Samuel P. 2004. "The Hispanic Challenge." *Foreign Affairs*, March–April, 30–45.

Hurtado Pérez, G. 2003. "Una defensa de la filosofía iberoamericana." In *El filosofar hoy*, edited by Oscar Nudler and Francisco Naishtat, 37–45. Buenos Aires: Editorial Biblos.

International Directory of Philosophy and Philosophers 2001–2002. 2001. Bowling Green, Ohio: Philosophy Documentation Center.

Jaksić, Iván. 2007. *The Hispanic World and American Intellectual Life, 1820–1880.* New York: Palgrave Macmillan. [*Ven conmigo a la España lejana: Los intelectuales norteamericanos ante el mundo hispano, 1820–1880.* Santiago de Chile: Fondo de Cultura Económica]

——. 1989. *Academic Rebels in Chile: The Role of Philosophy in Higher Education and Politics.* Albany: SUNY Press. [*Rebeldes académicos.* Translated by Francisco Gallegos. Santiago de Chile: Ediciones Universidad Diego Portales, 2013]

——. 1988–1989. "The Sources of Latin American Philosophy." *Philosophical Forum* 20, nos. 1–2:141–57.

Kitcher, Philip. 1999. "Race, Ethnicity, Biology, Culture." In *Racism*, edited by Leonard Harris, 87–120. Amherst, N.Y.: Humanity Books.

Kuper, Adam. 1999. *Culture: The Anthropologists' Account.* Cambridge, Mass.: Harvard University Press.

Lang, Berel. 1997. "Metaphysical Racism (or: Biological Warfare by Other Means)." In *Race/Sex: Their Sameness, Difference, and Interplay*, edited by Naomi Zack, 17–28. New York: Routledge.

Lange-Churrión, Pedro, and Eduardo Mendieta, eds. 2001. *Latin America and Postmodernity: A Reader*. Amherst, N.Y.: Humanity Books.

Llorente, Renzo. 2013. "Gracia on Hispanic and Latino Identity." *Journal of Speculative Philosophy* 27, no. 1:67–78.

Martínez Estrada, Ezequiel. (1933) 1971. *X-ray of the Pampa*. Austin: University of Texas Press.

McGary, Howard. 2013. "Gracia on Affirmative Action for Latinos." *Journal of Speculative Philosophy* 27, no. 1:91–95.

——. 1999. *Race and Social Justice*. Malden, Mass.: Blackwell.

Mendieta, Eduardo. 2006. "From Modernity, Through Postmodernity, to Globalization: Mapping Latin America." In *Cartografías y estrategias de la "postmodernidad" y la "poscolonialidad" en Latinoamérica*, edited by Alfonso de Toro, 61–91. Madrid: Iberoamericana y Vervuert.

——. 2001. "The 'Second *Reconquista*,' or Why Should a 'Hispanic' Become a Philosopher?" *Philosophy and Social Criticism* 27, no. 2:11–19.

——. 1999a. "Is There Latin American Philosophy?" *Philosophy Today* 43 (suppl.): 50–51.

——. 1999b. Review of *Hispanic/Latino Identity: A Philosophical Perspective*, by Jorge J. E. Gracia. *Hispanic Outlook*, December 3.

Mignolo, Walter. 1999. "Philosophy and the Colonial Difference." *Philosophy Today* 43 (suppl.): 36–41.

Mill, John Stuart. 2005. *Utilitarianism*. Edited by Oskar Piest. Indianapolis: Bobbs-Merrill.

Millán, Elizabeth, and Ernesto Rosen Velásquez. 2011. "Latino/a Identity and the Search for Unity: Alcoff, Corlett, and Gracia." In *Forging People: Race, Ethnicity, and Nationality in Hispanic American and Latino/a Thought*, edited by Jorge J. E. Gracia, 271–302. Notre Dame, Ind.: University of Notre Dame Press.

Miller, David. 1995. *On Nationality*. Oxford: Clarendon Press.

Mills, Charles. 1998. *Blackness Visible: Essays on Philosophy and Race*. Ithaca, N.Y.: Cornell University Press.

Miró Quesada, Francisco. 1979. "Posibilidad y límites de una filosofía latinoamericana." In *La filosofía en América*, edited by Ernesto Mayz Vallenilla, 167–72. Caracas: Universidad Simón Bolívar.

Morris, Thomas V. 1984. *Understanding Identity Statements*. Aberdeen: Aberdeen University Press.

Nozick, Robert. 1975. *Anarchy, State, and Utopia*. New York: Basic Books.

Nuccetelli, Susana. 2010a. "Gracia on Ethnic Philosophy." *Inter-American Journal of Philosophy* 1, no. 1:36–43.

——. 2010b. "Latin American Philosophy." In *A Companion to Latin American Philosophy*, edited by Susana Nuccetelli, Ofelia Schutte, and Otávio Bueno, 343–56. Malden, Mass.: Blackwell.

——. 2003. "Is 'Latin American Thought' Philosophy?" *Metaphilosophy* 34, no. 4:524–37.

——. 2002. *Latin American Thought: Philosophical Problems and Arguments*. Boulder, Colo.: Westview Press.

Nuccetelli, Susana, Ofelia Schutte, and Otávio Bueno, eds. 2010. *A Companion to Latin American Philosophy*. Malden, Mass.: Blackwell.

Outlaw, Lucius T., Jr. 2008. "Writing a Check That Philosophy Can't Cash." *International Philosophical Quarterly* 48, no. 2:239–45.

——. 1996. *On Race and Philosophy*. New York: Routledge.

Pappas, Gregory. 2001. "A Philosophical Perspective on Hispanic Identity." *Philosophy and Social Criticism* 27, no. 2:20–28.

Paz, Octavio. 1950. *The Labyrinth of Solitude*. Mexico City: Fondo de Cultura Económica.

Pereda, Carlos. 2006. "Latin American Philosophy: Some Vices." *Journal of Speculative Philosophy* 20, no. 3:192–203.

——. 1987. *Debates*. Mexico City: Fondo de Cultura Económica.

Piper, Adrian. 1996. "Two Kinds of Discrimination." In *Out of Order, Out of Sight*. Vol. 2, *Selected Writings in Art Criticism, 1967–1992*, 215–59. Cambridge, Mass.: MIT Press.

Ponce, Aníbal. 1974. "Las ilusiones de La Rotonde." In *Obras completas*. Vol. 3. Buenos Aires: Editorial Cartago.

Putnam, Hilary. 2002. *The Collapse of the Fact/Value Dichotomy and Other Essays*. Cambridge, Mass.: Harvard University Press.

Rabossi, Eduardo. 2008. *En el comienzo Dios creó el canon: Biblia berolinensis*. Buenos Aires: Gedisa.

Ramos, Samuel. 1962. *Profile of Man and Culture in Mexico*. Translated by Peter C. Earle. Austin: University of Texas Press.

Rawls, John. 1971. *A Theory of Justice*. Cambridge, Mass.: Harvard University Press.

Rosen Velásquez, Ernesto. 2009. "Politics and the Metaphysics of Latino Identity." Ph.D. diss., University at Buffalo, State University of New York.

——. 2008. "Hume's Racism and His Theory of Prejudice." *Southwest Philosophical Studies* 30:85–91.

Salazar Bondy, Augusto. 1968. *¿Existe una filosofía de nuestra America?* Mexico City: Siglo XXI.

Schutte, Ofelia. 1993. *Cultural Identity and Social Liberation in Latin American Thought.* Albany: SUNY Press.

Sellars, Wilfred. 1963. *Science, Perception and Reality.* New York: Humanities Press.

Snow, C. P. 1959. *The Two Cultures and the Scientific Revolution.* Oxford: Oxford University Press.

Sollors, Werner, and Maria Dietrich, eds. 1994. *The Black Columbiad: Defining Moments in African American Literature and Culture.* Cambridge, Mass.: Harvard University Press.

Stavans, Ilan. 2003a. *Dictionary Days.* St. Paul, Minn.: Graywolf Press.

——. 2003b. *Spanglish: The Making of a New American Language.* New York: Harper.

——. 2001. *On Borrowed Words: A Memoir of Language.* New York: Penguin.

Stavans, Ilan, and Jorge J. E. Gracia. 2014. *Thirteen Ways of Looking at Latino Art.* Durham, N.C.: Duke University Press.

Stavans, Ilan, and Iván Jaksić. 2011. *What Is la hispanidad?* Austin: University of Texas Press. [*¿Qué es la hispanidad? Una conversación.* Santiago de Chile: Fondo de Cultura Económica]

Strawson, P. F. 1959. *Individuals: An Essay in Descriptive Metaphysics.* London: Methuen.

Stubblefield, Anna. 2005. *Ethics Along the Color Line.* Ithaca, N.Y.: Cornell University Press.

Suárez, Francisco. 1982. *Francis Suarez on Individuation: Metaphysical Disputation V; Individual Unity and Its Principle.* Translated by Jorge J. E. Gracia. Milwaukee: Marquette University Press.

Tedlock, Dennis, trans. 1996. *Popol Vuh: The Mayan Book of the Dawn of Life.* New York: Simon and Schuster.

Vasconcelos, José. (1925) 1997. *The Cosmic Race: A Bilingual Edition.* Translated and edited by Didier T. Jaén. Baltimore: Johns Hopkins University Press.

Wittgenstein, Ludwig. 1953. *Philosophical Investigations.* Translated by G. E. M. Anscombe. Oxford: Blackwell.

Zack, Naomi. 1998. *Thinking About Race.* Belmont, Calif.: Wadsworth.

——, ed. 1995. *American Mixed Race: The Culture of Microdiversity.* Lanham, Md.: Rowman and Littlefield.

——. 1993. *Race and Mixed Race.* Philadelphia: Temple University Press.

Zea, L. 1989. "Identity: A Latin American Philosophical Problem." *Philosophical Forum* 20:33–42.

——. (1942) 1986. "The Actual Function of Philosophy in Latin America." In *Latin American Philosophy in the Twentieth Century: Man, Values, and the Search for Philosophical Identity*, edited by Jorge J. E. Gracia, 219–30. Buffalo, N.Y.: Prometheus Books.

——. 1948. *Ensayos sobre filosofía en la historia*. Mexico City: Stylo.

CONTRIBUTORS

Linda M. Alcoff
Professor of philosophy, Hunter College, and member of the Graduate Philosophy Faculty at the CUNY Graduate Center; past president of the Eastern Division of the American Philosophical Association

K. Anthony Appiah
Laurance S. Rockefeller University Professor of Philosophy and member of the University Center for Human Values, Princeton University; past president of the Eastern Division of the American Philosophical Association

Richard J. Bernstein
Vera List Professor of Philosophy, The New School; past president of the Eastern Division of the American Philosophical Association

Lawrence Blum
Distinguished Professor of Liberal Arts and Education and professor of philosophy, University of Massachusetts at Boston

J. L. A. García
Professor of philosophy, Boston College

María Cristina González
Professor of philosophy, Universidad de Buenos Aires

ROBERT GOODING-WILLIAMS
Ralph and Mary Otis Isham Professor of Political Science and The College, University of Chicago

JORGE J. E. GRACIA
State University of New York Distinguished Professor and Samuel P. Capen Chair, Department of Philosophy and Department of Comparative Literature, University at Buffalo; founding chair of the American Philosophical Association Committee for Hispanics in Philosophy

IVÁN JAKSIĆ
Stanford University Bing Overseas Studies Program in Santiago and Department of Iberian and Latin American Cultures

RENZO LLORENTE
Associate professor of philosophy, Saint Louis University, Madrid Campus

HOWARD MCGARY
Professor of philosophy, Rutgers University

EDUARDO MENDIETA
Professor and chair, Department of Philosophy, Stony Brook University; past chair of the American Philosophical Association Committee for Hispanics in Philosophy

SUSANA NUCCETELLI
Professor of philosophy, St. Cloud University; past chair of the American Philosophical Association Committee for Hispanics in Philosophy

LUCIUS T. OUTLAW JR.
Professor of philosophy, Vanderbilt University

GREGORY PAPPAS
Professor of philosophy, Texas A&M University; editor of *Inter-American Journal of Philosophy*

ILAN STAVANS
Lewis-Sebring Professor in Latin American and Latino Culture, Amherst College

NORA STIGOL
Professor of philosophy, Universidad de Buenos Aires

PERMISSIONS

The editor of this volume would like to express his gratitude to the authors of the articles and to the editors and publishers of the works in which the articles listed below were originally published for their permission to reprint them here.

Alcoff, Linda M. 2008. "Mapping the Boundaries of Race, Ethnicity, and Nationality: A Commentary on Jorge Gracia's *Surviving Race, Ethnicity, and Nationality.*" *International Philosophical Quarterly* 48, no. 2:213–38.

Bernstein, Richard J. 2001. "Comment on *Hispanic/Latino Identity* by J. J. E. Gracia." *Philosophy and Social Criticism* 27, no. 2:44–50. SAGE Publications.

Blum, Lawrence. 2010. "Latinos on Race and Ethnicity: Alcoff, Corlett, and Gracia." In *A Companion to Latin American Philosophy*, edited by Susana Nuccetelli, Ofelia Schutte, and Otávio Bueno, 269–82. Malden, Mass.: Blackwell.

García, J. L. A. 2001. "Is Being Hispanic an Identity? Reflections on J. J. E. Gracia's Account." *Philosophy and Social Criticism* 27, no. 2 (March): 29–43. SAGE Publications.

González, María Cristina, and Nora Stigol. 2013. "Gracia on Latino and Latin American Philosophy." *Journal of Speculative Philosophy* 27, no. 1:79–90. Copyright © 2013 by The Pennsylvania State University Press.

Gooding-Williams, Robert. 2001. "Comment on J. J. E. Gracia's *Hispanic/Latino Identity.*" *Philosophy and Social Criticism* 27, no. 2:3–10. SAGE Publications.

Gracia, Jorge J. E. 2013. "*Latinos in America*: A Response." *Journal of Speculative Philosophy* 27, no. 1:95–111. Copyright © 2013 by The Pennsylvania State University Press.

——. 2010. "Latin American Philosophy as Ethnic Philosophy: A Response to Susana Nuccetelli." *Inter-American Journal of Philosophy* 1, no. 1:44–55.

———. 2008. "The Foundations of a Philosophy of Race, Ethnicity, and Nationality." *International Philosophical Quarterly*, 48, no. 2:246–55.

———. 2001. "Response to the Critics of *Hispanic/Latino Identity*: Tahafut Al-Tahafut." *Philosophy and Social Criticism* 27, no. 2:51–75. SAGE Publications.

Llorente, Renzo. 2013. "Gracia on Hispanic and Latino Identity." *Journal of Speculative Philosophy* 27, no. 1:67–78. Copyright © 2013 by The Pennsylvania State University Press.

McGary, Howard. 2013. "Gracia on Affirmative Action for Latinos." *Journal of Speculative Philosophy* 27, no. 1:91–95. Copyright © 2013 by The Pennsylvania State University Press.

Mendieta, Eduardo. 2001. "The 'Second *Reconquista*,' or Why Should a 'Hispanic' Become a Philosopher?" *Philosophy and Social Criticism* 27, no. 2:11–19. SAGE Publications.

Nuccetelli, Susana. 2010. "Gracia on Ethnic Philosophy." *Inter-American Journal of Philosophy* 1, no. 1:36–43.

Outlaw, Lucius T., Jr. 2008. "Writing a Check That Philosophy Can't Cash." *International Philosophical Quarterly* 48, no. 2:239–45.

Pappas, Gregory. 2001. "A Philosophical Perspective on Hispanic Identity." *Philosophy and Social Criticism* 27, no. 2:20–28. SAGE Publications.

INDEX